Initiative And Response

CANADIAN PUBLIC ADMINISTRATION
SERIES

COLLECTION ADMINISTRATION PUBLIQUE
CANADIENNE

J. E. Hodgetts, *General Editor/Rédacteur en chef*

The Institute of Public Administration of Canada
L'Institut d'Administration publique du Canada

This series is sponsored by the Institute of Public
Administration of Canada as part of its constitutional
commitment to encourage research on contemporary
issues in Canadian public administration and public
policy, and to foster wider knowledge and understanding amongst practitioners and the concerned citizen.
There is no fixed number of volumes planned for the
series, but under the supervision of the Research
Committee of the Institute and the General Editor,
efforts will be made to ensure that significant areas
will receive appropriate attention.

L'Institut d'Administration publique du Canada
commandite cette collection dans le cadre de ses
engagements statutaires. Il se doit de promouvoir la
recherche sur des problèmes d'actualité portant sur
l'administration publique et la détermination des poli-
tiques publiques ainsi que d'encourager les praticiens
et les citoyens intéressés à les mieux connaître et à les
mieux comprendre. Il n'a pas été prévu de nombre de
volumes donné pour la collection mais, sous la direction du Rédacteur en chef et du Comité de recherche
de l'Institut, l'on s'efforce d'accorder l'attention voulue
aux questions importantes.

Canada and Immigration:
Public Policy and Public Concern
Freda Hawkins

The Biography of an Institution:
The Civil Service Commission of Canada, 1908–1967
J. E. Hodgetts, William McCloskey, Reginald
Whitaker, V. Seymour Wilson

An edition in French has been published under the
title *Histoire d'une institution: La Commission de la
Fonction publique du Canada, 1908–1967*,
by Les Presses de l'Université Laval.

Old Age Pension and Policy-Making in Canada
Kenneth Bryden

Provincial Governments as Employers:
A Survey of Public Personnel Administration
in Canada's Provinces
J. E. Hodgetts and O. P. Dwivedi

Transport in Transition:
The Reorganization of the Federal Transport Portfolio
John W. Langford

Initiative and Response:
The Adaptation of Canadian Federalism to
Regional Economic Development
Anthony G. S. Careless

Initiative and Response

The Adaptation of Canadian Federalism to Regional Economic Development

ANTHONY G. S. CARELESS

The Institute of Public Administration of Canada
L'Institut d'Administration publique du Canada

McGill–Queen's University Press
Montreal and London 1977

© The Institute of Public Administration
of Canada 1977
ISBN 0-7735-0280-7 (cloth)
ISBN 0-7735-0294-7 (paper)
Legal deposit second quarter 1977
Bibliothèque nationale du Québec

Design by Anthony Crouch MGDC
Printed in Canada by The Hunter Rose Company

Contents

Acknowledgements

During the preparation of the doctoral thesis from which this text is drawn, I was greatly assisted by Freddie Madden of Nuffield College, Oxford and Paul Fox of the University of Toronto. I was fortunate during this period of research to be a member of the Taxation and Fiscal Policy Division of the Ontario Department of Treasury and Economics. In this environment, and particularly with generous support from Terry Russell, its director, and his staff, I was able to pursue my studies in the midst of the daily requirements of a bureaucrat. Their willingness to sustain this project without in turn the certainty of a productive (or timely) result was very much appreciated. Of course, the opinions represented in this subsequent manuscript are solely those of the author and do not constitute positions of the government of Ontario.

In the preparation of this manuscript, Denis Smith of Trent University and Donald Smiley of York University have patiently offered valuable comments and perspectives. My deepest and most inadequate gratitude goes to my father, J. M. S. Careless. Throughout this entire project he selflessly offered support, precision, and numberless felicitous phrases. No author could be better served; no care could be better expressed.

Although this is neither a religious nor devotional text, our Lord's presence was nonetheless as immanent, even in this study of secular kingdoms.

Chapter One

Introduction:
Federalism and Policy Initiatives

1. THE NATURE OF THE ENTERPRISE

This book explores and comments upon public policy initiative and adaptation in the Canadian federation in order to demonstrate the transformation of the institutions, politics, and philosophy of one level of government by the direct or ancillary activities of the other. This phenomenon radically alters—if it does not render meaningless—the conventional notion of "jurisdiction" in the federal division of powers. Progressively, K. C. Wheare's "spheres of independent action" have been replaced by emerging *levels* of responsibility assumed by governments as now they both compete for a prime role in the same spheres or fields which comprise public policy in Canada. It might be said that a vertical distribution of powers, whereby a government had reserved for it full authority over a function and the processes it comprised, has largely been replaced by a horizontal distribution, whereby governments apportion between themselves these various processes or operations within a functional area. This competitive rearrangement of roles and authority is in its general tenor labelled either as a decentralizing or centralizing trend in Canadian politics. A major consequence is the change in provincial and federal capacity to take the initiative or to resist it. And this capacity may be determined by attitudes and practices quite remote from the understood requirements of federalism.

The principles of federalism, as found in Canada, have of course been subject to constant change—worthy of praise or condemnation depending on one's perspective. This author believes that federalism is of continuing utility to Canada, not so much to preserve the past but to respond to growing disenchantment with bigness, uniformity, centralization, and the effects of delegation in national government. Accordingly, a Canadian federal system ceases to be solely a reflection of tradition, regional intransigence, or Quebec, as its detractors would argue. Its enduring strength becomes its provision for a formal commitment to small-scale self-determination, and thereby a provision for more pervasive democracy. It affirms, through local-national compromises, that political power derives from the people and should arguably remain close to them in accountable forms. That federalism, in fact, may falter in no way means that measures to seek greater efficiency through uniformity can adequately replace renewed attempts at effective government policy making continually tempered by a formal recognition of diversity. Nor can federation be dismissed as an out-moded form of citizen participation in the new wave of pluralism for it allows for actual regional governments, not merely for the formation of regional opinion. Accordingly, one needs to watch economic policies which in pursuit of their goals alter basic principles of federalism without explicit debate and decision among the people and authorities concerned.[1]

The topic under study is the formulation of government policies on regional economic disparities, an activity no less significant for contemporary Canada in view of its broad ramifications than was the Quiet Revolution in Quebec. This study seeks to go beyond the economist's assessment of the success of various regional development policies. Current analyses have skipped over the significance for the federal system itself of government response to regional disparities in fiscal capacity, services, and economic growth. The present work adds two new perspectives; first, it delineates the legacies of opinion and action on which our most familiar current programs are based; second, it considers the consequences for government structures and functions of the policy process applied to regional development. It is hoped that the conclusions reached will contribute a new understanding of the changing rationales which buffet or mould our Canadian federation, arising both from designs to promote regional economic prosperity and from the increasingly systematic policy making process that is involved.

The narrative approach of this study is designed to highlight the workings of change across time or the continuing phenomenon of policy initiative and adaptation. When, indeed, federations are analysed simply in terms of normative or descriptive models, observations may tend to be abstract and categorical. The end result may be a "stop-action" picture of a structure of relationships caught at a particular point in time, but not one which reveals the flows and natural tensions inherent in the policy making process or the factors pertinent to the "living out" of policies. The Canadian federation has rarely demonstrated evidence of having achieved any enduring balance between provincial or regional interests and central authority, so that it particularly lends itself to this dimension of study through tracing its constant growth and change, rather than through a mere classification of the genus of its operations.

Moreover, those characteristics most significant in a flexible, working, governmental relationship may not be the same as, or fully encompass, those used regularly to identify it. For instance, the federal constitution in Canada only sets forth a primary authoritative division of powers; but both constitutional divisions and even intergovernmental consultation (as a much-noted form of adaptation termed "co-operative federalism") have now diminished as central factors in shaping national or provincial economic development. Now instead the importance of preemptive initiatives and of fiscal capacity for effective self-determination in Canadian government is basic, yet is still underestimated by theories that continue to stress the geographical and traditional attributes of regional jurisdictions.

Much useful critical analysis, it is true, has been directed at the intent, efficacy, or format of specific governmental policies in Canada. Nevertheless, there has still been insufficient attention paid to how the public sector formulates and then, in federalism, lives with the structures, techniques, and programs which it creates—whether wisely or not. An examination of the response of Canadian governments to a wide variety of changing problems or directives may therefore put into clearer perspective the strengths or limitations of factors in the operation of Canadian federalism which have not been previously considered or held to be significant: above all, the vital importance of policies for regional economic development in the working of the system as a whole.

2. REGIONAL ECONOMIC DISPARITIES AS A FIELD OF STUDY

In this inquiry into policy making, the problem of regional disparities in economic growth,[2] as recognized and treated by governments and their bureaucracies, supplies a highly suitable theme for treatment, since it provides throughout Canada's history a significant exemplification of the working out of stresses and discontinuities in the attitudes, structure, and operation of the country's federal system. In general, the effort to solve regional disparities has raised the question as to whether all provinces should be treated equally in an economic and fiscal sense, thereby reducing the scope for diversity among their various regimes, and as well, whether the central government should be the agent for redistributing wealth. The maturing of commitments to equity and unity has been a century-long process in the Canadian federation. Throughout, the issue of regional economic disparities has vividly mapped the ebbs and flows of feelings on the subject. Examining these developments in terms of their preservation of a federal process and system in Canada—that is, one which retains both aspects of unity and diversity, as well as the inviolable prerogatives of central and regional governments respectively—leads to the broad conclusion that a system which might now achieve a pervasive and efficient solution of economic disparities may not still be able to preserve the political diversities of the federal union and the self-determination of its component units.

More specifically, such an examination also can contribute to a better understanding of some of the most vital aspects or concerns of federal relationships in Canada. They may conveniently be indicated as follows:

1. the ever-present question of diversities in economic and financial capacity evinced among Canadian provinces and the resultant bi-lateral relationships that have emerged between them and the central regime at Ottawa;

2. the critically important nature of developmental or growth-oriented policies in the federation and their role as supplements to other policy pursuits;

3. the problems faced by traditional, administrative, and political jurisdictions in dealing with regional growth policies that function both within and between provincial and central levels of government;

4. the relative importance of ends, means, and personalities in the designing and implementation of policies for growth;

5. the various shifts, to be noted in the process, in the relations of one level of government to the other;

6. and, in conclusion, the character—and future—of intergovernmental co-operation in the federation as demonstrated here.

A particularly distinctive contribution of this study lies not in the selection of policies on regional disparities as the topic for study, even though most investigations thus far have examined such policies for their impact upon the disparities rather than on the federal system as a whole. It stems instead from an examination of what might be called the administrative political process in Canada, whereby the officials responsible for conceiving, implementing, and co-ordinating regional development projects have very largely determined the "how" of government response (assuming that politicians and public interest determine the "when"). These politics of officialdom do not appear in annual reports, cannot be measured by performance statistics, and are not adequately described by the formal intergovernmental institutions for policy implementation. Accordingly, the inquiry may appear interstitial and even gossipy at times. Yet the public record rarely deals directly with these pre- and post-legislative activities. Where indirectly it corroborates these operations, references can be made; but primary and secondary literature that illuminates the officials' part in the stresses and strains of Canadian federalism is all too scarce.

The public record and other standard references have been thoroughly reviewed in the course of the inquiry. What might seem a light acknowledgement of them arises from their primary focus on the program achievements of political decision making. Documentation of administrative politics, instead, has been established through extensive personal interviewing of bureaucrats, to complement the writer's own experience as a public servant in the field of federal-provincial relations.

This administrative process closely affects the mechanism and programs of government, and the power of personality in such a setting has notably influenced the ability of one level of government as regards the other. Whether or not problems of regional disparities have yet been solved, the interplay of agencies, analysts, and administrators related to this endeavour has profoundly altered the Canadian federation. In this respect, to focus on a review of "success" of a particular program would be to divert attention from the broader implications of its impact. From the ensuing inquiry into the policies adopted for reforming the rural economy, building regional infrastructure, or improving provisions for education, it will become apparent that all required incremental changes, *ad hoc* abridgements, and diversions in the traditional institutions and politics of the federal and governmental system, in order to produce the economic success that was sought.

3. The Essential Theme

A major change in the Canadian federation was wrought by the federal government's coming to grips with regional problems of economic growth largely after 1957, following almost nine decades of grudgingly yielding aid to reduce provincial differences in revenues and services. It amounts to a reassertion of strong central planning authority, which was fully evident by 1970 and which has been confirmed each subsequent year. As with the centrifugal fluctuations of much of the previous century, this latest phase has really been an extra-constitutional form of adaptation, achieved through the workings of "co-operative federalism," joint programs, and sheer economic power. It has not necessarily been a goal deliberately pursued by either federal or provincial levels of government, but rather is the outcome of further refinements in the means and techniques of carrying on intergovernmental financial relations. The latter process, in the presence of federal budgetary surpluses and the lack of the same at the provincial level, has led today to the central aggrandizement of services and decision making powers over the provincial sector, all to provide greater control for removing the disparities in wealth between the rich and poor provinces in Canada. Control is the technological answer to most problems. But the present result of such activities has been the emergence of a federation whose central and regional balance has come to be decided by fiscal power, not by constitutional design, where the ideal of efficiency has surpassed that of participation, and general survival rather than mutual respect appears to be the operative principle.

What we see at work, then, in the pursuit of regional development is a century of Canadian public policy derived from varied convictions, to meet a problem that is at once ingrained and pervasively complex. Matters of regional disparity more than defence, transportation, agriculture, or social welfare have proved insatiable in their appetite for public funds and creative solutions. Progressively, the best of our liberal-technocratic minds have been applied, with the result that the philosophies and structures of federalism, distinctive tradition, or parochialism have been confronted by policies espousing efficiency, integration, and uniformity. The lasting intransigence of disparities, however, has meant that the battle has long been less than casual; and the cumulative impact of responses to all facets may now have its own form of side effects on the political relationships of the federation.

Regional disparities have ostensibly been defined as economic problems requiring economic solutions. Nonetheless, whether by design or default, political modifications have resulted as well, without assessment of the implications. From the specific studies below, it would appear that economic, systematic reforms not only initiate but reinforce such modifications. Cyclical as many may be, this study in general argues that several century-long secular trends are evident.

4. The Trends and the Pattern

The responsibility for fostering both the economic stability and growth of the Canadian federation was originally bestowed upon the central government. So it was that the federal regime at Ottawa after 1867 opened the West, established national commercial policy, and furnished additional funds to provinces to meet their governmental costs. What was unexpected was the inability of all provinces to draw equal benefit and prosperity from Ottawa's national economic policies and its direct financial aid to every province. Various deficiencies stemmed from the differing nature of regional economies. Provinces which fell behind were not financially or otherwise equipped to cope, and they turned to Ottawa as the recognized stabilizing force to provide government revenues equivalent to those yielded in provinces having more productive economies. While over the years periodic grants, joint federal-provincial programs, and greater means of access to taxes were provided, this federal aid in finance or services did little for the renewal of a provincial economy, with the result that poor provinces experienced chronic problems of near-stagnation in growth and received continual fiscal transfers to compensate for the effects of underdevelopment.

The question of achieving growth in these poor regions only emerged into explicit consciousness after decades of ordinary, ongoing *laissez-faire* business activity had accentuated the differences between strong and weak economies in Canada, and as some provinces began to exercise their constitutional powers over their own resource sectors to try to influence their own rate of growth. As the gaps in income, services, and opportunities widened between provinces that varied in resources and advantage of location, the largely peripheral peacetime function of government (in dealing with infrastructure and the security of income) was brought into the limelight after 1945 at both the federal and provincial levels. Citizens demanded greater social services from the public sector (largely a provincial responsibility) and, in turn, the poorest provinces requested still more aid for their sluggish economies which were falling still further behind.[3]

The year 1957 is considered a watershed (in chapter 3 below), insofar as it marked a decisive redirection of interest at the federal level towards the understanding and alleviation of regional deficiencies in terms not simply of financial transfers but of improving economic potential as well. Consequently, (as chapters 4 to 10 will indicate) the early 1960s were characterized by endeavours at both federal and provincial levels of government to deal with the structural deficiencies of the economic system;[4] deficiencies, that is, which had resulted in low productivity, unskilled labour, lack of technological or commercial sophistication, the financial drag of the chronically poor Atlantic region, and the uncertain future of the whole agricultural sector of the Canadian economy. By the mid-1960s, the programs thus established were converted from broad national orientation to specific concentration upon the most glaring disparities in certain regions of the country. The change returned a good deal of power and initiative to the central government at Ottawa, which now began also to establish differential relations with the provinces.[5] This development further required an increasing disregard of existing constitutional jurisdictions, with the result that often only the soundness of a province's economy protected it from federal probing into those diversities which caused national stagnation and drag.

Throughout the whole process there developed in Canada a gradual recognition that the arrangements for the new federation, imbued with the spirit of pioneer individualism, had not recognized or provided for the problem of economic inequalities. Provinces had been given equal protection for their cultural, social, and political rights; but it was soon discovered that this equal protection could only presume, not secure, equal economic capacities. Accordingly, to the extent that economic equality (that is, equality in income opportunity) is today envisaged as a proper goal, it may well have to be achieved at the cost of older traditional "equalities" in the Canadian federation—above all, the political right to equally responsible provincial governments throughout Canada. Much of the discussion in the following pages, in fact, displays the persistent strains in efforts to adapt the political values of a federal system in Canada to the centralized regulating structure increasingly required by economic considerations and increasingly engaged in efforts to secure a levelling-up in regional economic growth. The consequences (assessed in the two concluding chapters) are surely of crucial significance for Canadian federalism today and in the future.

General Responses to Inter-Regional Economic Differences

Chapter Two

Vision and Reality:
Identifying Regional Disparities

Regional development policies may evoke memories of the significant federal initiatives of the 1960s: ARDA, TVTA, ADA, DREE, FRED.* In fact, these can more properly be seen as only a later stage in a century of confronting regional disparities. The costly commitments of the 1960s are remarkable when contrasted with the non-existent federal-provincial economic co-operation of 1867. Over the decades, Ottawa became more intimately involved with first the effects, and then the causes, of regional disparities. Simultaneously these central initiatives directed to the national interest put greater pressure on the provinces to respond to the federal solution as it bore consequences for its component parts. A most basic feature of these policies can be traced to the establishment and preliminary refinement of federal fiscal and economic policy.

1. THE SHAPING OF ATTITUDES TOWARDS ECONOMIC DEVELOPMENT

Within the years 1846 to 1912 British North Americans, and then Canadians, first established their attitudes towards economic development and the role of the state in that process. In the same period, changes in the international and continental economic climate created stresses which tested the adaptability of the financial arrangements devised for the Canadian federal union. During this time there were two developments

---

*See chapter 3, Appendix B

that came to have critical influence upon the issue of regional disparities and its solution. One was the establishment of the central, "Ottawa" view as predominant and right in financial and economic affairs; the other was the failure of governments to relate difficulties with finances and levels of services experienced by some provinces to fundamental economic disparities. Furthermore, during this period, efforts were made to bring both levels of government into closer contact with each other's affairs because of the absence of such provisions in the primary division of powers contained in the British North America Act.

Distinctive in the founding of the Canadian federation was the notably low-keyed debate over the allocation of central and local responsibilities. Perhaps the fight of George Brown and his reform following for Representation by Population was the only crusade for a fundamental principle at Confederation. Indeed, Confederation in a most significant way was a political union based largely on economic interests, created in response to the increasingly vulnerable economic position of the individual British North American colonies. The colonies, troubled by their loss of protected mercantilism, faced with the likelihood of considerable defence costs being placed upon them by Britain, and squeezed between static or falling revenues and rising expenses, turned to one another in their collective distress—and all turned West. Just as the three Maritime provinces of Nova Scotia, New Brunswick, and Prince Edward Island themselves contemplated regional union to co-operate in external trade, so the British North America colonies together came to consider a political counterpart to common economic interests. Increasingly, a federal union became attractive to the Maritimes on economic grounds, and on political grounds as well to the two sections of Canada, deadlocked in their existing union of English-speaking Canada West and predominantly French-speaking Canada East. Thus Confederation was in this respect a relationship based on differences, not similarities: each province was seen as a complement to the shortcomings of another.

When it came to the form of the proposed union, the decisions taken were less difficult than those based on economic considerations but nevertheless reflected a preference for central leadership. The Confederation debates in the province of Canada's Parliament in 1865 revealed that many considered this federal scheme to be largely a shift of the colonial pattern of control to North America.[1]

With this transposition of imperial-colonial relationships to the respective governments of the new federation, the reaction to contemporary American fragmentation in civil war, and French Canadian interest in finding a central arbiter, Canada sought to establish a definite balance between the forces of unity and diversity. Nevertheless, the attempt to find a balance which would be more viable than the American example produced a strong emphasis upon unity and the central government. This was challenged in subsequent years by rich and poor provinces seeking lesser or greater central influence, respectively, upon provincial welfare. The constitution became only a "primary authoritative division of power," beyond which non-constitutional adaptations were eventually undertaken to solve differences in fiscal needs, economic capacities, and levels of services. In the years following Confederation, therefore, governments were to test, challenge, and reinterpret the dimensions of a constitution that favoured unity and bestowed the philosophy of "Ottawa knows best" upon the federation.

The *per capita* approach to the financing of the Canadian provinces by Ottawa was a political compromise of economic needs. George Brown admitted as much in the course of the Confederation debates: ". . . some of the governments are vastly more expensive than others—extensive countries, with sparse populations, necessarily requiring more money per head for local governments [than areas] more densely populated. But as any grant . . . to one province must be extended to all on the basis of population . . ."[2] Alexander Galt, the influential Conservative finance minister, echoed similar sentiments, "it would be impossible to justify any distinction being drawn between subjects of the same country."[3] After all, in politics Rep by Pop had been the great leveller of privilege. The aid provided, therefore, was not based on realistic consideration of each province's need but was to be equal, and, moreover, tempered by the Victorian preference for thrift and self-reliance.

Support to the provinces, while it was fixed as a statutory subsidy and thus paid annually, was nonetheless static. It was given at a flat rate per head to all, in whatever province they might be, and it was tied to census figures already out of date in 1867. Thus there was no factor to account for increasing or differing costs.

The aid provided by the federal government to the provinces, while not even barely sufficient as a solution to financial disparities, was even less adequate for economic disparities. Within the fiction of assumed economic equality of the provinces, as reflected in *per capita* transfer payments, however, there was no need to make these federal-provincial transfers reflect much more than the revenue lost by a province upon transferring its customs duties to the new union. Thus the financial settlements of Confederation were to aid the revenue and not the expenditure side of the provincial budget. They were not development grants; there were no minimum national standards to be achieved or new projects to be encouraged. They were, instead, thrifty allotments to provinces to continue whatever they had previously done with customs revenues and certain revenue-producing public works. To the extent that the subsidy was not to grow disproportionately for some, it reflected a belief in comparability of equal provincial capacities or, at any rate, a lack of interest in the comparability of services from one province to the next.

Confidence in the resourcefulness of each province was misplaced. Canadian provinces both at the time of Confederation and later had been far from equally or similarly endowed in economic capacity. Each province entering Confederation had had properties and assets of a different order. The Maritimes then had a small, costly, vulnerable manufacturing sector, unable to compete with central Canada and its economies of scale; their agricultural sector was small and mainly geared to local consumption. Their large ship-building, shipping, and fishing industries had always been at the mercy of conditions in external markets. They now became subject to rapidly changing technology. The coming of depression in the 1870s, and the application of steel and steam technology, affected the Maritimes economy seriously, whereas the central provinces, with larger, more diversified manufacturing resource sectors, and with competitive agricultural products, proved to be more resilient. Later, the dependence of an emerging Manitoba or Saskatchewan upon wheat and international, not domestic, markets similarly made their capacities and their economic attitudes different from the central provinces.

Given these diversities, the uniformity and finality of the original Confederation *per capita* settlement were clearly unsatisfactory. Instead of acknowledging this, however, and establishing grants based on need rather than optimistic assumptions of equal capacities, the political enthusiasm for a new egalitarian nation infused the expectation of equal economic endowments across the country. This developed into an elaborate legal fiction. An eighty-year period of contrasts between myth and reality followed; provinces were all treated similarly under the constitutional formulae, although because of the poorer ones' blatant differences in economic and administrative capacities they had to be progressively assisted financially. These transfers, solemnly called "temporary," "special," or "final" were for "rectification of the inequalities of the original settlement." As such, they did not require and so avoided any understanding of causes. Each grant dealt only with effects that were but reflections of more profound differences in economic structure. It was elaborately pretended (until the 1930s) that provinces were indeed self-sufficient, but had not been equally compensated for by the terms of the original financial agreements.

Ottawa was not prepared to change its impression that all parts were fundamentally sound. Its policy was to disengage from an intimate involvement in the province's economic or financial affairs. Indeed, even until 1912, its practice was to use stopgap appeasement for dislocated economies. The federal regime was convinced that the provincial regimes were faulty in operation, not in nature; thriftiness was the solution. For their part, the provinces were slow to adjust to the difference between reality and the visions of Confederation. They too believed—with diminishing confidence—that Ottawa's aid would only have to be temporary.

As the financial and trade stresses of depression during the 1880s and 90s deepened, federal-provincial encounters grew sharper. At the federal level Ottawa, itself short of funds, became more unbending, using the legal fiction of equality to prevent any further bilateral adjustments with provinces. Thus it was stated by the Macdonald government in 1885: ". . . the question is not after all whether Nova Scotia gets more or less than its sister provinces. It is an undoubted fact that when all is said and done the province will barely be able to pay its way. . . . The question is one of granting better terms and if the principle is conceded in the case of Nova Scotia it will have to be conceded all around. . . ."[4]

There was evidence of a growing federal impatience with the province's plight. The following statement by J. M. Courtney, the federal deputy minister of finance, returned the blame to the provincial level: "I beg to point out that throughout [the Nova Scotian documents] lies the inadmissible argument that because the province is financially embarrassed the Dominion must come forward and rescue it from the unfortunate position."[5]

Ottawa here was getting down to fundamentals, querying whether these progressive enrichments did not constitute a new turn to Confederation. Probably because the federal tone indicated a rejection of such a new direction the provinces deliberately missed the point. They did not claim to seek a new era of federalism but still sought to pin adjustments to "terms of the original settlement."

Because there was no automatic formula for aid to provinces in times of financial troubles, and because the legal fiction elevated the political above the economic motive in federal-provincial transfers, this hard period of economic stress made poor provinces feel more at the mercy of the central government than masters of their own situation. Thanks to the federal superiority of attitude, and to their own temptation to seek "hand-outs," provinces were not encouraged to become independent agents. And in the Maritimes there developed the opinion that their problems stemmed from the lack of equal treatment at Confederation and that assuredly they deserved better terms. But the claim for "readjustment of the initial terms" to reflect equality had ceased to be a useful argument, since what was being asked for was really intangible, lost opportunities which could not be measured by economic standards. The division between rich and poor thus took root in psychological as well as fiscal terms.

When prosperity reappeared around the turn of the century, a further sign of its return, and of accumulating surplus, was the federal government's increasing mood of generosity. In a dominion-provincial conference of 1907, Ottawa did listen to complaints; and it changed the size, if not the philosophy, of its statutory subsidies. They were increased 34 percent overall. Nevertheless, while there was the introduction of some growth elements into the calculation of payments for original and new provinces, (now assessed according to the latest census and the size of population), they still were uniform in application. Hence the subsidies again proved a windfall to rich provinces, who received a 58 percent increase, and of little net gain to poorer provinces, who received increases of only 29 to 40 percent.[6]

These changes nonetheless constituted a first recognition of a continuing Dominion commitment to the economic success of a province, and not just to its initial establishment. And although the Laurier Liberal regime had now made some recognition of naturally increasing costs (as Galt earlier had not), *per capita* payments still suggested that the size of a province's population and not the degree of its government activity was to determine the assistance given.

In sum, at Confederation a constitutionally superior central government had been established, with responsibility for aggregate economic growth and development. No special or continuing attention of the central regime to the provinces had been expected. Both had their own exclusive jurisdictions quite independent of one another. Provinces were believed to be equally capable in politics and economics as well as self-sufficient, apart from the statutory assistance granted uniformly to all. When in some regions reality had proved increasingly unrelated to this myth, both levels of government had developed a schizophrenic behaviour towards disparities in growth. Neither level was able or prepared to look closely and systematically at the fundamental causes, even in the harsh years of the late nineteenth century, so that only *ad hoc*, interim adjustments were made on the revenue side of the budget. The federal government could not properly tell whether poor provinces refused to cultivate direct taxes for historical reasons or lacked the revenue capacity. Prosperity in the early twentieth century postponed the diagnosis but did not much improve the attitudes of either governing level. The consequence was simply indecision tempered by accusations—as the future would make still more plain.

By now, however, the whole idea of government activity was changing.

The question of services, not finance, became the central theme after 1912. Few provinces had really been satisfied with the size or nature of statutory subsidies since Confederation. The subsidies as revised in 1912 have endured to the present day; but a new form of aid—the conditional grant—was soon to be added. In some ways this new transfer was no better as a remedy for the poor provinces, because the fundamental problems of their economic position, during the whole of this first period down to 1912, had remained unexamined, much less solved. Governments whether by joint efforts or otherwise, still continued to deal with the effects and not the causes of disparity or even poverty.

2. THE CANVASSING OF OPINION ABOUT REGIONAL DISPARITIES

In the period 1912 to 1940, the federal government took a hesitant step towards a continuing involvement in the economic affairs of the provinces through the means of conditional grant programs. Although initially short-lived, they did, nevertheless, constitute a supplement to financial transfers and extended the examination of inter-provincial disparities somewhat into the field of comparable services. Canada's particular choice of political leaders during these three decades and the strains and uncertainties arising from war and depression worked against a very coherent policy response being made. But the accumulation of more detailed evidence about regional disparities, provided by a spate of royal commissions, and the arrival of new economic theories were definite preparations for a change to still closer and more enduring federal-provincial relationships at a later date. The events of this period, therefore, constituted filling and shoring activities by governments and advisers alike, in efforts to build a more elaborate intergovernmental structure.

i) Shared-Cost Programs. Industrial booms in the cities, and the moderation of the frantic agricultural expansion of the West before 1914, placed new employment, health, and educational strains on the provinces, whose revenue and planning structures were not all comparable. Ottawa found it increasingly more difficult to remain aloof from these problems at the provincial level. Its responsibility for trade and commerce was involved if the Canadian labour force was unprepared for industrialization, badly located, or in poor health, and if the products it made could not be shipped quickly and efficiently. Here, then, was a first instance of the fact that some regional problems had become so acute that they affected national prosperity.

Ottawa's new response under the Borden Conservative government after 1911 was to offer grants on certain conditions to the provinces in four specific areas—and thereby encourage more provincial expenditures. They were agricultural training (as early as 1912), technical training (1919), road building (1919), and employment offices (1919).[7] Several features of these conditional grants reveal the innovation in thinking that had occurred at this time. As a component of federal-provincial financial aid, they were a significant recognition of a need for specific provincial expenditures rather than for revenue, and hence denoted a change from the older block grants made to provincial treasuries. Unlike statutory grants, moreover, the conditional grants incorporated some concept of the cost of providing a basic, specific service. They constituted a recognition of the appropriateness of federal intervention to secure national goals, while reflecting a cautiousness about extending the federal jurisdiction in view of rulings by the Judicial Committee of the Privy Council. Initially, too, the grants were aimed at improving infrastructure and skills, both absolutely essential to a region's development of its economic potential, in contrast to later grants which sought basically to equalize and support income.

At the same time, the federal response was still in part traditional. Provinces were not treated differently, despite the evidence of differing problems and needs. Population remained still the only basis for payments and there was no discretionary adjustment for differences of topography, urban density, the cost of labour, the existence of provincial policies in the same field, or the priorities and plans of recipient governments. For example, agricultural "need" was not significantly related to the occupations of a provincial population. The heavily urbanized and industrialized provinces got more money for agricultural training than those sparsely populated and rural, where adjustment was more pressing. And federal assistance to roads clashed with provincial designs for their location and quality. Whereas Ontario wanted the money to develop a southern grid to serve its industrialization, Ottawa wanted to provide a northern link between the West and East.

As the cyclic downturn of economic activity returned after the First World War, the existing level and form of federal-provincial relations was soon brought under attack by provinces. This time, however, the federal response was not to ignore the problem but rather to divert it to Royal Commissions. A post-war contraction (after a brief inflation) was not an unexpected event. But two developments made adjustments in vulnerable regions—normally painful enough already—unduly difficult. First, the war-time boom had taken over the impetus of expansion from a waning National Policy with one significant difference: it required the regions to seek external and not domestic markets. This regionalization of Canada's economy meant that each province had its own special and distinct trade pattern. Each was increasingly unwilling, then, to submit to regulations that would jeopardize its security, while provincial tax and marketing regulations were devised to favour its own products.

Second, market adjustment in poor regions was exacerbated by monetary policy. Faced with inflation, immediately after the war the banks had taken the classical braking action of cutting back credit. Such a move was not designed to counteract the expected trend gradually, with the result that the whole economy was brought abruptly to a halt—hurting seriously those who were most dependent upon credit: the working man, the western farmer and the small Maritime businessman. Regional economies were now reinforced by regional identifications of interests, in terms of agriculture versus industry or debtor versus creditor.

The result of economic regionalization, and federal commercial and monetary policy was political fragmentation. In parts of the country there was deep disgust and disaffection, encouraged by a deflation that lasted until 1926. In the past, moreover, provincial disaffection with federal policy or lack thereof had resulted in largely empty threats of secession made by provincial governments to Ottawa. This time, after 1921, disunity threatened Prime Minister King within his own ruling Liberal party. The unruliness of Quebec Liberals and Western Progressives in Ottawa, or of Maritime voters and provincial governments elsewhere, made his parliamentary majority at times precarious.

ii) The Duncan and White Commissions. Given the degree of political fragmentation it was, of course, unwise for the federal government of the day to venture into new fields. King used the numerous royal commissions he appointed for the sake of political expediency to promote unity. Each region had to agree to the prime minister's cash solution of specific claims of other regions before he would accept the settlement of their own. In this way he refused to appoint the Dysart and Turgeon Commissions set up to deal with Western discontents,[8] until the West accepted the federal terms for settling the Maritimes' claims as proposed by the Duncan Commission.[9] The terms of its Report of 1926, however, by no means settled the Maritimes' fiscal and economic problems, as was shown when the depression of the 1930s struck, so that the financial needs of that region again were the subject of study by the White Commission of 1935—and a Nova Scotia provincial commission of 1934 also considered the question on its own.

In approaching the discussion of financial transfers to provinces, Duncan and the subsequent commissions touched upon various concepts which might at this point be usefully distinguished.[10] In treating regional or provincial disparities two modes of payments could be used: to the provincial governments to relieve disparities of services to citizens, or directly to citizens to relieve disparities in income (and ultimately in the services that they purchased). Increasingly the federal authority had to decide whether to deal with Canadians directly or through provincial authorities whose limited jurisdictions or capabilities might not provide the maximum social benefit from its expenditures.

In considering transfers to provincial governments there were at least three criteria that were most frequently discussed: i) payments in respect of the inequalities of past Confederation settlements, on the grounds that provinces had not all been given the same consideration; ii) payments in respect of fiscal capacity, to compensate for the inability of a provincial government to raise revenues equivalent to other provinces, using a comparable tax rate; and iii) payments in respect of fiscal need, to compensate for the inability of a province to provide a reasonably comparable standard of public services, in relation to other provinces, without an unduly high rate of taxation. It will be noted that each requires a different measurement: the first, a matching of terms of payment (*per capita*, debt allowances, grants-in-lieu of public domain) for all provinces; the second, equalization of the *per capita* revenues of similar governments; and the third, a complex measure of comparable program costs, comparable services, standards, and tax burdens to determine the need for financial assistance.

To put the following discussions in perspective, all the commissions of this era expressed an implicit or explicit preference for consideration on the basis of "fiscal need," while rejecting "historically unjust settlements." In fact, however, the fiscal need approach has proved to be too difficult and too contentious to measure comparably, and thus it has never been used except implicitly in shared-cost program criteria.

The most impressive feature of the Duncan Commission was the way in which it decisively served two purposes: it speedily provided King with the quick settlement of the Maritimes' rankling claims while denying any historical guilt of the federal government or lasting commitment on that ground; and, at the same time, it opened a debate concerning the positive role of the central government in a federation. Within its slim report, Duncan also skillfully grasped the conceptual nettles of equality, equity, needs, and capacities.

Undoubtedly to King's delight, the Duncan Report laid to rest the major provincial claims before the commission that past federal injustices against certain provinces could once again be compensated for. However, to fill the moral vacuum for the payments which were to be granted, Duncan introduced the important concept that government, and in particular the federal government, had an explicit commitment to promote equity and equality among provinces in their share of aggregate national prosperity. In the report there was, however, only an imprecise indication of the "need" for comparability in the performance of provinces, and of the need to end the relative isolation of provinces in their economic success or failure. Ottawa had to take a long term commitment of some sort to the adjustment of differences beyond provincial control. Duncan suggested that while "It is not possible . . . to maintain always an accurate balance . . . reasonable balance is within accomplishment if there be periodic stocktaking."

In measuring, if imprecisely, the gap between provincial revenue capacity and expenditure needs, the commissioners were implicitly committing one level of government to the assessment of the contemporary performance of another. They withdrew at this point, however, and avoided the unpalatable task of trying to establish, in a fragmented, regionalized economy, a new principle of periodically-revised, annual payments to the poorer provinces. The Duncan Commission passed such a long-term question on to its inevitable successor and suggested an interim "readjustment of the financial statutory agreements."

Generally, however, the succeeding White Report[11] written in the midst of the Depression of the 1930s was more cautious than Duncan or other contemporary commissions on the same topic.[12] While it refused to reconsider the Duncan settlement or other settlements of the past, arguing that beyond a certain point all finer and final judgements became purely arbitrary in their verdict as to fairness, it still was tempted to think in terms of a once-for-all settlement rather than a continuing federal commitment to deal with regional disparities. Provinces were still expected to be largely self-sustaining entities. The White Commission offered no elaboration of or contribution to Duncan's brief introduction of the concepts of equity and equality. Instead, much of its effort was devoted to dismissing the wisdom of the concept of fiscal need, which had been developed by Nova Scotia and constituted the core of the Maritime argument before the commission.

The Duncan Commission had not rejected the concept of fiscal need decisively enough to prevent further provincial development of the idea. The White Commission clearly attempted to lay the concept to rest. It felt it was a dangerous principle, because the federal government would thereby sit in judgement on a provincial government's need, passing reflections upon the thriftiness of its expenditures and the burden of its taxation. While the White Commission believed in a federal commitment to equity and equality, it could not see this as a "deliberate rule of action generally," and was shy of the idea that there should be a regular formula-like access of one level of government to the next. It was concerned about the opportunities for partisanship and the violation of jurisdictions that such regular payments might provide. Federal payments to provinces were apparently to rest upon Ottawa's own concern and generosity.

Nevertheless, the concepts of fiscal need or a regular federal commitment to provinces were not, in fact, completely dismissed. The White Commission assessment of equality was based upon the provinces' wealth, taxable capacity, and frugality of expenditures—all the required measurements for determining fiscal need. While admitting the impossibility of accurate calculations it did base its conclusions for payments upon a "remarkable disparity" of existing costs of government. Both the use of fiscal needs and the objective measurement of disparities were to reappear in the notable successor to the White Commission—the Rowell-Sirois Commission.[13]

iii) The Rowell-Sirois Commission. Most of the interwar royal commissions were part of a general ferment reflected equally in welfare economics, the social unrest of the Depression, and the growing evidence of chronic regional disparities in Canada. At issue was the role of central government in a federal state with regard to both classes and regions of depressed people. What was developing, to parallel Keynesian theory, was a view of the mutuality of federal and provincial interests. Should provinces be treated as mere subordinate jurisdictions, or should they still be recognized as sharing equally with the Dominion that important function of government which seeks to promote the happiness and welfare of the people? To what extent should federal policies have in mind provincial partners when they were trying to realize far-sighted national ends? To treat disparities in people's incomes, for instance, there was little need to make transfers simply to provincial *governments*. At stake then, in the questions raised by these commissions was not just the immediate size of the financial settlement but the utility of federalism to the urgent problems of economic depression.

In essence, there were two possible degrees of intergovernmental involvement based respectively upon equality or needs. All commissions of this period had rejected any further levelling out of past inequalities of Confederation, which therefore raised the question of the appropriate premises for continued federal attention to the provinces. Any further transfers would be going beyond the past concept that all provinces were merely being afforded equal treatment. Were subsidies to be paid to some provinces differentially on the basis of fiscal need or to all provinces in such a way as to preserve equality of treatment? In providing for increased debt allowances or reconveying Crown land, the commissions based their arguments upon equality. In urging or implicitly using the concept of fiscal need for the financing of "general government" they were giving the federal government the deliberate task of making differential payments.

The dilemma posed by the possible recipients (peoples or governments) of increased federal activities and the question of discriminating policies had remained unsolved by the above-mentioned commissions because they had approached the problem descriptively. The Rowell-Sirois Commission of 1937–40, on the contrary, took a definite stand at the outset—in favour of enhanced government roles at both levels—and in its study provided a clear blueprint for one possible solution. Its recommendations were based on an appreciation of the complex relationship between economic and political efficiency.

On the one hand, the commission opposed the regional fragmentation of the economy by arguing only central direction could provide tax reform, expertise, efficiency, and a new fiscal initiative: ". . . conflicts of policies between the Dominion and provinces have become a luxury which Canada cannot afford. The sterility of policy which chronic conflict was apt to engender might be an even greater evil than conflict itself. Fiscal policies must be in a single hand and responsibility for action must be assigned with unmistakeable clarity."[14] On the other hand, it clearly recognized the provincial "fact." Solutions had to be reached in terms of existing regional divisions and had to achieve effectiveness for their political units: "The Commission's recommendations are based in accordance with its terms of reference on the financial and economic analysis it had made. . . . It appreciates the existence of many non-economic and non-fiscal factors and its recommendations are not those which might have been made for a more homogeneous country. The Commission's plan seeks to ensure to every province a real and not illusory autonomy."[15]

The National Adjustment Grants (and Commission) proposed by Rowell-Sirois were to be a major, flexible tool to affirm both unity and diversity in Canadian federalism. Associated with a transfer of provincial debts to the federal level, as with taxes, this device would be separate from the measures Ottawa might otherwise take to ensure economic stabilization. The National Adjustment Grants scheme clearly protected the provinces' autonomy in expenditure while transferring to the federal government their major revenue sources. Based as they were upon need, the Adjustment Grants overcame the limitations of *per capita* subsidies and conditional grants. And the National Adjustment Grants Commission provided for independent adjudication of the need, a problem which had compelled earlier commissions to back away from making any wholehearted commitments.

The commission brought to a rigorous set of conclusions the many inconsistent policies which had been developed since Confederation to cope with disparities between provinces. Its Report of 1940 probed far below the superficial levels of disparities in finance and services to the fundamentally different nature of provincial economies. Its recommendations were indeed the first of any made to government that were founded upon a sensitivity to these basic economic disparities, and they stressed the necessity for continuing federal assistance wherever such fluctuating differences affected the level of services. But the commission staked its solution upon a comprehensive and carefully integrated blueprint in which the economic have-nots gained at the expense of the haves, and provinces received greater revenues from the centre. Because the rich provinces (by this time Ontario, Alberta, and British Columbia) would accordingly have received no grants, this represented a declared ending of equal financial treatment for all the constitutionally equal provinces. Given that both the rich provinces and the central government held the upper hand in their respective situations, prospects for the political success of the recommendations were doubtful at the least. But at this stage, the initiative for reform in the federal system, after more than two decades of examination by experts, now passed finally to the politicians.

3. The Polarization of Opinion over the Prospects of Equity Policies

During the 1920s and 30s, governments in Canada had permitted the delicate question of an extended and redefined federation to be explored. Whatever the various positions to be taken or reversed during the period following, 1940–57, one fact became undeniably evident: both federal and provincial governments were increasingly compelled by Keynesian economics to show a closer interest in the economic and fiscal concerns of one another. The Rowell-Sirois Report had only introduced the higher value of achieving uniformity of services and opportunities as more important than the exacerbation of extreme diversities through independent provincial growth.

i) Response to Rowell-Sirois. Various public explanations were given by governments for rejecting the report of 1940, from the priority of wartime problems or the inappropriateness of federalism evolved by the Royal Commission, to the need for "fundamental economic solutions first." Yet a basic reason common to Ontario, British Columbia, and Alberta was their unwillingness to accept a subsidy scheme whereby only the poorer provinces regularly received federal transfers based upon need, not share of the population. The rich took refuge in the tradition that Canada had no charter myth of collective aid to subscribe to; in fact, it had the legal fiction of equality as its own charter myth, so that no region would require abnormal help from the federal system.

The rich provinces pointed out with splendid detachment that, "There are five regions in Canada. Each of these units is distinctive and there is nothing to be gained and much to be lost in attempting to bring them to a common level."[16] Whether this form of logic was historically accurate or not, it was wholly irrelevant to many of the other provinces, which, far from wishing to remove Ottawa's presence and regain taxing powers, wanted to become even more closely attached to the federal regime's wide and wealthy tax base. The poorer provinces, like Manitoba, were also quite willing to transfer their share of power over direct taxation if it meant the end of the federal use of indirect taxes, which, being regressive, hurt exporting and import-dependent regions.

To bring the two provincial sides together would have required vigorous unifying action by the central government. Furthermore, there was the special problem of Quebec, which for cultural reasons preferred to re-move itself from any new fiscal arrangement in return for straight cash transfers from Ottawa and low-growth provincial expenditure. Prime Minister King, however, did not take any initiative towards reconciliation. He could not call upon any base of strong popular support: most voters identified with their province; there had been resentment with federal dithering during the Depression; and the provinces with the most votes were the rich—so very jealous of any loss of prosperity. In the throes of war, King was even less willing to guide a long process of modifying recommendations and especially did not wish to strain further a federation that was already headed into the emergency crisis over conscription. In any event, the prime minister did secure a transfer of taxation powers to Ottawa, and this was his main objective.

But the decision to suspend response to Rowell-Sirois during wartime nonetheless represented only a political solution to the theoretical and economic issues of the report, and the resulting interlude placed the poor provinces in an even more desperate position after the war. This was particularly so since the hostilities brought only temporarily greater in-dustrial activities. Investors recognized that the economic position of the Maritimes and Prairies had not changed except for the artificial and external stimulus of the war. Thus they strained existing capacities instead of engaging in new investment. After the war these industries contracted back to their output at less-than-full-capacity. Little had changed. Little could change without confronting the fundamental issues that Rowell-Sirois had indicated and King had avoided.

In 1945, King offered to the provinces those features of Rowell-Sirois which he felt were applicable to the post-war situation—particularly to meet the fear of inflation. His proposals contained an agreement for the continuation of the wartime transfer of provincial tax fields to Ottawa in return for various options of federal cash transfers to the provinces and a series of extensive proposals (known as the "Green Book" proposals) for federal implementation of social, welfare, health, and countercyclical policies in provincial jurisdictions.[17]

While the tax agreement thereby worked out in 1946 moved back somewhat to an earlier era of ignoring fiscal need (in that payments were to be based upon population), it did at least formalize the recognition of rich and poor provinces. It offered a choice of three options for joining the agreement, each of which was intended to appeal to provinces of varying wealth. Admittedly, the 1946 tax agreement (as its wartime predecessor in 1941) did continue to pay the richest provinces the most money, because the rental of lucrative provincial tax fields cost money. Yet it still was possible to say that since Ontario (and Quebec) refused to join the 1946 federal offer, Ottawa made its terms more attractive to the poor than the rich, for otherwise the latter could not be "b(r)ought" into the scheme. Given that the nature of the country's economy and finance would always make it difficult to please all provinces, Ottawa did, in 1946, take a small step towards giving special consideration to the poorer provinces. The length of its stride grew greater as the decades passed.

ii) The Federal Attitude to the Post-War Economy. The federal Green Book proposals of 1946 reflected the beginning of a serious concern for countercyclical economy policy as urged by Keynes. At times it overwhelmed Ottawa's more traditional reticence about extending its powers —particularly into the provincial sector. Rowell-Sirois' pressures for a strengthened central government were taken up with great enthusiasm at Ottawa, as indicated in the Green Book proposals. They culminated in the federal White Paper on Employment and Incomes, perhaps the most explicit statement of federal responsibilities in terms of the Keynesian perspective.[18] True to Keynes, Hansen, and to Rowell-Sirois, these policies were primarily for stabilization, not growth, and they reflected the fears of severe unemployment in a rapidly contracting post-war economy.[19]

The federal economists felt that problem to be inevitable. If investment was going to fall, the consumption side of the income equation had to be increased in order to preserve some degree of stability in the economy. It was hoped that private income through welfare transfer payments would prevent consumption from plummeting. Federal policies, thus, were aimed at providing social security benefits: mothers' allowances, unemployment insurance, miners' and fishermen's grants, disabled persons' assistance and, later, hospital insurance. All of these programs would reduce the income disparities between classes and regions and coincidentally lessen the impact of regional economic fluctuations. What was required, it was felt, was less government participation in industry and more stabilization to offset the inequalities of a free, capitalistic market. Any continuing expansion or employment was to be provided by private and corporate undertakings. Every effort was made at Ottawa to keep post-war estimates at an absolute minimum and to withhold approval of projects expected to compete unduly with private demands for men, materials, and equipment. What interventions Ottawa accordingly did undertake in regional economics at the time were mainly to provide income stability through welfare payments, public health programs, prairie farm finance, and export credits. Its concern, as stated in the White Paper of 1946, was primarily with individuals not regions: ". . . our objectives are high and stable employment and income and a greater sense of public responsibility for individual economic security and welfare."[20]

Thus fiscal and economic orthodoxy determined that the federal government's voice in post-war economic development would be a small one. A continuing program of development would indeed have stood little chance of surviving unscathed from countercyclical operations. The public works "shelf" of projects for countercyclical policy that was set up was a poor substitute for regular and high-priority development projects. They were not used, in fact, because the expected deflation failed to occur. They became a hard core of small, low priority projects that gathered dust and grew out of date in cost and technology. The period, moreover, did not require an active central government, when considered in terms of its traditional roles. The Liberal government under St. Laurent from 1948 to 1957, thus tended to supply more national connections (such as a Trans-Canada highway, oil and gas pipelines, microwave systems and railways), or monetary policy (bank rate, and national marketing boards), to provide for the freedom of action of the private sector and to furnish services where private initiatives could not or would not assemble sufficient capital (Central Mortgage and Housing Corporation).

While Ottawa paid careful attention to individual income and health security measures in the immediate post-war years, the poor provinces felt that more attention should be paid to establishing a sound foundation in certain regions for economic expansion. But generally, it was believed that a period of prosperity in the aggregate (and regional statistics were not well refined) would redound to the advantage of all regions.[21] As well, there was the continuing federal concern, as voiced in the 1920s by

Prime Minister King, that federal-provincial activity might not only extend federal interest outside of its constitutional boundaries, perhaps even unconsciously, but also abridge the due process of legislation through the cabinet and parliamentary system at both levels.[22]

Ottawa still argued in principle from a point of constitutional propriety. But change was on its way. Direct grants from the federal authorities to individual universities, started in 1953, were apparently not beyond their "interest" even though this was clearly a provincial jurisdiction. In the academic community, Maurice Lamontagne, later to be a federal Liberal minister, was arguing a coherent case for a dominant federal role in regulating aggregate demand along with a minor role in economic development.[23] Furthermore, while the central regime was still disclaiming that its concern for disparities in provincial services and revenues should next be extended to regional economic development and growth problems, the provinces were fast developing interests which required closer federal and provincial liaison. The theoretical mutuality of federal and provincial interests which had been deduced from Keynesianism was being made a practical reality. For the rapid expansion of provincial and municipal activities inevitably overlapped the enlarged spheres of specific federal interests in health, welfare, income security, and other aspects of stabilization policy.

iii) Provincial Institutional Innovations. As the fifties opened, the hostility between rich and poor provinces which had particularly been evident in federal-provincial conferences dealing with the Rowell-Sirois Report was being significantly reduced by the deliberate efforts of a new Conservative premier of Ontario, Leslie Frost, who took office in 1949. Gone were the bombastic performances of Hepburn and Drew and their simplistic statements of what "the provinces" wanted, for in their place was a different type of Ontario premier. While Ottawa was still unable to turn full attention towards regional solutions, concerned as it was with the effects of war, with stabilization and price controls, Ontario began to make initial conciliatory steps towards a flexible and integrated federation.

The Ontario regime had come to realize that, because of the uneven development of the country, problems had arisen which were now reflected in the different types of subsidy arrangements in effect. It admitted that certain provinces would suffer considerably if left to their own tax sources. Frost suggested, implicitly, that the fact of multi-faceted federalism be recognized. Claims of the rich and poor, (and those in between), he felt, should be made individually upon the federal government: "Some measure of assistance in the form of subsidies from the federal government to the provinces . . . is necessary . . . if for no other reason than to reduce marked inequalities in service which may arise because of variations in tax capacity. Probably there is no one formula which will meet the needs of the provinces desiring to come under such a subsidy formula."[24]

Perhaps it could be said that these observations of Ontario made in 1950 helped enable the federal government to make concessions to regional inequalities in a new equalization payments scheme of 1957.[25] In no small way did the relations between Ottawa and the provinces, and between all provinces, improve as a result of the example and lead given by Ontario's moderation. It answered the problem which had faced Ottawa in the past, of having to appear to treat all provinces simultaneously and equally. Ontario's aim, of course, was not purely altruistic, for if it could encourage Ottawa to have a special relation with each province then its problems as a particularly fast-growing province would be attended to separately. Ontario did, in fact, get a sufficiently "special" offer in 1952 to lure it into a tax rental agreement with Ottawa.

Interest in closer fiscal and economic relations with Ottawa was also a result of government activity in rich and poor provinces alike to stimulate and maximize economic growth within their territory. Limited funds and tight budgeting made Nova Scotia, Saskatchewan, and others interested in supplementing fiscal-need or fiscal-capacity cash transfers with internal reforms in the organization of government policy and for the encouragement of economic expansion. Most provinces spontaneously initiated several changes which eventually became more developed in the 1960s. Certain features were broadly common here. For instance, all established a post of economic adviser close to the premier and some provinces also appointed a staff of economists, such as Nova Scotia's Department of Economics, New Brunswick's Office of the Economic Adviser, Saskatchewan's Economic and Planning Board, and Ontario's Department of Economics. In most cases, however, the impact of the economic adviser and his staff was not immediately significant. The accountant's yearly budget was still the main "planning" document; and policy priorities largely depended on the linear and incremental growth of past policies, the political power of the minister in the cabinet, or more often on his personal relation with the premier. In most provincial governments the premier still acted as a one-man planner and as Treasury Board.

Saskatchewan went furthest in the 1950s in attaching to its Cabinet not only a Planning Board but also a Budget Bureau and a Cabinet secretariat. Some success was achieved by these bodies in specific program planning. But it never developed priority planning or an overall plan chiefly because of limited staff and inadequate statistics, the fact that a small provincial economy largely concentrated on wheat did not require sophisticated planning, and a firm belief that Ottawa had to be a forceful and joint partner in the process.[26]

In Ontario, the position held by the provincial economist, George Gathercole, was unique. Apart from being the deputy minister of the Department of Economics, he was a very close personal friend of Frost. The Ontario government of the 1950s was run very largely by these two men. This special access to the pinnacle of political power gave the economists in Gathercole's department a rare freedom to roam critically through existing or proposed government policies with a more integrated or long-run view than that of career civil servants in program departments, conscious (as were their ministers) of their own empires. So it was that Ontario's proposals for Hospital Insurance, set forth at the Federal-Provincial Conference of 1957, and most of the supporting statistics used by the conference for establishing a joint plan were developed in this Department of Economics, not in the provincial Department of Health—or in its federal counterpart.

In most provinces, however, the economists were few in number in the fifties and not yet central to the decision-making process. Often their energy was absorbed by efforts to diversify the provincial economy, predominantly by attempting to encourage industry. Saskatchewan operated incentive schemes to bring industry to the province and even attempted to run several industrial projects publicly, with little success. In 1958, Nova Scotia established Industrial Estates Limited (IEL) and to this day it provides—with only limited success—serviced industrial parks to attract business.[27] Both provinces attempted to encourage manufacturing, which was at best only a peripheral part of their economy. New Brunswick under Premier Flemming in 1952 established the New Brunswick Development Corporation with greater success, since it concentrated upon the province's natural resource sectors. A Voluntary Economic Planning Board was established in Nova Scotia. Neither Alberta nor British Columbia, however, used their economic advisers to any visible extent. In British Columbia the office was dropped upon retirement of the incumbent in 1957. In Alberta the Department of Economic Growth became progressively downgraded over the years, becoming Industry, then Industry and Labour, and, finally, Industry and Tourism. But because of their considerable wealth based upon primary resources, neither of these provinces had the need nor the inclination, given their highly conservative political views, to encourage industry by discretionary public policy.

In institutional arrangements the Maritimes went beyond provincial creations and established interprovincial fact-finding bodies. The privately-staffed and financed Atlantic Provinces Economic Council (APEC) was established in 1956 by Premiers Robert Stanfield of Nova Scotia and Hugh Flemming of New Brunswick—both of them new premiers elected on reform platforms. Together with the Atlantic Premiers Conference, and the Atlantic Provinces Research Board (governmental), APEC sought to take a new regional approach to problems of poverty.

All these organizations and institutions contributed a new statistical monitoring of economic performance to the federal relationship. Their sombre but persistent record of a region's or sector's under-achievement provided more reasoned material for each premier's assault on Ottawa. The poor provinces, moreover, expressed a mounting dissatisfaction with the paucity of the concept of fiscal capacity. Their concern with growth evolved from the fact that the welfare payments to the province (through the fiscal capacity formula) or those to the individual were not concerned with generating income locally to pay for services. The standard form of assistance treated symptoms, not causes. Beginning in the fifties, therefore, attempts were made to supplement this welfare tradition through pressure on Ottawa to secure development assistance, initially for infrastructure such as irrigation, roads, and power. The poor provinces thus asked for facilities necessary for economic expansion which in the rich provinces had already been supplied as a result of continuing economic growth.

iv) Summary. By 1957, regional economic disparities had been analysed by royal commissions to the extent of the statistical data available, but they had only been treated incidentally through federal initiatives towards tax sharing and personal income security. These policies remained incremental because of the bargaining required for entry into provincial jurisdictions though they were less and less improvised. As a successor to *per capita* statutory grants and shared-cost programs, the policy of interprovincial fiscal equalization had been far from fully comprehensive. Rowell-Sirois' blueprint for a balanced redistribution of privileges and responsibilities between federal and provincial governments had been set aside. In consequence, the process of intergovernmental bargaining, rather than applying blueprints or altering the Constitution, was to continue as the major adaptive feature of Confederation. In place of the Rowell-Sirois Commission's elaborate solutions were shorter-term and narrower tax rental and Green Book schemes, which were the product of federal initiative and provincial reaction instead of whole scale adoption of commission, or "third party" designs. While more specific and often bilateral these arrangements nonetheless carried forward federal assistance to deal with low points in personal social security and provincial revenues. The concentration of both these in chronically depressed regions of the country resulted in the new national "floors" having special relevance for such areas. Still, the next step in closer federal-provincial liaison would have to come through more intimate federal involvement in the economic activity of the province.

Already these federal initiatives were less unpredictable, less paternalistic, and more amenable to negotiation, increasingly conducted in the formal setting of federal-provincial conferences. They represented a significantly new peacetime extension of federal-provincial co-operation, but were products of philosophies which sought to fuse the political divisions of the federal system for efficiency in the provision of social services, income supports, university financing, and economic stabilization. In response, provinces which were equally uncertain about the preferred direction of federalism prepared to develop a position of strength from which to bargain. This was achieved, based on popular demand for their services and better knowledge, through research, of where they wished to go. Improvements in their statistical and analytical capacity particularly, and the provincial bureaucracy generally, together with the entry of new premiers upon the scene, resulted in greater competence among the provinces in assessing their situation.

This soon produced a growing challenge to the tradition that "Ottawa knew best."[28] The crises of war and depression—real or unrealized—had exhausted the ruling federal Liberal party (and officials) who had reigned almost continuously from 1921. Although there had been the growing commitment of the federal government to the affairs of the provinces, sparked largely by Keynesian philosophy, the latter were not prepared to accept uncritically Ottawa's proposals for them. The rejection of the Rowell-Sirois recommendations and the Green Book proposals, the winning of better terms in various tax sharing agreements, the disputes over federal aid to universities, and the federal concessions to provincial demands for a more generous national hospital insurance scheme, all demonstrated that Ottawa's peacetime role was in the process of being transformed.

In short, then, the events of this whole period from the twenties to mid-fifties represented a gradual equipping of governments to take a more energetic role in the field of regional disparities. What still was lacking was the will at the federal level to bend the collective efforts of rich and poor alike to the issue of regional growth. That situation was altered by four major events, next to be discussed.

Chapter Three

The Watershed to the Present

During the later 1950s, the federal government began to adjust to a new peacetime role partly on its own initiative and partly as a result of provincial pressures. A significant aspect of its altered role was a commitment to reduce regional differences in economic growth. This was not merely a further inevitable response to the stubborn questions of disparities in finance and services, but one also determined at this particular time by the new philosophy of economic growth, and by the policies of the new Diefenbaker Conservative administration.

The attempt to reduce regional disparities further by devising policies for economic development was one aspect of a more general redistribution of power, finance, and initiative, both between federal and provincial levels of government and between private and public sectors. What made it topical at this time were certain occurrences in the late 1950s which served as major catalysts in precipitating federal action regarding regional development. The Tax Sharing Agreement of 1957–62 represented a distinct recognition of different provincial fiscal capacities. The Royal Commission on Canada's Economic Prospects[1] challenged politicians to grasp Canada's vast economic potentials. The election of the Conservatives under John Diefenbaker in 1957 created a federal government which was pledged particularly to the cause of disadvantaged regions and their people. And the beginning of recession in Canada in the same year revealed the need for a new approach by government to economic regulation and expansion.

1. TAX RENTALS AND TAX SHARING

It will be recalled that the federal government had only tentatively ventured into the private and provincial sectors of economic activity,

believing them to be self-sustaining and self-regulating (apart from requiring certain fiscal grants, tariffs, market, and exchange controls). The
central regime generally was prepared to put forward capital where
private investors would not provide essential infrastructure to support the
incomes of citizens and to support the revenue of provinces, but it eschewed a positive role of directing economic or regional development.
Regions were left to develop their own potentials except where acute need
was demonstrated; even then federal aid was *ad hoc* and bore no implica-
tion for a permanent remedial treatment of disparities.

If provinces were to be left on their own to stimulate economic growth,
whatever the federal precautions to prevent the downward fluctuations
of revenues or personal incomes, they would require either greater access
to tax revenues (for the rich) or a greater levelling in the disparity between provincial tax yields (for the poor). Of first importance, then, to
a spirit of change was a new approach to intergovernmental sharing of
tax revenues. This largely was a brain-child of officials and ushered the
federal politician into a new era of a permanent, growing commitment to
poor regions—as well as providing greater fiscal freedom for the rich.
The Tax Sharing Agreement signed in 1957 for five years represented a
final adjustment to the form and philosophy of sharing revenues of a
common tax field between governments. Most of them, indeed, had been
dissatisfied with the Tax Rental Agreements of 1947 and 1952. Ottawa
disliked being accused of trespassing upon a provincial field of taxation,
which the rich provinces argued was theirs by right of first occupancy and
had only been leased or rented to the federal level for the duration of the
war. The poor provinces claimed that the options for rental payments
from Ottawa clearly favoured the rich and left no true option for themselves.[2] They were likewise concerned to see that payments were not tied
to the fastest growth indicators, and hence did not help the poor provinces
to stay even at their inferior level *vis-à-vis* the rich. Finally, they disliked
the absence of protection from stagnation or decline in growth elsewhere
that would be more seriously reflected in poor regions. All provinces
protested against what they considered to be the transfer to a peacetime
situation of a wartime formula based on buying provincial consent rather
than redistributing revenues.

In addition to the adverse opinions about the existing tax sharing of
the day, Rowell-Sirois' general criticisms still bore relevance. It had
attacked the tendencies of government to ignore special regional problems, to avoid formulae, to substitute politics for automatic support, and
to secure short-term bilateral "deals" in federal-provincial arrangements.

The 1957 Tax Sharing Agreement was designed to answer both the
immediate criticisms of governments and the conceptual criticisms of the

34

Rowell-Sirois Commission. In the new agreement Ottawa declared that it regarded income tax fields as shareable and not ones to be rented as the exclusive territory of one government. This attitude indicated a return to a more literal and strict interpretation of the BNA Act, that direct tax fields were open to both levels irrespective of first occupancy, and it also warned the provinces that Ottawa would no longer "share" its collections. While the central regime would abate certain percentages of its collections to the provinces to prevent double taxation up to an appropriate level, it stressed that revenues collected for and transferred to the provinces were, henceforth, a percentage of *actual* tax rates—not a *per capita* payment or special cash subsidy from the federal government. All provinces could set their own rates equal to or higher than the abatement; the responsibility for revenues and provincial tax burden would be entirely their own.

Having clearly allocated the power of direct taxation to both levels, and having ended the feuding over one level influencing the tax rates of the other, the agreement next granted all provinces greater tax room. This was of value primarily to the rich provinces. For the poor, however, a series of major principles of equity were included. All provinces were treated equally, whether in or out of the agreement. There was no range of options; non-participating provinces received from Ottawa escalation and stabilization payments upon their collections within the federal abatement similar to that paid to those in the agreement. Such payments were automatic, calculated on a visible formula and stabilized by being guaranteed to meet ninety-five percent of the previous year's revenue.

The federal payments were "equalized" annually by the following method. All provinces whose tax collections under the federal abatement failed to reach the *per capita* yield of a similar abatement in the two richest provinces would receive a new equalization payment to meet that level. Thus poor provinces were guaranteed a revenue yield not only equivalent to that of the wealthiest provinces but also one growing at a similar rate. In addition to equality and growth, the formula provided impartiality by the use of reliable, relevant statistics, and flexibility through a number of variables in its basic computation which could periodically be altered to suit the relationship between have and have-not provinces.

The 1957 Tax Sharing Agreement should be regarded as an important milestone in reducing financial disparities in two respects. First, it constituted at last a regular and flexible federal commitment to equalizing the fiscal incapacities of poor provinces, and set the theory and operation of revenue equalization (based upon the concept of fiscal capacity) and the practice of joint tax collection for the following decade. Second, as a supplement to *per capita* statutory subsidies and special grants, it represented the last and most major adjustment in this form of revenue support. While the size of tax abatements and the scope of equalization were increased considerably in the 1962 and 1967 Agreements, the major emphasis of this decade was away from innovations in a revenue access or support formula and towards economic development programs on the expenditure side of provincial and federal budgets.[3] The fiscal capacity principle of the 1957 Agreement was also supplemented on the expenditure side of provincial budgets through a modified form of fiscal needs payment by means of "implicit" equalization in shared-cost programs.[4]

In a sense, federal tax paternalism, which was reduced by the 1957 Agreement, was replaced during the 1960s with paternalism regarding expenditures. Having achieved a workable formula for reducing financial disparities, the federal government was prepared next to achieve uniform national standards through increased joint programs. Initially, new programs were designed to adjust further the discrepancies between surplus revenues at Ottawa and mounting costs of responsibilities for expenditures at the provincial-municipal level. Eventually they were modified to reduce also the differences in expenditure costs between rich and poor provinces, now that provincial revenue disparities were being reduced through equalization. This approach was supplemented in the late sixties by further attention to provincial disparities in potential for economic growth. In any case, shared-cost programs and direct discretionary policy for growth also supplemented the traditional forms of transfer payments to provincial governments. But more important, unlike unconditional transfers—whether statutory in character, tied to fiscal capacity, fiscal need, or tied to serving individuals—these programs of the 1960s were increasingly remedial rather than palliative in nature.

2. THE ROYAL COMMISSION ON CANADA'S ECONOMIC PROSPECTS

The new interest in economic potential was inspired by the Royal Commission of 1957, headed by Walter Gordon, which was concerned with national problems other than tax sharing. Disparities between regions, it was discovered once again, were not solely confined to services and revenues. During the 1950s Canada had readily filled the shortages of natural resources in the United States, such as in oil, pulpwood, gas, and hydro-electric power, and this had resulted in a booming economy. The Gordon Commission revealed the shallowness of this boom, its regional and sectoral concentrations, and forecasted the results for Canada's economic potentials. The activity of government had been to encourage resource development to the fullest, with little thought for the development of other sectors of the economy, the decline of the agri-

cultural sector, or the worsening competitive position of Canadian manu-
factured products as a result of outdated technology, high costs, low
productivity, poor market assessment, and the commercial resurgence of
war-torn nations.

Unlike the stabilization concerns of Rowell-Sirois and the wartime
Keynesians, however, the Gordon Report used new concepts. As well as
giving meticulous detail about inter-regional differences, it talked about
economic "potential" rather than the Keynesian notion of balance.[5] It
looked at potential or problems in a long-run sense and predicted what
changes were necessary for improvement. While praising the freer grants
of money to poorer provinces by the federal government without the old
constraints of the 1920s, it stressed that there were problems of incapacities and inefficiencies, of size, education, and skills that were not merely
to be solved by larger and larger grants. The report pointed to the need
for structural change throughout Canada that could only demand the
attention, money, and patience of the public sector; problems and
economies were not necessarily self-correcting. Implicitly, too, it reinforced the Keynesian approach to public policy—that the state of the
economy, not political partisanship, should be the basis for Cabinet discussions on expenditures. These decisions, Gordon indicated, had to have
increasing *economic* as well as political support.

3. DIEFENBAKER'S REGIME AND TECHNIQUES

The report was delivered to the incoming Conservative regime under
John Diefenbaker. His Cabinet was curiously equipped to respond to the
challenge. While Diefenbaker himself might have appreciated the clear
presentation of the long-run economic potential of Canada's regions
prepared by the Gordon Commission and the Maritime Studies done by
the Atlantic Provinces Economic Council, his disposition was to suspect
advisers and technocrats of political bias, especially those appointed by
others or by Liberal governments. He arrived at his distrusts honestly,
for the officials under his predecessor, Louis St. Laurent, had risen so
close to the actual making of policy during that increasingly tired political
regime, that policy initiatives largely depended upon their "withinputs."[6]
While in the Opposition, Diefenbaker had come to feel the policy makers
were not government MPs, but faceless officials. Peter Newman has
pointed out that Diefenbaker thought that the arrogant Liberals had
become isolated from public opinion because they preferred to listen to
their officials: "He, therefore, did not consult with his civil servants; they
in turn stood back and watched him conduct his regime without their
counsel."[7]

In consequence, a systematic dialogue between the policy-setting and executive levels largely failed to develop; neither Diefenbaker nor the officials who had become intimately involved in policy making under the Liberals managed to find a means of compromising their opinions to secure a productive rapport. The consequence was the absence of a clear direction in Cabinet policy making. As one minister observed, "Instead of discussing what we should do next, we spent most of our time arguing 'how do we get out of this one'?"[8] And the Cabinet's most ferocious internal struggles were indeed over fiscal policy.

The most notable characteristic of Diefenbaker's government was, in fact, the jeopardizing of attempts at a consistent and long-run policy (such as budgetary control, or adjustment of declining economic sectors) by *ad hoc* interventions for short-run and immediate political gain. Hence prairie farmers received cash support, thwarting whatever efforts were being made to encourage mobility of inefficient and small farmers to other sectors.[9] Gordon's approach to national economic readjustment was largely ignored during this term of office; the professional channels to the Cabinet were closed by the prime minister. The Cabinet stood at odds over immediate crises, and ministers attempting gradual reforms were unprotected from Diefenbaker's repeated interference in their affairs, and his indecision once he had interfered.[10] In such a climate, the bureaucrats pursued program operation and refinement with their provincial equivalents largely without a guiding political philosophy. The instability of federal intention in this period of administrative politics was in contrast wth growing provincial resolve. In fact, an opportunity was created for provincial self-confidence that did not have to face repeated federal initiatives at every point of provincial jurisdiction.

4. THE EFFECTS OF RECESSION, 1957–62

The biggest challenge to the Diefenbaker Cabinet was the recession of 1957–62. By 1963 the result of countercyclical policies instituted to correct this were judged to have erred fifty percent of the time.[11] In particular they revealed the lack of depth and systematic behaviour in government activities. Countercyclical fiscal and monetary policy had been developed in a period of prosperity and had remained largely untested for its effectiveness and sensitivity. Its outlook, moreover, was cyclical not secular, shaped by a belief in balance, not potential. But there was no comprehensive planning in peacetime government and only rarely even the most rudimentary "planning" for various processes. Co-ordination was frequently *ad hoc* and under the personal control of the first minister.[12] There was a lack of statistics, and of the bodies and processes required for a long-run projection of activities through the various planning stages of articulating goals, setting priorities, developing programs, and providing for finance and management.

The process of policy making was partisan and discontinuous. Cabinet decisions were frequently a result of a particular minister's power. The Department of Finance was poorly equipped or inadequately empowered to scrutinize plans before they went to the Cabinet. Finance also had little control of big departments or influential ministers. The national as well as provincial budgets were, accordingly, "expenditure determined"—with Finance having to find revenues for expenditure commitments.

Keynesian countercyclical policy failed its first real test in the recession partly because government did not appreciate the operational lags of these policies. Conservative ministers responded with the former approach of C. D. Howe, that of spending one's way out of a decline. This time, however, the injection of public funds (such as in Winter Works or Trans-Canada Highways) not only failed but played havoc with balanced budgeting. Canada entered a prolonged slump, worse than the American, and with the highest unemployment in the Western world. The country seemed unable to resuscitate itself.[13] Its economy continued to perform badly in terms of every economic *desideratum*: growth, stability, price levels, balance of payments, and employment.

A more serious problem arose not from a wrong timing of policies but from the use of wrong types of policies. The point made by the Gordon Commission was that investment, which had sparked the boom of the fifties, could not revive it without profound structural adjustments which had then been ignored.[14] Few politicians, at any level, had been willing to encourage labour training, organized marketing, consolidations of enterprises, or improved productivity, instead of more visible development projects which produced resource exploitation on an impressive scale and created jobs (even if only semi-skilled ones). Canada had sought flashy signs of development and had allowed the essential intangibles to deteriorate seriously. There was little new secondary industry. Few persons had the answers, and the probing for solutions only resulted in hesitancy and clashes. In one instance, Ottawa tried to stimulate private investment by loans and special funds, while the Bank of Canada raised interest rates to the highest level in forty years.

Ironically, despite their own self-willed isolation from expert advice and their highly crisis-oriented operations, two creative influences emerged in the Conservative Cabinet, John Diefenbaker and Alvin Hamilton—the Minister of Northern Affairs and later of Agriculture. They, in fact, fashioned a political environment that allowed for attempts at new regional policies. Diefenbaker's interests (and hence often Cabinet policies) were not primarily national, but were really oriented towards his favourite clientele, the disadvantaged, in this case the Prairies and the Maritimes. The Conservative leader was greatly impressed by the work of Dr. Merril Menzies, an economist who had attacked the Liberals' *laissez faire* attitude to resource exploitation, the relegation of a responsibility for economic growth to private enterprise, and the government's worship of national GNP statistics. Diefenbaker took up Menzies' cause: that the Liberals' welfare and short-run stabilization policies were inadequate, and that they ignored not only the preservation of a Canadian national identity, because of resource exploitation by foreign interests, but also the failure of certain regions to share in overall prosperity. This thesis was a politically useful tool. It had served during the 1957 election to stress a contrast between the two "old-line" parties when the third, the socialist CCF party, argued that one did not exist. The Conservatives had consequently portrayed themselves as a real alternative to the Liberals, who had stood for re-election largely on their past record.[15]

Despite the volatility of his policies, Diefenbaker in office did switch the direction of government activities away from a tenacious concern with national and maximizing policies and left for the federal governments of the sixties a commitment to less prosperous regions. The Atlantic Provinces Adjustment Grants and several power projects which he instituted were useful means of moving capital and infrastructure into certain regions of the country. While these actions were largely empirical responses to political issues of the moment, they nevertheless left an unfulfilled but very real enthusiasm at Ottawa for a vision of similarly prosperous regions in all parts of Canada. If nothing else, Diefenbaker gave to government the visionary spirit of discovery.

Alvin Hamilton contributed some of the policy and administrative machinery that this vision required as well. Although he vehemently disagreed with his leader's emphasis upon the short-run and political, Hamilton was able to take advantage of the highly unregulated or unsystematized behaviour of the Tory ministers to assemble, without concern for the precedents of past executive-administrative relations, a novel mixture of expertise and enthusiasm that effectually produced a major exploration into the regional and sectoral problems of agriculture.[16]

5. THE SUBSTANTIVE ASPECTS OF GOVERNMENT CONCERN FOR GROWTH

Thus at this point philosophies, personalities, and politics all combined to focus government action upon regional disparities. "Control" again appeared to be the issue; free market and social forces, both national and international, were not eliminating regional disparities, and these contributed to a poor national performance. Economic activity was henceforth to be encouraged and eventually specifically directed by government —a reversal of the postwar policy.

Predictably initiatives emanated from Ottawa rather than the provinces, although progressively the areas of activity were central to provincial jurisdictions. These initiatives did not, however, threaten but rather enhanced provincial government, since tax sharing, hospital insurance, and infrastructure support all constituted financing of provincially designed activities. Nevertheless, it should not be assumed that in this interlude Ottawa politically and administratively acquired an altruistic commitment to federalism for the long term, so that it undertook to underpin provincial governments. Instead the transfer of funds to the provincial (and private) sector was an economist's response to allocate resources to "bottlenecks," in this case the lagging partners in the traditional federal division of responsibilities. Moreover, Quebec's detached and protectionist position made Ottawa reluctant to propose any radically altered division of responsibilities which might open profound rifts across the country. Much could be done first before this redistribution became the only alternative. Thus the provincial governments reaped the current rewards of Ottawa's interest in greater public activity because it was conceived still within the traditions of Canadian federalism.

Regional economic development did not become an overnight commitment of the federal government after 1957. In fact, the specific concentration upon "slow" regions was only an eventual result of a prior concern for national economic growth in certain sectors. It can be seen generally that Ottawa had in earlier years only gradually faced the issue of regional disparities. But it should be recalled how very far it had progressed from the Victorian view of government frugality held by Galt and Brown, through the caution of Prime Minister King, to the elaborate post-war proposals for a federal reduction in disparities of services between provinces, and finally, to the Tax Sharing Agreement of 1957 and the new attitudes of the Diefenbaker Conservative government. One may contend that throughout this time the fact of regional economic disparities, although ignored at Confederation, had nevertheless relentlessly forced itself upon the federation, and had progressively won concessions not only in the priorities of government but also increasingly, in the structure of the federal system itself, as witnessed by the regular federal-provincial meetings, the joint programs, and research organizations. What once had been treated as disparities in government revenues or levels of services had thus by the 1960s been recognized as merely symptoms of the basic differences in income, productivity, and economic development among Canadian regions. The solution required greater attention to the quality of their resources, labour, and capital supply, all problems far beyond existing transfers of welfare funds.

In any event, economic growth was now to become a central concern of Canadian federalism; the policies engendered to promote it and remedy regional disparities would henceforth be of major consequence. Across the watershed, in the sixties, Canadians were increasingly to entrust the federal government with power to enter into a series of highly significant regional development schemes.

These schemes are set forth in the following chapters of this study devoted to the character of the growth programs that thus were instituted. From these, four programs pertaining to manpower, agriculture, industry, and the particularly disadvantaged Atlantic region, have been selected for closer examination, in order to trace how goals, methods, and co-ordination were developed in the Canadian federation of the 1960s in the process of designing policies to deal with sluggish aspects of economic growth.

Two general patterns might be identified at the outset as indicating the trend of government thinking throughout the new and important period of the 1960s. The first is that attention to economic growth increasingly became centred upon specific regions. During the period, policies diverged from earlier decades in their concentration upon *structural* aspects of national growth: labour skills, industrial location and productivity, and the controlled adjustment of naturally declining sectors. Besides, by 1967 most of the programs had been revised or replaced to secure a disproportionate concentration of funds in areas where below-average performance was indicated.[17]

A second pattern was the change in government expenditures, from the traditional welfare support to cope with the effects of dislocation in the early sixties to the critical treatment of their presumed causes by the end of the decade. In this regard, it was notable that despite popular feeling that the economy had to be stimulated into action after the recession years of 1957–62, the Liberals, who returned to office in 1963, along with their officials, began seriously to question the usefulness of past habits of dispensing welfare and the treatment of effects rather than causes.

Hence greater attention to economic growth moved government activity from generally encouraging investment and providing infrastructure at a national level in the mid-fifties, to treating national structural problems in the early sixties—to dealing with causes of improper resource use as well as inadequate decision-making procedure—and, finally, to a concentration on structural and infrastructure problems in depressed regions towards the close of the decade. That is the process we now turn to observe.

Appendix A

The Measurement and Magnitude of Regional Disparities

Because the following chapters deal primarily with the stress and strains of programs for regional disparities it might be useful at the outset to provide a quantitative indication of the problems that had to be solved. They can be divided into categories which correspond with chapters 4 to 8: the poverty of manpower skills, rural areas, industrial productivity, and the entire Atlantic region. The figures used in the following sections have been kept largely to magnitudes in percent to facilitate comparisons with other countries.

1. RURAL POVERTY

As with most problems, the selection of relevant data to a very large degree determines both the definition of the problem and its solution. In the context of the early 1960s, therefore, the agricultural problem was defined as a "rural income and poverty problem." The reader is referred to the study by Helen Buckley and Eva Tihanyi for a discussion of what constituted "income" and "poverty."[1] If the Canadian average urban income of 1961 were given an index of 100 per family, the rural non-farm average was 69 and the rural farm average, 63.[2] Rural-urban disparities were compounded by geographic variations. If a criterion of poverty of a rural family is established as defining "poor" those farms with a total capital value of less than $25,000 but gross sales of $3,750, not only did 44 percent of all families residing in rural areas of Canada fail to rise above the poverty line but in the Atlantic provinces this increased to 68 percent and in the Prairies to 50 percent. Perhaps the only encouraging aspect of these 1961 statistics was that the concentration of extreme poverty in specific regions eventually led to comprehensive programs especially for these areas.

Moving to the rural-urban context, the continuous pressure to reduce labour inputs and increase capital and managerial inputs for greater productivity in the primary resource sector not only released 330,000 farmers into the non-farm rural sector during the 1950s but also considerably increased the supply of low-skilled rural labour into the urban market. Thus the rural poverty problem emerged as a specific case of a more general phenomenon: the limitations in people for adjustment to rapid change.

2. Manpower Deficiencies

The adaptability of the labour force depended considerably upon its skills. The manpower problem which arose in the late fifties was not simply one of high unemployment resulting from a declining rate of economic expansion. Indeed it was that, but more permanently it was a structural problem of manpower unskilled for changes in the basic structure and technology of the economy. In fact slower economic growth meant a lessened ability to make the adjustments which were required. In specific terms, during the 1950s not only was there a 32 percent decline in employment in the agricultural sector but labour eventually had to adjust to a swing towards "white collar" occupations which was associated with a shift from direct production labour to indirect labour of 15–20 percent and a shift from non-office employment of 16 percent.[3] Of importance here is that the changes in technology altered substantially the character of job opportunities leaving a gap between the training and experience of workers and the skills required by the new technology.

Inadequate education was the most serious handicap in the labour market of the late 1950s. The unemployment rate for people who did not complete primary school was more than double the rate for people who completed primary but not secondary school and six times the rate for people who completed secondary school.[4] The rate of unemployment was greatest, correspondingly, in the primary resource sector, the Atlantic provinces and Quebec (Atlantic unemployment 1961, 10.0%, Quebec 9.1%, Canada 7.0%). Moreover all regions reflected evidence of "creeping unemployment" where despite boom and bust in each successive period of the 1950s, the percentage of people out of work had been higher than in the preceding, equivalent period.[5] The Select Committee of the Senate on Manpower and Employment offered the following warning in

1960: "This situation must be viewed with a sense of urgency. Without any question we must devote a much larger proportion of our resources to education and training of all kinds. . . . An immediate programme must be initiated and no effort must be spared in making the public aware of the situation and the need for remedial action."[6]

3. INDUSTRIAL PRODUCTIVITY AND TECHNOLOGY

Once again, the issue of economic productivity was closely related to the level of unemployment (i.e. demand for products) and the presence of skilled manpower to operate, manage, and direct research in Canada's secondary industry. Productivity lies at the heart of a country's economic welfare and the prosperity of its people. The Economic Council of Canada stated, "Without adequate productivity growth an industrial nation's competitive position and its international payments position may be subject to disturbing pressures and strains."[7] In terms of "labour productivity" (i.e. output per employed person or per man-hour), Canada's 1955–65 performance placed it in fourteenth position among the industrialized nations of the Western world. In terms of total output, Canada's rate of GNP growth exceeded that of both the United States and Britain but when the more rapid rate of population growth was taken into account it fell behind these and twelve other countries. Compared to its own past efforts the increase in productivity in Canada, 1950–55, was 3.5 percent whereas it slumped seriously to a level of 0.9 percent during the 1955–60 period. While much of this slump was due to a necessary adjustment of productivity in agriculture (a drop in 1955–60 to 3.0 percent from 9.1 percent in 1950–55), and to the economic recession of 1957–62 which created slack, nevertheless non-agricultural output dropped from a rate of 2.3 percent in 1950–55 to 0.4 percent in 1955–60.[8] In terms of a potential rate of growth in output, Canada achieved (1955–63) a rate of 1.0 percent per year against a projected potential of 1.9 percent per year.[9] As the Economic Council observed, "Annual productivity gains are generally measured by very small numbers and changes of a few decimal points . . . may well spell the difference between having a dynamic economy and a slack and sluggish one."[10]

What was disconcerting to the Gordon Commission and government economists during the late 1950s was that heavy unemployment was not the only or prime cause. Certainly the fluctuations in aggregate demand since 1955 had prevented the full and efficient use of plant and equipment but Canada also lost competitive strength because of an inappropriate fixed dollar exchange rate during this period. While there was expansion during this time it was confined to the service sectors of the economy with little conseqence for productivity. With a slack economy neither efficiency nor labour mobility for its most productive uses were pressing objectives. In fact industries in Canada complained of a shortage of specialized research staff, statisticians, scientists, and managers. While Canada was a capital intensive country in business investment—often above the level of the United States—it could not purchase comparable efficiency because of short production runs, frequent changeovers of assembly lines and an inability to spread design and engineering costs.[11]

5. THE ATLANTIC ECONOMY

It has been customary to begin a discussion of regional disparities with a definition of the magnitude of disparities in terms of income *per capita* and from that enumerate the components of the low *per capita* income in the Atlantic provinces. Personal income *per capita* as a flow of income to individuals has, as its largest component earned income which reflects the productivity of labour and capital. It is thus a useful indicator of the level of economic output produced in each region. Since 1940, personal income *per capita* in the Maritimes has been about 70 percent of the all-Canada figure. While the growth in *per capita* incomes has been similar in all provinces over this time, the absence of a higher rate in the Maritimes since 1946 means that they have been unable to reduce the gap in disparities. The Economic Council stated that ". . . it would be hazardous to assume that rapid economic activity [after 1946] although providing a favourable environment would be sufficient in itself to reduce interregional income disparities significantly."[12] It was this failure of the Atlantic economy to be able to grow in a favourable economic climate and narrow the gap between poor and rich, as it had prior to 1946, which eventually led federal officials to turn to the structural incapacities of the Maritimes.

The Atlantic region has demonstrated a persistent under-utilization of manpower resources by virtue of both a high seasonal unemployment rate (amplitude of Maritime variations, 1955–59, 13.4 percent, Canada 7.4 percent) and a low labour force participation rate (45 percent Maritimes, 55 percent rest of Canada). Low levels of business investment in the Atlantic provinces during the 1950s (only 57 percent of total new investment *per capita* in Canada) prevented a new source of continuing employment in the region.[13] Investment in housing, spending by institutions and by government departments, had a limited impact in stimulating continuing employment.

While most attention could be placed upon the difference in structures of the economy in various regions of Canada, the Economic Council emphasized that, *"It is the regional differences in industrial productivity rather than in economic structure which exert a major influence on regional income disparity."*[14] Once again this returns the issue to rates of participation, of unemployment, investment, and educational training. Further, and finally, it might be observed that regional public expenditures on growth–related services, including education, health, transport, and resource development has been consistently and substantially lower than in other Canadian regions.[15]

6. Financial Magnitudes of Programs

In the four studies which follow, attention has been directed to non-financial aspects of each program. To assist the reader in appreciating their fiscal and economic impact a rough indication of the expenditures in each of the four programs is provided. Program modification and National Accounts revisions make a precise longitudinal analysis complex; accordingly these figures are intended to give only a general picture of magnitude.[16]

i) Agricultural rehabilitation (ARDA) and intensive regional development (FRED).
ARDA, commenced in 1962, was supplemented after 1966 by the more comprehensive FRED funds in selected areas (Gaspé, Manitoba's Interlake, Mactaquac, and Bay of Chaleur Regions in New Brunswick, and PEI). Under both agreements, long term commitments (up to ten years) were undertaken between federal and provincial governments, some continuing to this day. Ottawa shares 50 percent of costs under ARDA, and a variable amount under FRED. Total federal commitments, to March 1975, amount to $853 million. Actual federal expenditures, between March 1962–March 1975 amount to $669 million.

ii) Manpower.
The cost-shared Technical and Vocational Training Assistance Act 1960–67 was superceded by the exclusively federal Adult Occupational Training Act (OTA) in 1967. Transitional payments between the two acts for capital projects were also made available. Total payments under TVTA, including transitional grants and the value of tax abatements to Quebec (in lieu of a shared-cost program) 1960–69 were $1,526 million. Under OTA, payments between 1967–74 amounted to $2,482 million, on an expanded program.

iii) Atlantic Development.

The Atlantic Development Board's program expenditures on infrastructure were made between 1962 and 1970, at which time its projects were merged into the DREE administration. Total expenditures by ADB over this period amounted to $141 million, including a special Ministry of Transport cost sharing of area trunk roads.

iv) Industrial Incentives.

By 1975 this program had two distinct streams: the original assistance to industries seeking expansion, new plants, or new locations; and, assistance in special areas to faster economic and social development projects critical to general growth. The original industry support program commenced in 1963 had by 1975 spent $614 million, while the Special Areas program (now the General Development Agreements) spent $563 million between 1969 and 1975.

In terms of the overall federal budget, DREE and Manpower programs comprise 2 and 4 percent of total expenditures by all departments. Although a seemingly small proportion of total federal dollars, their highly discretionary character, especially in low-budget provinces, made an impact of considerable significance, year over year.

Appendix B

Acronyms of Frequently Used Phrases

ADA	Area Development Agency
ADB	Atlantic Development Board
ADIA	Area Development Incentives Act
ARDA	Agricultural and Rural Development Act
APEC	Atlantic Provinces Economic Council
BAEQ	Bureau d'aménagment de l'est du Québec
BNA Act	British North America Act
CIC	Community Improvement Corporation
COEQ	Conseil d'orientation économique du Québec
CPAR	Comité permanent d'aménagement des ressources
DREE	Department of Regional Economic Expansion
EIC	Economic Improvement Corporation
FRED	Fund for Rural Economic Development
HRDA	Human Resources Development Authority
MDA	Manitoba Development Authority
NES	National Employment Service
OEA	Office of the Economic Adviser
OPQ	Office du planification du Québec
OTA	Adult Occupational Training Act
PDA	Program Development Agency
PPBS	Program-Planning-Budgeting-System
PCO	Privy Council Office

RDIA	Regional Development Incentives Act
SPS	Special Planning Secretariat
TVTA	Technical and Vocational Training Assistance Act
VEP	Voluntary Economic Planning

The Operation and Control of Specific Programs for Reducing Disparities

Chapter Four

Policies for Manpower Training

When one surveyed the lack of growth in Canada, or more especially the difference between regions in the 1960s, it was evident that a highly skilled and readily mobile labour force was, as a productive resource, a crucial factor for the presence or absence of development. One of the first tasks facing governments, then, was to cure the growing deficiency of skilled manpower in the country. While insufficient training was a nationwide problem, it was particularly severe in Quebec and the Maritimes causing unemployment there to be close to double the normal rate in the rest of the country. Lack of skills, unemployment, and underemployment were, indeed, the main factors explaining the differences among regions in economic potential during the 1960s. It is therefore appropriate that the study of programs to reduce economic disparities begins with government policies to improve the quality of manpower in Canada. And so, although never explicitly designated as a regional development "tool," federal manpower policies implicitly were conceived to "level up" skills in depressed areas as a basis for development in that very area.

The problem had begun in the preceding decade. Canada had depended upon the flow of European immigrants into the country to provide skilled labour for its rapidly expanding industrial sector. The labour required had to be increasingly better trained as the economy moved towards greater processing of its resource exploitation. But as the European nations began to recover from the war and retain their own skilled labour, the quality and quantity of immigrants to Canada became insufficient for industrial demand. Furthermore, although there had been veterans' retraining programs in Canada they had been concentrated in manual skills, and unemployed workers were just not capable of filling the specialized job vacancies. Finally, in addition to the adult training and skills required by the existing workforce, there was clearly insufficient vocational capacity to handle the wave of students who were the emerging product of the post-war baby boom.

1. THE TECHNICAL AND VOCATIONAL TRAINING ASSISTANCE ACT

The response of the federal government was the Technical and Vocational Training Assistance Act (TVTA) of 1960 which enabled agreements to be signed with each province providing for an equal sharing of costs incurred by the provinces for technical training of youths or adult retraining, a higher proportion of sharing for capital expenditures and a sharing of living allowances for adult trainees. The original initiative was not joint but arose from several sources within the federal government. Not surprisingly the American experience provided a prior and important "demonstration effect."[1] The link with the American research, which never resulted in as comprehensive or as continuing a program as that formed by the ten sections of TVTA,[2] was provided by Ross Ford, an Albertan education official who had worked several years in the late fifties with American authorities and was eventually called to Ottawa by the Department of Labour to draft a training program that would meet the incapacities of the Department of Immigration.[3]

The federal Labour department had only limited data on labour need or supply, and therefore had to devise a program based upon existing statistical knowledge of the problem or objectives. Economists with a knowledge of labour statistics, theories of the firm or economic forecasting were not plentiful and could be found primarily in the Departments of Labour or Trade and Commerce.[4] The Dominion Bureau of Statistics and Department of Labour both felt the other should tackle the very large and complex task of gathering and measuring data on the workforce and the issue was not resolved.[5] The National Employment Service (NES) which had been established in the 1930s was situated outside the government in the Unemployment Insurance Commission (UIC) in an inferior position with little access to management or the unemployed (as will be explained later). Hence the initiative for TVTA came primarily from the Labour officials and was unsystematic because of the lack of data on performance and needs.

While the provinces were not jointly involved in the formation of TVTA, their attitudes and activities were sympathetic to such an innovation. They all had worked with Ottawa since the war under the Vocational Training Co-Ordination Act of 1952, which had provided a forum for like interests and personnel (though the grants available were not always fully taken up by the provinces—Duplessis, for instance, had prevented any acceptance by Quebec). Quebec had developed its own youth training institutions since the war. Premier Duplessis' isolationist policy and use of the French language had both combined to place Quebec outside most interprovincial and international migration. In an effort to obtain a highly skilled, but self-contained French-speaking labour force, the province had thus established, and could well boast of, numerous trade schools, institutes of technology,[6] apprenticeship centres, and specialized schools.

Alberta, under the influence of Ford prior to his transfer to Ottawa, had begun as well to expand its vocational training plant by setting up the Northern Alberta Institute of Technology in 1961. The province already had an enviable record of a well-educated population. Ontario, under Stanley Randall, who became minister of development in 1963, had begun to assess the adequacy of its high school program—in short, whom it caught and taught—and was on the edge of a major capital program for applied arts and technology institutes. In the Maritimes there were neither the funds nor the expertise to provide new initiatives, but the activity of the Atlantic Provinces Economic Council continued to stress the importance of education and training for higher incomes and a more buoyant economy.

The Canadian Vocational Training Branch staff produced the Technical and Vocational Training Assistance Act in this setting. Its aim, basically, was to give provinces large cash assistance to encourage rapid expansion of capacity for technical and vocational training as designed by each province. The role of the federal government was restricted to providing funds, setting general guidelines, accumulating some operating statistics and acting as an adviser when requested. It was primarily interested in making funds sufficiently attractive and restrictions sufficiently few to encourage all provinces to take up the program—and immediately. The division of expenditures within capital construction, and between youth or adult training—as well as the criteria for success—was left in provincial professional and political hands. There were few other federal controls, apart from the Labour department, upon the program. The Department of Finance in Diefenbaker's time still exercised little discretion over program design or size; in the Cabinet each minister proposed and defended his policy suggestions with individual prestige counting significantly for acceptance. Moreover, the concept of TVTA was sufficiently exciting and new to suggest a sensible solution to the mounting crisis. Thus, the TVTA agreement was operated without financial encumbrances exclusively by those civil servants who had been professional educators.

The merit of the program, in contrast to American and later Canadian examples, was that it was multifaceted and comprehensive—sufficiently general in objectives and flexible enough to cover a variety of applications according to age, skills, needs, region, and the requirements of other policies. While the individual provincial-federal agreements were identical, the funds, with Ottawa's assistance, were applied to a varied range of capital and training projects (though some bordered upon educational and cultural). The timing of the new programs was appropriate, for most provinces were able to make immediate use of its provisions. Some provinces were able to use the federal funds to fill out their own medium-term building plans which already had been prepared. Ontario and Alberta both undertook extensive school construction projects; these provinces quickly used up their financial allotment for capital spending.[7] In Quebec, it took almost three years to reverse the policy of Duplessis in the 1950s and devise capital projects eligible for TVTA grants. In the Maritimes, the tighter financial situation necessitated a hurried reshuffling of provincial priorities to release revenues from other fields to match federal money before the initially high rate of sharing capital costs was cut back after 1963. These provinces, in fact, were not able to match the federal funds allocated to them under TVTA during the life of the agreement.

Poorer provinces, therefore, built fewer capital projects and concentrated upon youth and evening training in existing schools as a cheaper alternative to the costs of adult retraining and living allowances (even though Ottawa paid 90 percent of training allowances after 1963). Alberta, likewise, concentrated two-thirds of its money in youth training projects, largely because its young and small industrial sector did not pose massive retraining problems. Ontario and Quebec, both with existing and varied secondary school and youth training schemes, concentrated most of their money upon adult training.

2. OPERATIONAL SUCCESSES AND CONCEPTUAL FAILURES OF TVTA

In operation the program was characterized by harmonious relations between governments but more difficult relations within government. It was natural that TVTA, which spent $1 billion in six years, should considerably enlarge the functions and enhance the prestige of the federal Labour department and its provincial equivalents. The Department of Labour had long held a second-rate position in the federal hierarchy. Section 92(13) of the BNA Act limited the field for innovation of the federal labour department more than most, and all provinces possessed their own active labour department or equivalent thereof.[8] The size of TVTA and its protection from Finance, because the Act was not subject to annual or budgetary limitations, provided a period of prestigious, open-ended development and high morale for Labour. At the provincial level, the program improved the budget of education or labour departments; in Ontario, for instance, the traditionally unchallenged priority of building highways was confronted by increasingly large expenditures upon education. Moreover, participating departments at both levels could argue before their Treasury Board that because of equal federal-provincial sharing of costs they were spending only "50¢ dollars."

Success was further secured by the presence of educators at both levels in charge of administering the Agreements. With a program designed by an acknowledged leader, Ford, with seemingly unlimited funds and only general guidelines, the professionals could explore and experiment in the field of youth and adult training. There were very few instances of federal vetoes; "success" (if money buys power) for federal officials came from encouraging provinces to spend money. Provincial officials emphasized the willingness of Department of Labour personnel to provide expert advice and research. Every effort was made at Ottawa to work as many projects under TVTA coverage as possible; the more questionable training proposals were merely financed under a "pilot project" designation.

Conceptually, however, TVTA suffered from what eventually proved to be a fatal weakness. Unlike other federal programs, there was never evident either within the federal Department of Labour or between governments a dialectic concerning the program, philosophy, or technique that would have encouraged reassessments, new policies, or better discernment of overall direction. Because the Agreements were not specific about the end results, the federal officials exercised a minimum of influence on provincial administration. In accordance with the intent of the legislation and conservative federal views about their jurisdiction in education,[9] no attempt was made to control the operational or conceptual details of programs. Ottawa did not try to develop an education empire; the size of the federal TVTA staff was small (forty-seven in 1965) and there was no felt need to duplicate or simulate provincial activity in training—not even when a provincial education or labour department was clearly felt to be mediocre. In fact, little was done to reduce the very considerable differences in the use of TVTA funds by provinces or in the ability of provinces to take up their allotment. But this absence of constraints, both operational and financial, created a sense of ease within the federal-provincial program departments and prevented a healthy development of tensions. Consequently, the shortsightedness which occurred prevented TVTA officials from seeing the growing dissatisfaction in other parts of government with the perception of labour problems and their solution as provided by TVTA.

The responsibility properly fell to Labour and the National Employment Service to rid TVTA of operational ambiguities and provide a clear direction of programs towards market demands or long-run future requirements. In the past, federal programs had often consisted of reducing the effects of a problem rather than its causes so that funds frequently developed or supported difficulties rather than readjusted them. Many of the agricultural programs during the 1940s and 1950s had displayed these strong characteristics of welfare, as political "boondoggles." Set in this tradition, TVTA required stern direction and evaluation to prevent massive transfers to symptoms and not causes. Quebec, for instance, was permitted to select its trainees rather than use applicants to NES (as other provinces had to) and in mailing the training allowance cheques to the "trainee" (rather than paying him in the classroom) denied Ottawa the opportunity of checking whether its money was being spent truly upon training or rather as welfare. With a lack of terminal criteria of success, Ottawa felt the latter form of expenditure was most prevalent.

The terms of the Agreement empowered the federal Labour department to undertake research to provide the program with operating and long-term guidelines. From the outset, however, Labour provided a minimum of guidance because of the belief that education was a provincial responsibility. Thus the establishment of training objectives was left with those responsible for education; although the federal government supplied at least half the funds, it felt at the time reluctant to define and measure programs within the provincial jurisdiction. An analysis of economic factors and employment needs was not made regularly; nor was an assessment of provincial standards, course content, or trainee needs. Little effort was taken at either level to provide for the mobility of trained manpower. All these considerations concerning the quality and depth of TVTA were set aside in the rush to build physical plant. This was an understandably attractive alternative to the difficult task of working out needs and objectives of training. Moreover, Ottawa had wished to encourage a quick response to TVTA and had offered to finance 75 percent of capital cost until 1963 (thereafter 50 percent). The generous size of these funds encouraged provinces to concentrate interests upon the short-run objective of building with the result today that several provinces have, like Alberta, a surplus of physical capacity for the scheme.

The partnership of NES with the Department of Labour to provide data for TVTA was not successful. The NES played an integral part in all training, to the extent that eligibility under TVTA required prior registration with the Service. The history of the NES had been one of underperformance. It had been placed under the Unemployment Insurance Commission in 1940 beyond the direct control of government to reduce the element of "porkbarrel" in welfare. Such an environment crippled the NES as a positive force; it reached persons only once they were unemployed. It was considered a last resort for those seeking jobs; it was an obligatory channel for welfare payments although only a voluntary centre at which to register one's unemployment. Hence, its remoteness as a tool of government, its lack of respectability or reliability, and its lack of staff, due to inferiority, prevented it from becoming a significant service to labour, management, and the unemployed in organizing the employment market and providing for optimum utilization of manpower resources.[10] Writing of it in 1964 the Economic Council of Canada declared: "The (analysis and development) division has been plagued by staff vacancies over extensive periods of time . . . which have necessitated much doubling up of the available staff's responsibilities. The result is that only the most rudimentary labour market analysis has been attempted and this for internal administrative use almost entirely."[11] One result of recommendations of the Economic Council and other inquiries was that the NES was moved within the Labour department in 1965.

Economists, and those concerned with a long-run integrated government policy for development—among them the Economic Council of Canada, the Ontario Department of Economics and Development, and the federal Department of Finance—expressed an increasing concern that an overall manpower policy should replace mere technical training. They argued that training, by itself, was of little value. For the market needs in Canada, and a "return" on training expenditures, a full range of manpower tools was required: continuing training with education, guidance, counselling, placement, incentives to mobility, and regional development. TVTA, moreover, was not sufficiently "geared to the training of unemployed persons and was reaching far too few of those who had inadequate basic education and training."[12]

In the light of this evolution in thinking, the expensive and unco-ordinated activities under TVTA appeared more and more vulnerable. Most disturbing was the rapid escalation in costs of the program and the lack of federal control over its expenditures. The devolution of responsibilities to municipal boards of education in some provinces further thwarted the opportunity to direct training toward national market needs and increased the possibility of training being used for cultural, educational, and prestige purposes. Moreover, the continuation of federal sharing to 75 percent of capital costs past 1963 did not solve the problem that poor provinces, most in need, were still least able to use the program fully. Under TVTA the rich provinces took up by far the largest proportion of funds. This was not necessarily a reflection of greater problems of unemployment in these provinces but rather the greater wealth of the province and the ability to "bring forward" future planning to make it eligible for TVTA funds. If anything, therefore, the application of TVTA heightened the disparities between rich and poor in their attention to the unskilled. Without labour mobility or adequate national statistics, however, it was simply not known whether problems in poor regions were solvable or not.

It took two years for the thinking at Ottawa and elsewhere to result in new federal legislation on manpower. The responsibility for moulding a fresh policy out of this discontent fell to the new Liberal government, under Lester Pearson, which had taken office in 1963, and in particular to Tom Kent, a Liberal policy adviser. Although TVTA officials were most bitter about his "hatchet work" in terminating TVTA, undoubtedly Kent was assisted by Finance, Treasury Board, and equivalent sympathy in the provinces. His methods, however, were highly secretive and the handling of the federal transformation of its training program is of importance for an understanding of the influence of Kent and his views on federal-provincial relations.

Tom Kent was probably the Liberal party's most outstanding and important adviser during the 1960s. His paper, "Towards a Philosophy of Social Security," formed a central part of the intellectual rejuvenation in 1960 at the Kingston Policy Conference of a tired Liberal party reeling from their 1957 electoral defeat—the first in twenty-two years. Kent joined Lester Pearson (who had become the new Liberal leader) as a policy adviser in 1961 and wrote much of the party platform for the elections of 1962 and 1963, in the second of which the Conservative regime was beaten. He moved into a quasi-political/quasi-official role in his efforts to redirect departmental activities. Placed in charge of the Special Planning Secretariat to the Cabinet[13] in 1965 with the massive task of co-ordinating all of government activity to the poor, he organized the War on Poverty Conference, a unique, mid-decade meeting of governments to discuss policy priorities and co-ordination. Kent convinced Prime Minister Pearson that while government had to rationalize the provision of services it had also to fill out policies for individual social security and income support which had been started after the war but had been severely tested by the recession of 1957–62. Both the Canada Pension Plan and a new manpower policy were largely his creations. He was soon made deputy minister of a new department of Manpower and Immigration and in 1969 moved to start another—the Department of Regional Economic Expansion (DREE). Both times his minister was Jean Marchand, an equally outstanding and senior figure, and a tough politician.

The unusual "visibility" of Kent made him a very political civil servant with frequent and easy access to Cabinet and an authority to deal personally with both federal and provincial ministers. Accordingly, his intimacy with the pinnacle of decision-making in the federal government did not endear him to officials of equivalent rank but less influence in other departments and governments.

Given Kent's intellectual contributions to the ruling Liberal party, his interest in social adjustments and his capacity for solving problems, it was not surprising that his talents should be directed toward the problems of labour training. His experiences with the War on Poverty Conference put him in direct contact with critical analyses of the Technical and Vocational Training Assistance Act. Moreover, his futile endeavours in the Special Planning Secretariat trying to co-ordinate and direct federal policies, reinforced his distaste for parochial, short-sighted empires created by self-aggrandizing departments. Kent had no patience with large staffs, traditional relationships, unnecessary linkages, and obscure services. He himself was a remote and often blunt man to the officials below him, keeping each apprised of only a portion of the total situation and quite prepared to replace those who thought differently or to bypass those who were redundant. When applied to federal-provincial relations, this approach sought closer relations between the ultimate consumer and the provider of services and was impatient with overly-governed programs or unnecessary tiers of co-ordination.

Because of his position of influence in a quasi-political role, supported by a strong minister, Kent's rationalizing approach had harsh and often disastrous consequences for officials and programs at both levels which fitted his category of misguided or unnecessary. It was probably what Kent represented rather than quirks of his personality that failed to endear him to his bureaucratic colleagues. He was in the vanguard of a new rationalism and control in federal policy which was to become the fashion in the late 1960s. Because he represented an agent of change, his relations with the more traditionally-minded provinces were made all the more difficult. Federal-provincial relations in his presence underwent very severe strains.

3. THE CONCEPTION AND INTRODUCTION OF THE ADULT OCCUPATIONAL TRAINING ACT

The Liberal decision to create a new department of Manpower and Immigration (hereafter called "Manpower") in 1965 was undertaken only after considerable debate about the wisdom of linking the two functions so intimately. This had an immediate twofold result: manpower policy became an integral part of immigration requirements and the Department of Labour, deprived of TVTA and with a confined constitutional role, dropped into a position of a third-rate department. While the Labour minister and his deputy quite approved of developing a better manpower policy, others felt that a new department under Marchand and Kent promised a new, more comprehensive, tougher, and result-oriented approach. Evidently Marchand and Kent were convinced that a new program could not be run in the relaxed manner of TVTA and they were instrumental in advising the Cabinet of the need for a complete change.

Marchand was not slow to act once entrusted with his new mandate. In January 1966, only a month after the decision to create Manpower was announced and nine months before his department was officially formed, he and Kent (and not the Labour minister or his deputy) represented Ottawa in a TVTA meeting with the provinces. Within a year Kent secured the departure of all of the top federal TVTA officials and replaced them with new economists, analysts, and technicians. Also, in June 1966, Kent informed all the provincial officials publicly that TVTA had been a waste of money and that it had nothing to show for six years' of government financing.

During the initial months of transition, officials at Ottawa were unable to inform their provincial colleagues of Kent's plans for changes in TVTA, due to expire in March 1967. The older federal officials either did not know of the changes contemplated or were not now able to maintain a close relationship with their provincial colleagues—a situation that made them clearly uncomfortable. The new appointees of Kent did not feel the same obligation to be helpful since they looked to Kent rather than the provinces for their new ideas and rewards. These new men lacked the professional camaraderie with provincial officials; their training emphasized departmental performance in greater isolation from external factors than TVTA's philosophy had encouraged.

The provincial program officials were not prepared for a major change. In the past, aspects of TVTA had been periodically renewed and the absence of any federal pronouncements to the contrary as the deadline approached this time seemed to indicate that renewal would be automatic. Hence one province confidently renewed its leases on rented training facilities for five years.

Perhaps, however, this was a sign of provincial shortsightedness rather than trust because there were some definite indications of a reform. In addition to the critical analyses of TVTA mentioned earlier, journals began to carry remarkably similar criticism of TVTA, which suggested calculated federal leaks of change. At the same time, provincial and federal treasurers were meeting in an effort to control rapidly escalating costs in joint programs, like TVTA, which were playing havoc with their budgets. Particularly the rich provinces, which carried most weight in conferences, were dismayed at the uncritical demand for funds made upon them by their labour or education departments and the absence of any controls at the federal end. Finally, Kent had already indicated his clear disgust with TVTA. All these events, however, were taking place without official communication from Ottawa.

The storm broke at a federal-provincial conference in October 1966. At the conference, Marchand and Kent reiterated the failures of TVTA mentioned above and particularly indicated that its massive costs could not continue with such questionable results.[14] They emphasized the need for a program that provided operational and terminal criteria of performance and uniformity. Then Marchand announced to stunned education officials that Ottawa would not renew the TVTA Agreements. There could be no discussion of the decision, only discussion of the timing of the "phase-out." In its place, Ottawa proposed the Adult Occupational Training Act (OTA) which put the design, performance criteria, and funding of adult retraining completely at the federal level. Eligibility was to be handled by Canada Manpower Centres (CMC), a replacement for the NES. Provinces would be asked to provide facilities and courses, as Ottawa saw no need to duplicate provincial functions. However, the OTA program was not to be a replacement for TVTA but only a selective enlargement (albeit to national criteria) of the adult retraining portion of TVTA.

If provincial program officials (but not treasurers) had felt bitter about the abrupt termination of TVTA without consultation, they were outright hostile to its replacement, OTA, which they considered ill-conceived and insulting. Kent's closely guarded efforts devoted to creating his department and dumping TVTA had not produced a sufficiently tested alternative in OTA. His impetuous nature had failed to provide an immediately workable replacement for TVTA and the conference became a rout; federal officials were totally unable to answer the barrage of technical questions from provincial TVTA professionals. An emergency meeting was held the evening of the first day but little progress was made. Technical and definitional questions continued to plague the passage of the Act until the point of third reading in the House, April, 1967, and most provinces delayed signing the Agreement for technical reasons, and in protest, until September 1967.[15] This was not only a delay (as Marchand claimed) arising from the pettiness of provincial TVTA officials in losing their program.[16] There were in fact significant differences over the philosophy and practice of OTA.

4. Conceptual and Operational Difficulties with OTA

The setting in which OTA was to be designed and administered was not conducive to harmony in the first place. While Kent had enlisted new types of officials to design and direct OTA, the provinces continued to use their TVTA professionals to supply the required services under the new program. This was scarcely a relationship of equal and likeminded civil servants; the TVTA officials continued to draw comparisons between OTA and the now defunct TVTA, both in philosophy and their positions of importance. Under OTA the provincial TVTA officials had the humiliating and unexciting duty of simply fulfilling federal requests. Not only was this a source of bitterness, but also there was a fundamental difference of attitude between the federal and provincial officials.

The federal staff selected by Kent believed in optimal resource planning, use, and management. This indeed had become particularly necessary as the training program expanded in cost. Also the popularity of the Planning-Program-Budgeting System (PPBS) approach to budgeting by objectives encouraged concentration upon measurable results.[17] Hence individuals in the scheme became raw numerical data; there was little room for special cases or flexibility and programs were designed to show a "profit." Trainees were not given a choice of courses but rather asked to fit into those offered for definite job vacancies.[18] In this respect provincial officials labelled the OTA as impersonal and crassly market-oriented. Both the Adult Occupational Training Act and Agreements were unusually detailed and specific documents, leaving little opportunity for administrative flexibility. PPBS was narrowly conceived and encouraged self-contained departmental activities with little provision for any intra- or interprovincial programs that would thwart its measures of efficiency and accountability.[19] The need for, or use of, federal-provincial committees or informal links was thus lessened by such specificity and by Kent's inclination to design and execute a program within his department and from his office. He tended to tell the provinces what they should provide or what would be revised rather than seek their opinions. Provincial officials felt this form of approach was a source of continuing strain under OTA.

Because both levels of government contained different types of officials under OTA acting within different constraints, conceptual and operational disagreements were understandable. Provincial training officials operated within an education objective; the relationship between training and education was seen as intimately linked. New immigrants or unskilled persons, it was felt, had to be given a basic citizenship and creative education if any training added thereto was to prove adaptive and responsible. One provincial official observed that more people lost jobs through their behaviour and attitude than through a lack of skills. The federal government, however, concerned with its jurisdiction and costs, had to regard training as part of its responsibility for national economic stability. The unskilled person was seen largely as an economic weakness which required special training for specific labour market shortages. Hence Ottawa argued that training and education could be divided between jurisdictions. Provinces such as Ontario and Quebec claimed training was education and, therefore, conversely, federal funds should be transferred to provinces for fulfilment of the latter's constitutional duties in education.

The situation was further complicated by a dilemma within the Manpower department as to the appropriate use of the OTA program which, in turn, produced an ambiguity in relations with the provinces and other federal departments.[20] The quandary at Ottawa developed somewhat from the secrecy of the original OTA design, the lack of practical experience of officials under Kent, and his determination to work out problems without consulting his experienced provincial counterparts. The other aspect of the confusion was that the unemployed were not only unskilled but frequently uneducated, so that half of retraining expenditures often involved first providing a basic grade ten or twelve general education even before training could begin. This led to a confusion of objectives at Ottawa. Was the manpower program a short-term tool for labour market adjustment and stabilization or a human resource development program based upon long-run cost-benefit criteria? If the program could have been operated as designed, it would have provided periodic and short-term retraining of the work force to stabilize unemployment. In fact, often fifty percent of federal money was spent on basic education—making up for the deficiencies in provincial education of a decade earlier—before skill development could begin. Federal officials spoke simultaneously of requirements of the long-term and short-run, education and training, benefit-cost and social adjustment, without demonstrating a clear understanding of the direction that they wanted for the OTA program.

Placed in a federal-provincial context, this confusion continued to reinforce provincial beliefs that education and training were indivisible. They felt more confident about the usefulness of direct contact with trainees and resented the absence of federal consultation.

Regional and national priorities were issues in the clash of governments over the mix of youth and adult training under the new Act. The Maritime and Western provinces had put most of their TVTA money into vocational training for youths. The Maritimes found this a cheaper program than the cost of adult retraining and provision of living allowances; youth training was considered a "preventive" approach to adult retraining. In Alberta and British Columbia their small, young industrial sector did not present a major problem of updating a large, old workforce. Immigrants there were primarily Canadians and did not require basic language or citizenship training. The primacy and rapid expansion of the natural resources sector, furthermore, called for only moderately skilled adult workers. Hence both provinces concentrated efforts upon improving youth vocational training.

Ottawa, however, was concerned with a mobile and national labour force and wished to see a major concentration upon adult retraining. Kent complained in a public speech that, ". . . the average age of the unemployed who came to our offices for jobs was 36. But the average age of (provincial) trainees was 23. One in every five of the people who needed a job was over 34 years . . . only one person in 40 of that difficult category . . . was in training."[21] The new Act, in fact, placed much vocational training beyond federal aid as eligibility for training required the trainee to be an adult at least one year out of high school. To receive training allowances he now had to be three years out of the labour force. The provinces, therefore, had to carry the burden of both youth training and operating costs of facilities which had been supported under TVTA. This burden was particularly heavy for the Maritimes.

The Occupational Training Act was designed to reflect the interest in manpower mobility. This included both occupational and geographical mobility to deal with structural unemployment. Manpower officials frequently moved trainees across the country to secure the necessary courses, and it was firmly believed that this would form a pattern for labour mobility. Mobility incentives, however, did not become an operational part of manpower policy because Ottawa was reluctant to adversely influence provincial economies. To the extent that mobility was inter- rather than intraprovincial, such a policy could hasten the already large natural migration from the Maritimes, and this was politically unacceptable. The Maritimes argued that industrial location required a skilled labour force, and mobility of labour lost to the Atlantic provinces that in which they had invested. On the other hand, labour, it was claimed, would not remain in a depressed area without new jobs. If new industries were slow to move to a centre of skilled labour that labour would move itself. Rather than engage in this vicious socio-economic circular argument the issue was avoided. Today, the mobility program is small and rarely mentioned.[22] Most politicians, even from rich provinces, have preferred instead to add money to the new venture of regional development rather than demand, as do officials, better returns from present manpower expenditures through mobility.

66

Numerous misunderstandings arose under the OTA program because of insufficient provisions for a frank and regular flow of information and opinions between federal and provincial operating departments. During Kent's time (he left Manpower in 1968) provinces were not consulted by the central federal office, conferences were few and, when held, were largely for information, not discussion. There was not the same informal federal-provincial contact under OTA as with TVTA. Federal officials had first to work out among themselves the appropriate goals of Manpower. Relations with the provinces were thus further strained to the extent that confusion of goals led to opposing federal-provincial stands. The "labour market adjustment" approach was primarily the federal aim, while provincial education officials, who were not "optimalizing" economists, stressed the "human resources" aspect of training. The most frequent provincial complaint, in fact, was not about the inflexibility of the program, but the obscurity of federal thinking and the uncertainty of their demands.

Under Kent and a more scrupulous Treasury Board,[23] OTA officials were prevented from making extensive, definitive commitments to the provinces. Conflicts over what provinces might claim as legitimate costs delayed repayment by as much as three years. With the addition of regional Manpower directors as well as local CMC offices, the provinces had extra levels of delay added to their channel for request—particularly to the extent that regional directors were obliged to refer to Ottawa for decisions. The Western provinces and Ontario found especially that, in this situation, consultation with Manpower made the possibility of planning adult training courses for longer than six months remote.

Several specific difficulties between federal and provincial departments suggested the effect of the dead hand of secrecy upon productive relationships. Manitoba, like most provinces, had mixed relations. Premier Roblin moved the province out of vocational training when OTA was established, largely in response to what he thought were Kent's extensive assurances that Manpower and CMC would handle all training problems. Roblin missed the point that Manpower, in competing for the federal budget, had to show results. The OTA program (unlike TVTA) was provided with funds to meet national, not provincial, training needs and according to national budgetary constraints. Thus only the best trainees were selected for adult retraining and there were few of these in Manitoba. The remainder had to be covered by the province. On the whole, Manitoba in its Interlake (federal-provincial rural development) program and New Brunswick (in a similar program) found that Manpower provided a useful though limited training service related to the development and relocation of industries and people.

In Quebec, a dispute over the federal manpower role in the Gaspé area (another rural development project), resulted in special federal-provincial relations being worked out. Since Quebec had provided its own youth training and placement service for twenty years, the advent of Manpower's OTA in 1967 was seen as a parallel and unnecessary program. For "provincialistic" reasons, the training of labour for the needs of the Quebec economy was a crucial issue and mobility an unacceptable concept. The rural development plan for the Gaspé contained an important retraining component and on this Quebec decided to stand and demand provincial control over manpower policies, with federal funding. This was unacceptable to Marchand and Kent for reasons of uniformity, accountability, and labour mobility. The conflict raged at the political level, although official relations remained co-operative. Eventually, the stalemate was relieved by federal proposals for a joint Quebec-Ottawa manpower committee to resolve differences.[24] This committee became permanent and regular, and provided for a smoothly operating manpower program. Through it Quebec secured a unique training program under which the province selected both its own trainees and courses. The province, and not the CMC, also certified construction workers for job vacancies or retraining. Quebec thus developed a special and harmoniously-operating relationship under the OTA agreement.

Relations between the Manpower departments and other federal departments reflected an unevenness similar to that with the provinces. Kent's particular style of operation made it difficult for his officials to meet with their equivalents from the other departments and give decisive operational or policy commitments. The importance of hierarchy was such in Manpower that regional officials had repeatedly to refer requests from other federal field staff to Ottawa. Field officials were not kept informed of the labour requirements of other federal programs (ADA, ARDA—to be discussed below) and departments complained of the inability of the Manpower program to adjust to the demands of certain regional projects.[25] This was not necessarily a criticism of Manpower *per se*, as its national policy objectives did not fit certain regional peculiarities. But because few but Kent were fully aware of the direction of policy, officials in his department had to be evasive and non-committal. The consequence was, therefore, that the reliability of Manpower programs was uncertain as was their adaptability to those of other departments.

In terms of the campaign against regional disparities some initial conclusions can be made about the two programs studied. The introduction of new training schemes in the 1960s reflected a concern with national structural deficiencies. OTA, however, was more consciously and narrowly aimed towards the economic disparities between regions. Whereas TVTA had, in effect, distributed its funds on the ability of provinces to match their allotment (predominantly the rich), OTA resulted in the spending of federal funds in the Atlantic region at a rate more than twice that in the rich provinces.[26] Thus OTA was a clear indication of a discretionary element entering into federal spending to counter deficiencies in economic growth—in this case the low productivity of labour.

The return of manpower policy to exclusive federal control (which was what OTA signified as a replacement for TVTA) did not merely provide Ottawa with an opportunity to enter into discretionary spending. More than that, it began a phase of bilateral relations whereby individual adjustments of a national act were made by Ottawa for each province. Quebec especially enjoyed considerable flexibility in being able to choose its retraining candidates and to spend OTA money with a freedom not found in other provinces. While this provided a useful adaptability to national legislation it might also have enabled a "divide and conquer" policy to be adopted at Ottawa, on which more will be said in a concluding chapter.

The OTA legislation represented two further changes in Ottawa's attitude to the usefulness of joint programs. Under the TVTA program the federal government evidently received little political return for buttressing provincial expenditures (often as high as 90 percent). The OTA legislation ensured, however, that the consumer knew directly who was financing the retraining programs. As well, TVTA had been haphazard or varied in its objectives—depending on the province—and OTA was a definite attempt to provide an objective of market-oriented training (although in application there has been considerable ambiguity about the interpretation of this latter goal). Both of these changes, it should be noted, reflected a more relaxed federal attitude to the earlier inhibitions about entering new jurisdictions.

One final observation might be made on these policies to ameliorate national deficiencies and regional disparities in the economic structure essential for growth. It was evident that personalities played a crucial role in the implementation of policy and operation of programs. They frequently set the pace of development, the tone of relationships, and the extent of working compromises within the framework of a federal-provincial agreement covering (in this case) abutting fields of interest. Individuals not only operate a program, they interpret it, and it has been shown how, with both OTA and TVTA, that the possibilities of duplication, revenue losses, and lack of objectivity were all consequences of the presence or absence of smoothly operating personal relationships.

These characteristics of Manpower programs were but reflections of a more extensive government policy aimed at reducing regional disparities in economic potential. It is appropriate to turn next to another component of that policy, the efforts to grapple with the perplexing problem of rural poverty.

Chapter Five

The Search for Solutions
to Rural Poverty

The productivity, size, and occupation of the rural population were major factors influencing the ability of certain regions to reduce their disparities in growth potential. Basically over-populated, underemployed, and immobile, the rural people formed the core of regional poverty and constituted the most intractable problem for development economists. Nevertheless, very great efforts were made to reduce this aspect of regional economic disparities during the 1960s by means of a federal package of programs for the adjustment of rural poverty—with significant consequences for co-operative relations between governments.

It is not possible in a single or even several chapters to cover the myriad aspects of the federal Agricultural and Rural Development Act (ARDA). Several excellent studies provide a full view of the creation, validity, and operation of the ARDA concept during the last decade.[1] This chapter is concerned with the process, within and between governments, of developing programs to deal with rural poverty under the very general administrative and financial provisions of the ARDA legislation. The ARDA agreements signed with the provinces since 1962 have reflected a variety of attitudes and emphasis. During the decade their characteristics changed and it is the process of refining ARDA concepts and structures in order to cope better with the rural aspects of regional disparities which the chapter examines.

The major events that shaped the ARDA approach to regional problems can be briefly summarized. It began with the Agricultural Rehabilitation and Development Act, passed in June 1961 by the federal parliament to enable Alvin Hamilton, the Agriculture minister in Diefenbaker's cabinet, to explore jointly with the provinces the means of achieving parity in income levels in the agricultural sector with other sectors of the economy. This very general legislation reflected both a desire for joint collaboration with the provinces and an uncertainty, in the light of past failures, as to the best approach to regional disparities. A Resource for Tomorrow Conference, sponsored by Ottawa in the fall of 1961 provided considerable private and expert advice concerning the optimum use of Canada's natural resources. The federal ARDA administration was established in January 1962 within the Department of Agriculture. In October of the same year the first of the general ARDA agreements was signed with the provinces. The ARDA program was launched early in 1963 at the provincial level with Ottawa sharing half the cost. These agreements lasted until 1965 and concentrated largely upon an agricultural program of developing alternate land use, soil and water conservation, and farm consolidation. Provision was made for research into alternative employment opportunities, but initially little use was made of this section of the agreement. Most projects concentrated upon dealing with land and resources in order to improve the farmer's well-being.

The second set of agreements, of 1965–70, continued joint financing, provincial design, and land-oriented development projects. However, several changes reflecting a shift in emphasis from the largely unrelated agricultural assistance projects to planned regional development were incorporated in the legislation, amended as the Agricultural and Rural Development Act. In 1964, the federal Liberal regime placed the Act in a new department of Forestry and Rural Development under Maurice Sauvé. This transfer recognized the growing evidence that rural poverty embraced more activity than just farming and that labour displaced by farm consolidation lacked the skills and mobility to find alternative employment. Finally, a special Fund for Rural Economic Development (FRED) was created within the Act to assist rural areas that were so lacking in social capital, education, and wealth that no ordinary ARDA program of resource and rural manpower development could fill their needs. To be eligible, an area had to demonstrate both widespread low income and a reasonable economic potential which would benefit from joint, integrated, and diverse programs to develop infrastructure, occupational training, and labour mobility, to foster housing, education, health facilities, and administrative reorganization. Each province proposed a FRED designated area to Ottawa. Those actually developed lay in Manitoba, New Brunswick, and Quebec and one constituted the whole of Prince Edward Island.

The entire ARDA-FRED program was but one of the central government's regional programs which were transferred to a newly-created Department of Regional Economic Expansion (DREE) in 1969. Jean Marchand and Tom Kent then were moved from the Department of Manpower and Immigration to head this new effort at co-ordination as minister and deputy minister respectively. Under the new department's policy all FRED projects were to be terminated and ARDA largely curtailed, reflecting the increasing concern to provide urban and industrial development for depressed regions. In fact, several FRED projects survived, and a third five year ARDA agreement has since been signed with all provinces. However, rural projects formed only a small and unattended aspect of DREE's operations and they are, today, largely preserved through provincial political efforts.

1. THE ESTABLISHMENT OF THE ARDA CONCEPT

Traditionally Alvin Hamilton has received the credit for the creation of ARDA. More accurately, his chief contribution was the creation of an institution in which the contemporary thinking about rural development and adjustment could be collected, tried, assessed, and refined.[2] Hamilton's own thoughts about the solution to rural poverty were not particularly novel; what was new was his vision that this required a joint, vigorous, and definite action of governments to encourage self-help as a replacement for welfare. Hamilton crystallized the ferment of the time by the creation of his ARDA branch in which, by judicious selection of staff, he could capture a variety of different opinions about rural poverty. Appropriately the director of ARDA was a former resource official in the Department of Northern Affairs (A. T. Davidson) and Hamilton's personal advisers (Maxwell Mackenzie, Merril Menzies, and Baldur Kristjanson) were economists and analysts, also from outside the purely agriculture sector. S. C. Barry, the deputy minister of Agriculture, had little influence upon or interest in the ARDA approach. He, as did many critics, thought that the program would degenerate into a rural "boondoggle." It was to the credit of the ARDA staff at Ottawa that this strong political temptation was, by and large, resisted.

By the opening of the 1960s the main issue in agricultural matters in Canada centred on the nature of appropriate governmental policy for supporting the forty percent of farmers who failed to make an adequate income on their farms and yet possessed potentially viable farm units. Initially it was wondered whether development policies could replace a tradition of welfare; by the mid-sixties it was questioned whether seeking adjustment and mobility for the farm population was not a better policy.

And by the late sixties it was asked whether any rural spending should affect the natural drift to the cities, apart from supporting those too old or unwilling to move. The ARDA programs operated within this full circle of changing contexts.

Since 1912 the federal government had helped agriculture adjust to change. The financing of agricultural colleges was followed by the provision of marketing boards, farm price supports, farm credit, crop insurance, and conservation aids, largely directed at helping farmers remain profitable as farmers. After the Depression, direct relief payments and intensive land care under the Prairie Farm Rehabilitation Act of 1935 helped to make the farmer more productive in the face of rising costs. The result of these tactics, the latest of which was the costly South Saskatchewan Dam irrigation project (1962), was to stabilize income and agricultural land occupancy but not to improve income or reduce poverty. The federal approach was one of implementing local resource developments to stabilize the farmer, in the belief that changes to the land directly affected his well-being. Often this was unsubstantiated in economic fact but was based upon political, not economic, assessments. While it was possibly an appropriate attitude in the time of the Depression or drought, it could not answer the problem of a general decline in the agricultural sector during a period of prosperity.

One line of response to the growing disparity in farm incomes was found in the Senate Committee on Land Use of 1960–61 and the Resources for Tomorrow Conference of 1961, both of which respectively influenced the ARDA Act and Agreements.[3] Neither body broke with tradition, to the extent that emphasis was placed upon resource development, but both rejected the use of welfare payments to support a persistently uneconomic situation. While mobility was implicitly regarded as a tool, greater emphasis was placed upon the efficient development of resources. If resources could be exploited with less conflict in their use, a farmer would be able, by his own efforts, to receive his fair share of national income. If farms generally were too small and overstaffed to be efficient, then the consolidation of land and release of surplus labour could be directed towards other rural activities. Thus in the tradition of past programs land was to be reworked; grass pastures, reforestation, blueberry patches, and fish breeding were expected to adjust the farmer to a new role—but still as a rural citizen.

During the same period the American Rural Agriculture Development Program expressed a similar faith in self-help. Its approach was more complex and included provisions to raise social horizons and prospects in the depressed low income farm areas. Great emphasis was placed upon community action in "fix-up, paint-up, clean-up" projects for the rural areas: better roads, new buildings, and generally a better morale created by small rural industry. In the American program, responsibility for planning was placed at the local level and the rejuvenation was to cover political and social as well as economic aspects. This was "rural fundamentalism" and it had strong support in the Canadian provinces and in certain parts of the federal government. It did not regard the agricultural or rural problem as one of overpopulation created by advancing technology and costs. It did not foresee an underserviced rural population as a result of rising costs and economies of scale. The solution, it believed, to rural problems was not outmigration but alternate unsophisticated rural projects and better farm management.

The provincial contributions to thought about low rural incomes reflected a largely uninspired and unchanged approach. Representation in provincial legislatures expressed the strong and traditional rural influence. Because of a lag in the redistribution of seats, the population shift to urban areas (and their consequent problems) was not properly displayed in the legislature or in the relative weight of government departments. Hence the influential agricultural and resource departments in most provinces emphasized support and development of rural areas, not their adjustment. Naturally these departments sought to protect those traditional, vested interests that constituted their clientele. There were exceptions, however; in Ontario and Manitoba there were indications that efforts were being made to measure the extent of rural poverty and alternatives, while avoiding policies which encouraged irreversible rural development.

At Ottawa, the ARDA Branch had no more certainty about the direction of its policy than was found in the many opinions on the subject. Before this time, help for the rural regions had largely been concerned with symptoms. When the approach was directed at causes, much more data was required concerning land use, inefficiencies of scale, mobility, and public participation. Hamilton had not given strong direction in the original Agricultural Rehabilitation and Development Act. He had said: ". . . the bill does not state what the Act will do. . . . This is true Mr. Speaker, because no one in the provinces or in the farm organizations or at the federal level knows yet what the Bill will bring forth and the extent to which we are going to use this Bill."[4] Nevertheless, despite the magnitude of the task and uncertainty about techniques, Hamilton communicated enthusiasm and trust to his officials and created an easy-going environment where new approaches could flourish.

At the same time, the minister himself had opinions about his ARDA program. He was from Saskatchewan and had observed the plight of his fellow farmers; not surprisingly his emotions reflected a rural fundamentalist faith in the rejuvenation of the farmer. His solutions were not a break with the past tradition of farm resuscitation and local projects. While the preamble of the act suggested a recognition of changes, Hamilton's speeches did not, as the following contrasting extracts show:

> Whereas agriculture in Canada is undergoing technological changes that necessitate adjustments on the part of many Canadians engaged in this basic industry in order to maintain their standard of living . . .[5]

> We believe that this parity of income should not be allowed by charity but by providing opportunities for the farmers to help themselves. . . . If any person tries to divorce this [ARDA] from the overall agricultural policy of the government that person does a great injustice to what we are attempting to do here.[6]

Hamilton travelled about the country promising that whatever was needed for the rural area, ARDA would finance. He sought to encourage provincial interest and participation by sharing costs and leaving the terms very general. Because he wanted agreements with traditionally-minded provinces, and because he believed it, he promised that not one person would have to move because of ARDA. Hamilton did believe marginal lands should be converted to other uses but not with a loss of rural population. He saw farmers running forestry projects, local sawmills, growing worms and blueberries, and making shoes or cider. He felt farmers could be thus re-employed on their own lands or used in rural community projects which he had studied in the United States. As one official observed, Hamilton was very much a "grass-rootser" while his Liberal successor, Maurice Sauvé, was a planner.

Hamilton's views neither oppressed nor influenced his staff, for his rule over ARDA lasted only about a year; he fell ill during 1962 and the Conservative party lost power in April 1963. His immediate Liberal successor, Harry Hays, had no knowledge of or interest in ARDA and his short stay was uneventful and unimpressive. When ARDA was moved into its new department in 1964, under Sauvé, eighty pieces of legislation remained to be signed. Sauvé was new to ARDA but keen to learn of its application. He listened closely to his officials, and was often prepared to revise his opinions and to support them fully—both in Cabinet and in public. There was a completely free flow of ideas between Sauvé and his ARDA staff—they were brought to Cabinet meetings and he in turn protected them in difficult political situations. Sauvé was strong in Cabinet while ARDA, being small, posed little threat to other departments. In this secure, confident environment new ideas and policies were encouraged.

A. T. Davidson, the director of ARDA, was determined that his funds should not be used solely for rural welfare.[7] His staff contained no rural fundamentalists and it was to their credit that they had been able to resist the strong provincial pressures—even those of Hamilton—to convert ARDA into a tool of patronage. Unavoidably some money was spent on projects having little impact upon rural incomes but these expenditures were regarded as a greasing of the provincial machinery to secure co-operation. Most of the federal staff agreed that adjustment, not development, was the key to rural poverty. This would include providing for mobility to the urban areas. As Davidson observed: ". . . the chances of simply growing out of this problem with little effort on our part in the next two or three decades are slight. We cannot assume that increased efficiency within agriculture alone will be the complete salvation of rural areas. We must do something about it. One of the main purposes of ARDA is to help meet this problem of adjustment."[8]

Once the federal staff had agreed that ARDA required integrated provincial planning for adjustment, the contentious issue became how to encourage this response at the provincial level. Hamilton had aroused interest by the promise of funds for almost any activity, but Davidson and his staff wished to reorient the interests of the provinces and equip their staffs to plan. Three factions formed in the ARDA staff: one was concerned with the social implications of development programs; a second believed that spending money gave a program power, and sought to service any provincial project; while a third was concerned with the development of planning. The three often conflicted. The head of the planning group wished a planning framework to be placed upon *ad hoc*, poorly integrated, and haphazard projects for spending money, and he considered that federal willingness to spend on blueberry patches, cider mills, rural roads, reservoirs, and improved land use without a direction to policies would never solve rural poverty. The second group argued that the ARDA program spending could not be suspended while a framework of planning was made operative. The third group wanted development to keep pace with community expectations. A certain amount of unregulated spending was inevitable, but so was encouragement of provincial planning. Eventually provincial treasurers themselves began to be concerned with the excessive number of unrelated projects under ARDA, by which time the federal officials were ready to finance, and staff if necessary, provincial planning bodies to secure some control and rationale in provincial expenditures under ARDA. In this way Ottawa assisted planning in Prince Edward Island, Nova Scotia, New Brunswick, Quebec, Manitoba, and Alberta.

At times, however, alternative land use, and soil-and-water conservation projects in the provinces became so large and numerous (greater than

70 percent) that they threatened to consume most of ARDA's funds at the expense of research or the search for alternative employment opportunities. The federal staff, after moral suasion failed, limited soil, drainage, and pond projects to 50 percent of available funds in the second agreement. Saskatchewan's community pasture projects were limited until there was activity in other fields. Many of Quebec's projects likewise were not new approaches to rural poverty but continuing welfare programs (often highly political) written on ARDA forms. At one time up to ninety percent of these kinds of projects were not approved at Ottawa until a decision was made on how to handle these funds.[9] Caught largely unprepared, provinces at first used ARDA to extend their existing program; only eventually did some begin to *alter* their approach to rural areas.

2. INTERGOVERNMENTAL RESPONSES TO ARDA-FRED

To reduce rather than subsidize rural poverty required considerable adaptability at the provincial level—and policies were conceived which varied considerably from one government to the next. Apart from their rural bias, the response of provinces to ARDA depended considerably upon the size and composition of their ARDA staff. The small provinces usually had one official in their Agriculture department serving as co-ordinator, sometimes only part time. This official would process ARDA applications from other departments and, by consultation, allocate ARDA funds amongst these departments. But these smaller provinces could not keep up with the federal changes or integration or carry out research because they lacked the organization and manpower which could react quickly enough. Most of the Atlantic provinces' proposals were small scale and isolated programs, such as pig breeding in New Brunswick or forestry work in Nova Scotia. Since more federal money was available than could be matched by the Atlantic provinces, the enterprise became not one of carefully arranged priorities, but adoption of each and every project that a department could afford and put on an ARDA form.[10] The conservatism of the Maritime provinces produce little enthusiasm for federal attempts at innovation, such as introducing beef cattle grazing in Nova Scotia.

The FRED program, however, enabled the federal government to assist in rationalizing the provincial approach. Eventually it encouraged planning bodies in Nova Scotia, the Program Development Agency (PDA); in New Brunswick, the Community Improvement Corporation (CIC); and in Prince Edward Island, the Economic Improvement Corporation (EIC). This represented a victory for federal ARDA influence in the provinces. Not only did they secure provincial planning but they were, by the device of FRED, able to move the planning unit out of the provincial agriculture department and into the premier's office where there were more likely possibilities of balanced, cost-conscious, comprehensive planning not primarily directed at farming *per se*.

The lack of planning and co-ordinating experience raised difficulties. In New Brunswick, for instance, the CIC had "a tendency to develop plans and projects on the assumption that people will somehow fit into them."[11] The CIC also went beyond its role of co-ordinating "line" department programs in the ARDA areas and tended to propose programs parallel to those of departments. It was inclined to interpret its position as one of exercising power rather than supervising co-ordination, and it duplicated departmental efforts rather than improved their research capacity. It also threatened to reduce the significance of rural departments. The result was deadlock and hostility.[12]

In Alberta, ARDA activity was largely routine. Alberta had a number of its initial applications rejected primarily because they were poorly planned and costed.[13] By the second agreement of 1965 this problem was solved although, by intent or default, the province did not fully match its ARDA allocation.[14] The comprehensive ARDA project at Edson encouraged good citizen participation and the selection of projects was well prepared at the local level, with realistic goals, a good understanding of problems involved, and agreement as to what had to be done. The downfall of the program, however, came at the interdepartmental level, where officials and politicians were unwilling to make special arrangements for Edson that would have necessitated changes for the other provinces; they were not prepared to make government policy flexible for specific regions.[15]

Ottawa could not rely upon much control being imposed upon the choice of ARDA projects within the Quebec government as it could increasingly in most other provinces. For political reasons the federal ARDA staff was unable to treat Quebec applications with the same severity as those of other provinces and this regime received probably a greater amount of money for empirical, haphazard development projects than most. The provincial ARDA committee, CPAR (Comité Permanente d'aménagement des ressources) was composed of the deputy ministers of seven influential rural and resource-oriented departments under the chairmanship of the tough, aggressive deputy minister of Agriculture, Jean-Baptiste Bergevin. The committee, as in most provinces, jointly generated projects which looked eligible for ARDA funds. These unco-ordinated scattered proposals rarely went through a provincial Treasury Board or Finance scrutiny but were sent quickly and directly to the premier's desk through his special adviser, Claude Morin. In the peculiarly dynamic, exciting situation in Quebec of the early sixties as the new Lesage government pursued its "Quiet Revolution," there were few established administrative or policy channels, procedures, or regulated expenditures. Each department counted on obtaining its individual successes with the Cabinet and premier. Bergevin's personal friendship with Premier Lesage and the influence of seven deputy ministers' signatures on ARDA proposals usually secured their approval for CPAR within a day.

On the other side, Ottawa had few relations with CPAR because of the intense nationalism of the French Canadians. Also the fluid situation in the province defied regularity. Quebec felt it needed no advice; its planning experiments were just as novel as Ottawa's, if not more so. As long as the federal government was prepared to fund without influence, Quebec exercised its independence.

When an intensive and excitingly novel study and "social animation" project was suggested for the Gaspé region of Quebec, officials at both governmental levels jumped at this proposal for a FRED expenditure (run by the BAEQ: Bureau d'aménagement de l'est du Québec).[16] Ottawa was eager to divert Quebec's allotments into a project which might eventually secure rational, integrated ARDA expenditures, and almost certainly would encourage closer planning consultation. Both CPAR and COEQ (Conseil d'Orientation économique du Québec: the official planning body for the provincial government) were intrigued by this experiment in regional development planning. Large, but backward, Gaspé contained a number of federal and provincial seats, which made it politically attractive; yet it was not economically a key area, which made it a good laboratory for new experiments. Hence there could be attempts at community action and education without the furor that might be raised elsewhere. The concept of *animation sociale* was to be tested in this region in the belief that change began with community comprehension of and desire for renewal. The BAEQ project financed by Ottawa and Quebec was staffed by a group outside the civil service, primarily university sociologists.[17] The only government link was through Bergevin, chairman of the board, deputy minister of Agriculture and chairman of CPAR. The federal government was not involved, apart from financing, though it would have liked to have had closer consultation.

The massive report of the BAEQ study covering every social, political, and economic aspect of the area, was produced in 1966. Its greatest success was the accurate measurement of the problem in Gaspé and its acceptance by local people through exhaustive public education and participation programs provided by *animateurs*. Its failure was its impracticability. Confronted with a carefully-documented gap between jobs and people (even after assuming a realistic amount of mobility), it had no acceptable solution. Solutions to the problem of outmoded occupations, low skills, inefficient economies of scale, and poor municipal organization, had been proposed by those who knew little about development economics and politics. Faced with inefficient and overpopulated farming, lumbering, and fishing industries, they fell back upon highly expensive subsidies to these inefficiencies as supposed substitutes for welfare. The proposals were economically and politically unacceptable: the projected new regional system of government jeopardized the status and functions of existing officials and politicians;[18] an expenditure of a quarter of a billion dollars affording subsidies, jobs, and relocation for only four percent of Quebec's population was unrealistic in the extreme. It was forgotten, too, that the provincial government would not be happy with proposals of increased labour mobility into the Montreal area as it wished to deemphasize the growth of that strongly anglophone centre.

Daniel Johnson, the newly elected premier whose Union Nationale party had replaced the provincial Liberal regime in 1966, received the report with mixed feelings.[19] He could scarcely ignore the interest and support which the BAEQ project had generated, but he had strongly opposed, while in Opposition, its technique of independent planning. There was an immediate scramble within his government to control the implementation of the BAEQ study. Bergevin felt his CPAR group should direct the design and implementation of FRED projects stemming from the study, as they had with ARDA. Roland Parenteau, the director of COEQ, the official but privately-staffed planning body for the government, thought his planners should be entrusted with the study. Johnson accepted neither opinion; he phased out CPAR and restricted COEQ to an analytical role. CPAR had served its usefulness in setting the future allocations of the second ARDA Agreement funds. COEQ he never trusted very much, as its history had been unimpressive and it was outside government control or influence. Because of his wish to oversee the BAEQ plan of which he was suspicious, Johnson moved its director, Guy Coulombe, and his staff into the premier's office to effect and expedite its implementation.[20] After Johnson's death in 1968, implementation was handled by a new regional body, ODEQ (L'Office de développement de l'Est du Québec).

Organizing to implement the BAEQ plan, while complex and time–consuming, was dwarfed by the problems of securing broader consent to the plan. The actual impact upon intra- and intergovernmental relations of the BAEQ study was a good example of the many operational problems encountered in trying to implement the FRED plans. There were varied and hostile reactions from provincial departments to the report. Some argued that its proposals had been prepared in total secrecy and without their consultation. Others balked at the new programs or relations with other groups which they were required to provide. In actual fact what had occurred during the formation of the report was that departments which had been unwilling or unable to co-operate with Bergevin and the BAEQ were implicated regardless of their wishes. Often departments could offer BAEQ their "rule-book" services but were unable to provide programmatic advice outside traditional functions and methods.[21] The BAEQ frequently found no willingness for an innovative or integrated response to issues beyond current administrative objectives. In this situation there was little opportunity for dialogue between government bodies.

This gulf was deepened by the issue of status, or "who comes to whom." Bergevin had felt he was not compelled to work with deputy ministers who were remote and unco-operative, and he had instructed Coulombe not to overexert his staff in attempts at liaison while assembling the plan. Some departments felt they were senior and should direct Bergevin, otherwise they would "sink" him. Bergevin, however, was in a powerful position with CPAR and close to Lesage and his influential adviser, Claude Morin. Generally he avoided bureaucratic fights by listening to those who co-operated, such as Education, but presenting unco-operative departments, such as Lands and Forests, with *faits accomplis*. Premier Johnson extended this breakdown of departmental empires by implementing the BAEQ plan from his office. Nevertheless, some departments had legitimate objections to the report, particularly Industry and Commerce, which flatly rejected the feasibility of rural industries outside the industrialized corridor between Montreal and the city of Sept Isles.

In addition to the intragovernmental negotiations over the BAEQ study, as a FRED project it required close relations with Ottawa. Quebec repeatedly insisted that Ottawa's role was to finance, not design the FRED plan.[22] Ottawa replied that this arrangement of the early 1960s no longer applied; if the federal government was to spend its money it would also design its expenditures. The issue extended to every field, not just ARDA; Ottawa insisted on a federal presence where federal funds were concerned and Quebec asserted that only the provincial government could represent the Quebec people. The issue culminated in and contributed to a confrontation at the 1968 Federal-Provincial Constitutional Conference between Justice Minister Pierre Trudeau and Premier Johnson—with little resulting success for Quebec.[23]

Despite these political conflicts, officials set to work jointly to implement the plan. On paper the federal ARDA staff were to deal, in committee, with Coulombe at the provincial level, in assembling departmental programs. In reality, relationships were not that straightforward. Federal officials found it necessary to work directly with provincial departments.

In so doing they arbitrarily cut across the lines of authority that Coulombe was attempting to establish over highly independent departments. This led to confusion in some instances when similar federal and provincial departments felt their functions jeopardized by the FRED project. The federal ARDA staff's instructions to the Quebec Department of Fisheries were contested by the federal Department of Fisheries which felt that wrong demands were being made by the BAEQ plan upon St. Lawrence fishermen. This and other problems meant that it took almost three years to achieve initial implementation of the plan in Quebec and even then departmental contributions were frequently below projection.

3. INTRAGOVERNMENTAL RESPONSE TO ARDA-FRED

As the preceding section has illustrated in detail, ARDA-FRED projects unavoidably took a lengthy time to implement given such a highly complex policy-making system with two levels of government, many departments, political suspicions about extensive negotiations, and the necessity to consult all involved on every change. At the federal level consent between departments became progressively a more time-consuming process as ARDA and the FRED concept matured.

Since its inception, ARDA's relation with other federal offices had been harmonious, primarily because the former did not constitute a threat to the latters' own priorities or finances. Most departments applauded the attempt to end the welfare approach in rural areas and to encourage self-help and mobility, and admired a small staff attacking such a massive problem. Initially ARDA was prepared to finance the activities of other departments which offered good rural programs and this additional subsidy was attractive for departmental empires. The Department of Finance eventually stopped this internal financing and ARDA switched to persuasion to urge other departments to bring some of their priorities and practices into harmony with its projects. The greatest problem for ARDA was that these departments or their agencies, such as the Area Development Agency or the Central Mortgage and Housing Corporation, were sympathetic but inflexible.[24] They were afraid that special concessions in one area would necessitate, for political reasons, the same concession being made nationwide. Hence, for example, federal housing loans were tied to a certain set of house designs that applied everywhere, despite the fact that in poor regions such housing might be far too expensive for the local population. The uniformity problem was exacerbated by the tendency of ADA, CMHC and Manpower programs to be centrally directed: for political, economic, and administrative reasons, field officers were not permitted to make local adaptations.

ARDA relationships changed with the extent of its activities and the size of its budget. Initially Finance and Treasury Board had feared ARDA would be unable to resist political pressures and would degenerate into welfare support. These departments had little hope of financial regulation of ARDA's daily operation, protected as it was by a five-year budget, an agreement to match provincial spending, and a strong minister in Cabinet. Treasury Board was uneasy with the lack of political control in ARDA; both Hamilton and Sauvé gave their officials considerable freedoms. Sauvé transferred the minister's discretionary signing power (without Treasury Board pre-audit) beyond Davidson, to his field directors. Sauvé, indeed, had little interest in administrative details and he quickly approved the proposals of his officials. This fast "turnaround" time in ARDA applications worried both Finance and Treasury Board. In 1967 the Economic Council of Canada produced a study which revealed the absence of cost-benefit analysis[25] in ARDA programs, reflecting also a general concern about ARDA's expenditure rationale.

Finance and Treasury Board became visibly happier with ARDA as its staff succeeded in encouraging provincial planning and the development of a rational approach to expenditures. As Davidson and Poetschke (in charge of the FRED initiative) turned their efforts towards comprehensive planning, Finance and Treasury Board gave strong support in Cabinet to a FRED fund. Their motives were primarily negative—nothing much was expected to result from attempts to grapple with the mammoth problem of comprehensive development—but ARDA expenditures, which were unavoidable, were best made upon some rationale. ARDA did, in fact, produce five FRED projects by 1968. The first two were pleasant surprises while the remaining three quickly assumed nightmare proportions in terms of the cost and extent of federal commitments. These projects were located in PEI, Quebec, New Brunswick (two), and Manitoba.

As the FRED planning at the provincial level with the aid of ARDA experts began to produce policy proposals, a FRED Advisory Board of deputy ministers was established at Ottawa to design and co-ordinate finance and other departmental programs. The work of the Board met with great success initially; the uniqueness and modest size of FRED experiments encouraged officials to participate as individuals and not as representatives of a departmental view. There was a real willingness to look at a problem without the blinkers of existing program constraints. Departments were prepared to examine a problem and its solution and then adjust existing programs to secure corrective action. For instance, the Department of Finance reversed its firm policy of not assisting education in the provinces and did so for the sake of comprehensiveness in the FRED plan in New Brunswick.[26]

While the New Brunswick and Manitoba FRED projects were somewhat startling because of their size, the BAEQ application which followed was horrifying. No one had grasped the integrated size of the federal commitments to the Gaspé project until the individual ARDA negotiations were assembled and set before the Advisory Board. Several features were disturbing. Finance was increasingly aware that this system of procedure was unable to control expenditure. The research and social animation process generated such expectations that a heavy commitment was laid on government before the whole package could receive financial scrutiny. While the Department of Finance supported the FRED approach, the uncontrollable political situation engendered a massive block commitment to expenditure. The BAEQ plan was followed by an even larger Prince Edward Island application.

It was difficult to cut into these FRED plans because they had been carefully assembled as integrated packages. Thus by the time the later FRED plans were being reviewed by the FRED board the matter had gone so far politically that it could not consider the size, but only the quality of the plan. Program departments, such as Manpower, became increasingly concerned with each new FRED plan about the size of their own commitment. This planning process was beginning to compete with and shift their own priorities, whereas earlier the ARDA requests had been small or accompanied with ARDA funds. By the time of the final FRED plan review (for Prince Edward Island in 1968), the concern with expenditures and priorities had caused the approach of board members to become strictly departmental.

What had happened was that the ARDA-FRED program, at first dismissed as a boondoggle or as incapable of tackling a complex comprehensive development plan, was shaping a process which had a growing influence on government policies. The small ARDA staff were developing a rural adjustment technique that laid out education, training, housing, and health plans as well as providing for administrative and institutional changes in government operations. In their component parts programs looked tolerable if not amusing; assembled into a plan, they were potent.

4. FEDERAL RATIONALISM AND REGIONAL DISPARITIES

One of the most profound personal influences upon policy was exerted by Tom Kent when he assumed the post of deputy minister of Forestry and Rural Development in July 1968, and in 1969 of its later successor, the Department of Regional Economic Expansion (DREE). Kent's arrival brought abrupt changes to every feature of ARDA-FRED. The problem of rural poverty had found no assured answer. It was simply not known whether funds, education, new industries, mobility, or infra-structure were individually or collectively the solution. Depending on the time period available a variety of approaches could be tried .(Time period became a very crucial factor in the highly political approach of DREE). The creation of the Department of Regional Economic Expansion in 1969, in fact, reflected a new sense of urgency in the federal thrusts to end rural disparities, and reflected also the dissatisfaction with single functional (i.e. rural) solutions. The aim of the new department was similar to those of the programs—ADA, ARDA, FRED, ADB—it re-placed or took under direction: to narrow the income gap between have and have-not regions through providing more jobs; that is, through self-help and not welfare or mass migration out of the region. Its methods were greatly different. Policies were devoted to large regions of slow growth (seventy percent of DREE funds expended went east of Ottawa) giving assistance to private industrial development plans. Emphasis was placed upon improving urban infrastructure, to serve as a lure for new industries and to encourage rural-to-urban migration. Both Marchand and Kent brought to this department, as they had to Manpower earlier, a discipline that was political, secretive, quantitative, and innovative.

Once again Kent was provided with an opportunity to exercise con-siderable political authority, as he had in earlier posts. Marchand devoted his own energy largely to Quebec, both for DREE's purposes and as a general trouble shooter for the new Liberal prime minister, Pierre Trudeau, elected in June 1968. Because of the burden of Marchand's responsibility, Kent was left to handle negotiations and policy for the rest of the country, although only a deputy minister and therefore, strictly speaking, impartial and anonymous. Policies, consequently, were not "depoliticized" at the deputy minister level, as is usually the case, thus preventing a healthy tension from developing between official and minister. Instead the tension appeared to shift into the lower civil service echelons—between Kent and his officials.

Kent's attitudes towards programs and officials brought under DREE appeared to be similar to his earlier techniques with TVTA. According to those who worked with him in the federal regime or dealt with him from the provinces, he removed most policy decision making to his department in Ottawa and to his office within the department, frequently leaving his wider staff and the provinces bewildered as to his motives or future in-tentions. The regional officials of ARDA-FRED lost their signing powers and were placed on strict budgets, closely directed from Ottawa. The regional officials were not informed until the last minute of their annual budget size, guidelines or program renewals, and they were unable to assist their provincial counterparts in their own budget making. Even when budget details were given to field officers, they were not permitted to take notes or learn the size or national distribution of DREE funds. It was made clear to them that development of new strategy or policy commitments to the provinces would be executed in Ottawa and that decentralization was to cover only administrative and tactical matters. This proved to be too rigid, at least in the case of the administration of the development plan for Prince Edward Island, where increasingly the DREE representative had to apply policy to changing local situations.

As for the central staff in his department at Ottawa, Kent once again bypassed those with whom he could not work or who did not leave his service. As had been the case with OTA, most of the senior ADA and ARDA-FRED staff indeed left or were removed to the provinces.[27] Few agriculturalists remained in DREE. Those who left complained that Kent had broken the department into numerous sections with poor lateral communications. Information was directed primarily to his office; he streamed and filtered all requests from below or outside.[28] Only Kent had a complete picture of the department's policies and priorities. Some of his staff were not permitted to establish lateral relations with other departments. Field officers complained, for instance, that regional representatives of other federal departments had, for information, to consult DREE in Ottawa, and not its regional offices. Regional staff were instructed not to work along with provincial planning units which had been assisted by FRED funds.[29]

The FRED projects under the new department fared little better than the ARDA program had done. Soon after Marchand declared them to be "almost dead."[30] Had DREE been unopposed, these projects would now be fully terminated as Marchand announced was his intent when the new department was formed. But provincial governments in Manitoba, Quebec, and Prince Edward Island were successful in their strong protests against this. DREE efforts to discredit the operations of the Manitoba FRED project, the most effective of all these schemes, were stopped when the new premier, Edward Schreyer, secured a promise from Prime Minister Trudeau and Marchand that the program would be continued.[31] In Quebec and Prince Edward Island similar strong provincial protests achieved the retention of the FRED projects, although the "mix" of policies to be shared was redirected towards infrastructure and not to those policies for social or institutional change. Kent also had to yield eventually to strong political pressure from Ontario and reverse his decision not to sign a third five-year ARDA Agreement. Clearly both FRED and ARDA as rural reforms were considered by DREE to be low priorities and received both little support or service at the federal level— short of requests (felt in some provincial administrations to be almost unrealistic), that all expenditures under FRED and ARDA be shown and evaluated on a quantitative basis.

The FRED and ARDA projects (and TVTA) had fallen victim not so much to the seeming perversity of Kent in administration or decision making as to a general change in the federal attitude towards the development, implementation, and assessment of its programs. This began in the mid-sixties and progressively encompassed all federal policy.[32] A change in style and scope more so than goals was the unique contribution of DREE's policies to the various ARDA-FRED programs. While both the new DREE program and the earlier FRED approach were concerned with jobs, parity of income, social adjustment, and labour mobility, the scope of methods for achieving these goals was different.

DREE saw the future of Canada in industrialization; and it entertained none of the variety of views found in ARDA during the sixties. The new federal program was a great deal more unilateral and single-minded. In an earlier relaxed period, ARDA and FRED had almost the luxury to pursue various enquiries about the depth and nature of rural adjustment. As noted, Sauvé and Hamilton were "participative and grassroots" planners. Like the TVTA officials, they did not just deliver services from a rule book or according to pre-established criteria. Sauvé sought to service the provinces; they were considered as completely joint partners in confronting a problem that ignored jurisdictional boundaries. He was even prepared to admit he was wrong. When his officials demonstrated to him that poverty existed outside Quebec and that agricultural programs should be broadened, he accepted their position.

In sharp contrast, DREE made a hard-headed political decision to focus upon jobs, the provision of infrastructure and public works, and to avoid dissipation of effort on the rural areas, big bureaucracies, and multi-faceted approaches. DREE staked its future on the provision and generation of jobs, trusting that attitudinal and structural changes would eventually follow. DREE was also more passive, preferring through industrial incentives to restructure the economy only on the initiative of private industries and not on its own aggressive planning—as had been the case with FRED. This line of procedure inevitably led to abrupt and arbitrary decisions about what development meant. Thus ARDA and FRED (at the federal level) scarcely survived the new DREE techniques.

From this change in the scope of policy to reduce regional disparities there followed a change in style which reflected Ottawa's greater concern for federal control of its expenditures in the provinces according to its own standards of "efficiency"—both economic and political. Without going into the detail of later chapters, suffice it to say here the centralization of political and economic criteria for directing ARDA and FRED programs, as described above, reflected the new belief that federal spending must have federal objectives and be in accord with such goals. In such a setting (as will be demonstrated more fully later) there was little room for the politics of consultation, joint inquiry or compromise. Not only did ARDA-FRED projects fail to fit the new rationale, but they also involved aspects of joint consultation which were regarded as inefficient and unworkable. The new pre-packaged, pre-financed approach of Ottawa now meant that provinces became recipients of, not partners in, federal expenditure decisions.

The detail given in this chapter has been required to point to two facts often overlooked by more abbreviated and categorized accounts of these programs. The first was, once again, the evident importance of personalities for the extent of program commitments and the nature of inter- and intragovernmental relations—as indicated also in the preceding chapter. The second was the very considerable variation in provincial response to ARDA and to Ottawa in that connection. Depending upon its own political regime and its plans for the economy, each province achieved very different results with its expenditures under ARDA-FRED —from an incremental assistance to farm projects to evident reduction of the stagnant poverty of the rural population. The histories of ARDA-FRED, and then DREE, seem to reflect, once again, a growing policy concentration upon certain regions in Canada and stronger moves towards bilateral federal-provincial relations in an endeavour to reduce the worst aspects of regional poverty. In the process, the structure of policymaking and even of federal-provincial relations, has been very significantly altered. In fact, given that the poor provinces were so dependent on federal aid, DREE's approach, eschewing joint policy making, raised the question about the continuing role of such provinces in the federation, the fuller impact of which will be assessed subsequently.

There has been no measurable end result of the alterations in programs of the sixties on regional poverty in Canada. The recent stress upon urban and industrial growth, as a new lure for redundant rural population, serves to recall that disparities are not simply a question of poverty and adjustment but of potential and growth as well. It is, in fact, to this attempt to encourage growth within the urban centres of high unemployment through industrial expansion that the following chapters must turn.

Chapter Six

The Pursuit of the Private Industrialist
by Government

Federal government interest in the growth and welfare of industry developed during the 1960s as a result of two concerns. One was the need to rejuvenate generally the industrial complex after the eclipse of its talents, research, and competitiveness during the 1950s by other trading nations through Canada's having given excessive attention to the exploitation of its natural resources. The other concern was more directly related to the differences in potential for economic growth among regions. While the recession had created centres of cyclically high unemployment, throughout the country certain regions had, in addition, chronically high rates of unemployment, a consequence not of the eclipse of industry but its absence. It was to solve the disparities between regional employment opportunities, which made poor regions especially susceptible in times of recession, that the federal government entered the field of industrial incentives in the 1960s.

During this decade the federal government offered industrial incentives —either through profits tax holidays for corporations or cash grants—by means of three different pieces of legislation: the Area Development Agency (ADA), 1963–65; the Area Development Incentives Act (ADIA), 1965–70; and, the Regional Development Incentives Act (RDIA), 1969–   . Gradually government overcame its timidity in dealing with the private industrial sector. What began in the late 1950s as location, market, and managerial advice to industry by the provinces became by 1970 discretionary and selective industrial incentives offered by the federal government.

Industrial policies, of whatever nature, operated in a field interlaced with various goals and methods of both central and provincial regimes. The provinces' earlier experience in providing incentives stemmed from their ownership of natural resources as well as the recognition, especially in poor provinces, that industrialization was a solution to most government problems of insufficient revenue. Consequently; there were many provincial observers who were very sensitive to any policy, or promise thereof, for the fostering of industry by Ottawa. The rich provinces, by and large, had little need to entice or deal with industry outside of establishing basic regulations for it, although subsequently attempts were made to affect the location of firms. For its part, Ottawa was a late starter; constrained as it was by a traditional respect for the basic inviolability of the private sector[1] and only eventually motivated by a concern for the loss of Canada's competitive trading position in the world—once again, as with agriculture and manpower, a deficiency not met by the boom economy of the 1950s. During the 1960s, the topic of industrialization became the focal point of frequent intergovernmental conflict over what constituted the appropriate federal policy for economic growth—of both the nation and its constituent regions.[2] As well, industrial growth became the centre of competition for the economic prominence of governments within the federal system. It became the hope of the poor to catch up with central Canada and the expectation of the rich to move to full potential. Ottawa's attempt to mediate the clash of these conflicting desires—as well as to respect the private sector—shaped the difficulties in this aspect of regional development to which we now turn.

1. THE NEED FOR ASSISTANCE TO INDUSTRY

The concern for a rejuvenation of the secondary industry sector in Canada was stimulated, as in other fields, by the example of a previous American activity. In the United States under President Kennedy during the early sixties, there was a strong and urgent feeling that the national economy had to be reactivated after the recession of 1957–61. His Council of Economic Advisers stressed the use of potential and growth as targets, rather than a point in the business cycle.

Canada's recession had been more severe than the American, thereby making the questions of business and individual incomes all the more pressing. Businessmen discovered Canada to be losing its place in world trade for a variety of reasons. Traditional industries met increasing competition from the resurgent and modernized industries of countries damaged in the Second World War. The economic recession of the late fifties indeed revealed the failure of numerous marginal firms in an overly fragmented, Canadian manufacturing sector. Major industries were technologically out of date; textile manufacturing, for instance, used heavily recycled equipment and was only able to remain competitive through a move from Ontario to Quebec, although this merely secured cheaper labour rather than improved productivity.[3] The lag in productivity and lack of aggressive selling in Canada was attributed to the mentality of a branch-plant economy. The parent American or British firms provided innovations, entrepreneurial talent, new market enterprises, technological sophistication, and research; these activities were not the prime responsibility of a branch plant. Hence when a new chemical industry was developed in the late fifties in Canada, it represented a type of innovation and source of new jobs which business interests felt was needed in increasing numbers.

Besides the need to improve the quality of Canadian industry, the recession and a tendency towards an inferiority complex in Canadian management made urgent the discovery of an ability to manipulate the capacities of industry. The country had long had an awareness of chronic unemployment in certain provinces and regions, and better research revealed an increasingly stark picture.[4] Moreover, the depression in automotive and farm implement sales, as well as the completion of the St. Lawrence Seaway, put several large urban centres within Southern Ontario (Windsor, Brantford, Cornwall) into a state of severely high unemployment which required new forms of large-scale, highly-skilled enterprise in these areas.

These types of problems produced demands for more industrial research, greater assistance for innovations, new incentives to attract industries, aggressive export promotion, and better solutions for the burden of unemployment and low incomes. The answers to these demands required measures of co-ordination and provision of funds beyond the capacity of the private sector. The federal government was urged by businessmen to promote these industrial interests with a new department, just as traditional government departments had served farmers, fishermen or primary resource industries.

For their part in this ferment, the provinces passed on to Ottawa as a national problem the discontent arising from their own industrialized cities and regions. Although the rural-urban shift and the depressed economic conditions put pressure on their municipalities first, few provinces had devised corrective policies, largely for reasons of political philosophy or financial constraint. Saskatchewan had experimented with industrial incentives, including nationalization in extreme cases, but with little success. Most provinces provided advice on location, market, or organization, but no financial support. Ontario, with more staff, could additionally provide projections for markets and labour force. The poorer provinces with their traditional limitations of little skilled manpower, distance from markets and lack of ancillary services experimented with limited success at the periphery of their resource base.[5] The two Western-most provinces, their Social Credit regimes firmly wedded to a principle of non-interference in industrial activity, allowed whatever secondary industry that wished to enter the province to service their booming primary resource industries.

The development of resources by government had constitutionally and traditionally fallen to the provincial sector. Even if there had been no very active provincial innovations, Ottawa would not then have been disposed to assert itself forcefully in the field. The federal government of the fifties, it should be recalled, had felt that its activity should be minimal in regard to the private industrial and commercial sector, and in the early sixties it felt that its primary contribution should be to provide a favour-able research environment, basic infrastructure, and a trained labour force. Consequently, there was little scope for joint federal-provincial action or planning within this narrow definition of the federal responsi-bilities. In Diefenbaker's Cabinet, moreover, the making of economic policy was not considered a joint power with the provinces. Prime Minister Pearson also not only subscribed to this philosophical view but attempted to carry into practice a number of federal policies without prior provincial consultation. He met with considerable difficulty because of an underestimation of the need for provincial co-operation in order to obtain the effective administration of certain aspects of these federal policies. Thus the prospect for either individual or joint government activity regarding industries in the early sixties appeared to be limited. The provinces were not able, inclined, or requested, to participate in a new industrial policy. Their most frequent dialogue with Ottawa con-sisted of protests about unemployment and cautiously conservative re-quests for federal activity, provided that natural market forces were not upset.

For its part Ottawa had not been wholly unaware of the need for encouraging innovation in industry. In 1961 the Department of National Revenue began to administer an amendment to the Income Tax Act as a program of the Department of Trade and Commerce which encouraged industrial production and innovation by granting double depreciation allowances on certain classes of industrial machinery and equipment that produced new products in areas of concentrated unemployment. Special research grants were also announced in the Speech from the Throne in 1962. The spirit of change and a new thrust in Canadian trade was generated by the enthusiastic Conservative minister of Trade and Commerce, George Hees, whose motto was "YCDBSOYA—You Can't Do Business Sitting On Your Ass." At every opportunity he exhorted business to examine and improve its productivity and competitiveness. At the National Productivity Council, the Industrial Promotion Conference, and the Export Trade Promotion Conference he provided meetings in which public and private officials were brought together over mutual industrial problems. Furthermore, the businessman's requests for his own government department and better market and labour force statistics were reinforced at the public level by the recommendations of the Glassco Commission of 1962,[6] which suggested a department of industry providing research, incentives, and promotion, supported outside the civil service (and their daily problems) by a research body of economists with a longer term perspective.

Innovation, research, and production were also traditional concerns of the Department of Defence Production, a research and development body as well as a supply department for government defence activities. Its responsibility for the allocation of military contracts naturally developed a concern for the competitiveness of Canadian companies and the presence of talent or deficiencies of skills, quality, and innovation in the country with regard to other nations or certain regions in Canada. The Defence Research Board and National Research Council were two of the few supporters of pure and applied research in the largely branch-plant Canadian economy.

The Department of Labour through its labour market studies rounded out the productivity, export, and market research of Defence Production and of Trade and Commerce. Finance had relatively few economists for its largely budgetary role; but it was the new Liberal minister of Finance, Walter Gordon, and his advisers who, in the light of his earlier Royal Commission Report and of American experience, argued for a broad regional approach to meeting the income gap. For the problem of unemployment, under-employment and low incomes Gordon proposed a broad program to cover ten percent of the population by designating large regions for industrial development. These could have included all of eastern Canada to Three Rivers in Quebec, as well as Northern Ontario.

Opposed to this proposal was the Department of Labour which took an area (sub-regional) approach. Senior Labour officials argued that federal aid should concentrate on only carefully-defined, very poor areas —which would thus narrow the coverage proposed by Finance to a few centres. They believed public action should be concerned less with potential and growth and more with stabilizing the areas of acutely high levels of unemployment. Rather than a broad designation, Labour urged the use of National Employment Service (NES) areas and statistics to direct federal money by the criteria of unemployment, underemployment, and slow growth income.[7] The differences of opinion were exacerbated by the arbitrary administrative boundaries of NES, which bore only coincidental relations to growth, industrial potential, population density, and hence, to pools of skilled labour or economic regions. NES and Labour statistics proposed as criteria were in fact crude and uncertain. While Ottawa abounded with agricultural statistics, "theory of the firm" micro-economists were few and the data was not available to map progress or needs objectively.[8]

The creation of the Economic Council of Canada and the Department of Industry in 1963 were the immediate results of the ferment about industrial growth and economic planning. The Council was outside the daily crises of government departments and fulfilled the need for an expert group to assemble statistics and to reveal long-term trends and needs. The new Department of Industry was provided with the research staff from Defence Production and Trade and Commerce, to supply sector-by-sector analyses and expert advice for private industry. The services of the Labour department became an essential input for the Department of Industry; their greatest contribution was to provide the criteria that would make areas eligible for a new series of industrial incentives, which were to be co-ordinated by the new Area Development Agency (ADA) within Industry.

2. The Extent and Scope of the ADA Incentives Program for Industries

It was hoped that ADA in a unique way might offer development policy which was unconfined by precedents of welfare or adjustment grants to industry. While ARDA and TVTA had been administered by existing departments and first had had to break with traditional behaviour, the creation of a new Department of Industry aroused expectations for long-term, growth-oriented, industrial policies. Perhaps the political enthusiasm of its minister, C. M. Drury, and of Prime Minister Pearson, in the first flush of their election to office, resulted in statements somewhat overly energetic and ambiguous, which generated an expectation that was not matched by the legislation. The greatest problem with ADA was the gap between what it did and what those outside it felt it should do.

Difficulties with ADA stemmed first from uncertainty about its role. As an integral part of the Department of Industry, there was no specific act establishing ADA that tied theory to practice. Differences between pronouncements and practice soon created disappointments. Despite its broad-sounding title, the agency did not constitute the establishment of a spending program by government. ADA was not planned to make a fresh incursion into the private sector but rather to provide a better co-ordination of existing industrial incentives—tax holidays, winter works, accelerated public works—within a more rigorously-defined context. ADA was, typically, announced primarily as an emergency, short-run experiment to increase employment in designated chronic areas, in contrast with the more long-term and growth oriented aspects of most of the policies of the Department of Industry. The agency administered largely automatic criteria for eligibility and automatic formulae for assistance. Its approach remained primarily a welfare or supportive one. Hence the designation of recipient areas and industries was not on the basis of creative, discretionary policies for economic growth but by virtue of their level of unemployment or stagnation (which very likely was good reason to question the economic potential of the area). The National Employ-ment Service, a body concerned with unemployment, not economic growth and development (as was the Economic Council of Canada) determined the boundaries of regions. The resulting program represented a social policy of employment, not an economic policy of development.[9]

Provincial interests in the new provision of federal incentives were, however, whetted by the experience of joint ARDA and TVTA programs, and by the absence hitherto of any exclusively federal industrial program to restrict the scope of ADA. In fact, ADA was designed to be far less energetic or daring than ARDA or TVTA although it had the benefit of their experience.[10] Initiative under its program was not really federal, provincial, joint, or co-ordinated, but private and corporate—as was the planning. While industrial growth was to be encouraged, ADA did not contribute its own views about a development plan to reduce regional disparities. It shunned the development of mobility concepts as used by TVTA and, instead, encouraged the taking of jobs to people in marginal areas. Above all, assistance was not to direct the free market forces but to provide "one-shot" aid to starting firms, evidently a response to busi-nessmen who feared creeping socialism.

Many in government at both levels, however, felt that much more than this was required to deal with unemployment and regional depression, and to promote sound industrial growth. For a number of reasons, such as a conservative interpretation of its legitimate jurisdictions, the federal government had denied to itself this task, but not without the occasional titillation of grander visions, thereby creating an ambiguity as to ADA's real role. The title of the agency itself encouraged wild speculations and this was reinforced by misleading generalizations in the House of Com-mons. For example, in introducing the legislation, Pearson said: "The areas we are concerned with are those in which unemployment is heavy and chronic in its nature, where special government action is therefore called for in order to encourage economic *development* or industrial adjustment."[11] In the same debate, Drury alluded to "economic development" and "planning" as well as indicating the executive role of government in the process.

> . . . [the agency] will have authority to authorize and direct departments, branches and agencies of the government to undertake special measures as may be appropriate to facilitate economic development in designated areas . . . it will be possible to plan and implement coordinated programmes involving the facilities of a number of departments.[12]

Elsewhere his statements seemed to indicate retraction of the above:

> This particular programme is directed . . . not towards industrial development *per se*, or economic development *per se*, but to the relief of chronic high level unemployment. Because unemployment is a federal government responsibility there is no need for joint federal-provincial programmes.[13]

The Departments of Labour and Industry intended these statements to be read narrowly; other federal departments preferred the broad implications. Provinces did likewise; their experience with regional growth made an extensive program either a necessity (in poor provinces) or a consultative program a philosophical *desideratum* (in rich provinces).

Unlike the generally favourable response to ARDA and TVTA, the attitudes of the provinces to the new federal legislation posed a second major difficulty in the use of industrial incentive policies to reduce disparities. All generally felt the federal program to be too narrow, largely because provinces had had a longer history of a concern for growth and jobs. Most had the advice of economists who encouraged a broad approach to problems of unemployment. Accordingly, provinces considered the federal approach a stop-gap solution to unemployment rather than an attack on a basic economic problem. Beyond this, however, reactions differed according to the wealth or planning experience of a province. The poor provinces (the Maritimes, Quebec, and Saskatchewan) and those without industrial development problems or preferences (Alberta and British Columbia) questioned not so much the propriety of federal action but its narrowness. These provinces urged that the area program be made regional, that unemployment criteria include a criterion for economic growth, and that the passiveness and jurisdictional cautiousness of the federal government be replaced by active and preventive planning. The traditional response to symptoms and not causes of problems, the focus upon areas of high unemployment which often concentrated efforts in "hinterlands" rather than growth nodes, and the failure to concentrate labour and capital in the areas of greatest proven potential, were all considered marks of an outdated approach.

The same group of provinces argued that federal inhibitions were producing a program with potentially harmful results; the conflict between TVTA-ARDA mobility requirements and the ADA approach of "jobs-to-people" was seen as an indication of the most basic lack of co-ordination. Their protests were somewhat vindicated by subsequent federal changes: the relaxation of NES boundaries in the Area Development Incentives Act legislation of 1965–70 to include contiguous counties in designations, and the giving of complete discretion to the minister in the Regional Development Incentives Act legislation (1969) for the designation of broad regions, not areas. Under the latter act there was also provision for "special" designation of certain urban growth centres which enabled federal financing of infrastructure projects necessary for economic growth and social progress.[14]

While Ontario (and to a lesser extent Quebec and Manitoba) shared in some of these provincial protests, in essence their complaints were of a different nature. Poor provinces and those without their own industrial development plans regarded ADA as insufficient both in its geographic coverage and its passive approach. Ontario, however, was less worried about the extent of the program and more concerned about its supposed neutrality and objectivity.

Ontario rejected the federal government's claims that its incentives were neutral and simply confined to labour market adjustments; instead it argued that federal policies were diverting the natural and most efficient location of industry, labour, and capital. It warned that the "welfare" ADA policy would impede efficient overall growth. It pointed out (as did a special study for ADA of New Brunswick) that capital was not the only factor retarding activity in certain regions but that a lack of labour skills and entrepreneurial talent along with distance from markets provided sound reasons why intelligent industries would not locate there. The issue was not the extent of ADA but whether such a program should be permitted to exist, given that it prevented the natural flow of labour and capital to its most productive use in Canada. The ADA program, Ontario claimed further, did not maximize economic or social productivity by its policies; in fact, it served as an expensive "mislocation agency." Welfare grants, together with the working of the natural mobility of labour and capital, could have given comparable income and services to these designated poor regions at a cheaper cost to Ottawa and with higher productivity for all Canadians than under the ADA scheme.

Ontario's objections became more vocal after the Area Development Agency was replaced by the Area Development Incentives Act of 1965 and subsequently by the Regional Development Incentives Act in 1969. These changes were a deliberate attempt to favour the poor regions with special industrial attention which the impartial criteria of ADA had failed to achieve. Under ADA, Ontario had three of the sixty-five designated regions in Canada (Cornwall, Windsor, Brantford) that alone took three quarters of ADA funds between 1963 and 1965. This was because these areas suffered primarily from high, exceptional (but not chronic), unemployment and thereby had a ready pool of skilled labour, good transportation facilities, and good entrepreneurial talent. They also had the advantage of being located within the central Canadian market. The ADIA, however, in 1965 "dedesignated" these three prosperous centres and added more remote Ontario areas which reduced the attractiveness of the province compared with regions elsewhere. The ADIA legislation also moved towards a relaxation of the unrealistic NES boundaries by adding the "contiguous counties" surrounding a NES area. The province disapproved of this move away from narrow areas focussed upon NES districts, which tended at least to be urban-centred. The more diffused approach dispersed urban-centred industrial activity. Under the RDIA legislation in 1970 Southern Ontario still was not designated for industrial incentives.

It was these federal attempts to reduce regional economic disparities through the industrial policies of ADA, ADIA, and RDIA that again began to divide provinces into camps of rich and poor reminiscent of the forties. Ontario's protests were derived from what it considered to be an increasing burden of the rich provinces to provide for the poor. Because Ottawa had made the commitment to secure a rough equality in the standards of living of all Canadians, this in effect required a fiscal transfer from the rich provinces to the poor (calculated by Ontario to amount in 1970 to a net outflow of funds from Ontario to Ottawa of $1.4 billion).[15] While Ontario did not begrudge this flow of funds to achieve a rough equalization in Canada of tax burdens or the levelling-up of services, it did very much resent this added federal interference in the economy which it viewed as a warping of the natural economic forces and flows which had made the province so prosperous. To Ontario the federal industrial incentive policy was so adversely weighted against the most productive regions that it was akin to "roasting the goose that laid the golden egg."[16] While there were already distortions on the fiscal side of the economy, to interfere with economic forces would remove from the prosperous the opportunity to generate the amount of wealth that could provide the tax revenues needed for fiscal redistribution. Ottawa, however, did not agree that the breaking point had been reached, and it continued to try to lure potential industry through incentives away from central Canada.

3. The Problem of Uniformity as an Unrealistic Criterion

The ADA program was similar to the initial designs of TVTA and ARDA in that it reflected the post-war caution of the federal government in intruding on provincial and private areas of operation. Just as these latter two programs had avoided influencing provincial decisions in order to secure ready participation, so ADA had equivalent provisions. Automatic and uniformly applicable criteria such as those used by ADA for area eligibility and dedesignation, and the size of the industrial incentive provided removed the possibility of accusations by other governments and business of partisanship or favouritism to regions or industries. The narrowness of ADA, too, was meant to purchase a neutrality in its impact upon provincial competition for industries. Drury, the minister of Industry, expressed this belief to the Commons and its Standing Committee on Industry, Research and Energy Development:

> . . . to have incorporated a concept of growth and a measure of income [in the ADA criteria] would have complicated the problems of defining areas and have introduced an added element of uncertainty and subjectivity with political implications.[17]

> . . . it is an arbitrary set of criteria that just applies to any given place where there is a need for them to go. It is not anything that you deliberately go out and plan to do.[18]

No province, however, accepted the implicit federal assumption that an automatic and objective program would have uniform impact across the country. Rich provinces believed that poorer regions which were designated could unnaturally siphon off talent, labour, and capital from more favourable locations which were not designated. The Western provinces complained that ADA did not provide the same opportunity for expansion in their provinces as elsewhere because certain natural resource industries were not eligible and they possessed a small secondary industry sector. Poorer provinces argued that the incentive of a tax holiday could, in fact, be used only by the high profit companies which would go to the central provinces in most cases. Later, under the Area Development Incentives Act, Ottawa responded somewhat to these complaints by broadening the industries and areas eligible for incentives and adding cash grants as an alternative to the tax holidays.

Apart from challenging the concept of uniformity written into ADA, provinces questioned the supposed objectivity and reliability of Department of Labour statistics actually used to decide on eligibility, designation, and dedesignation. The National Employment Service (as indicated earlier) lacked adequate staff and was a last-resort welfare agency in the eyes of the skilled unemployed. If anything, its sampling and reliance upon voluntary reporting overestimated unemployment and underestimated under-employment.[19] Ontario argued that the ADA program was premature; although funds were allocated, neither DBS nor Labour could provide reliable statistics—particularly on income levels—to operate an objective program. T. N. Brewis has observed:

> With a little juggling of the criteria and the adoption of different but equally valid techniques of statistical calculation one could present a kaleidoscope of different pictures of which areas should be included and which eliminated. It would change the picture for example if the number of years in computing the average were altered, or if the rapidity and direction of change in employment were considered or if in some cases nodal or median incomes were selected as a criterion for designation rather than the arithmetic mean.[20]

Aware of this vulnerability of their statistics to interpretation, the federal government was secretive and reluctant to discuss decisions with provinces. Ontario, for one, doubted the objectivity of area designation; the inclusion of its Southern Georgian Bay region in 1965 was not based on any of the three criteria of eligibility as far as the province could see. More likely this region which could not properly qualify was included for political reasons to assuage hostile provincial feelings towards the new ADIA legislation which ended the province's lucrative designation under ADA. As a consequence of these suspicions, Ottawa did not fulfill an earlier promise to evaluate the ADA program after two years of operation, largely out of concern that better statistics would reveal the arbitrary ministerial decisions of earlier years.

Poor provinces argued that their designated areas had no hope of competing with those in central provinces under the uniform ADA incentives. For one thing other provinces were located closer to the markets of central Canada. Because industrial incentives under ADA and ADIA were uniform, remote regions also did not have their urban centres designated and thus could not make their area designations additionally attractive. In 1970 this particular argument was answered by the RDIA which did designate urban centres, as well as giving designated regions pre-dominantly in eastern Canada the highest level of incentive grant, thereby consciously weighting the incentives program in favour of peripheral provinces. Nevertheless the later designation of Montreal in 1971 as eligible for a low rate of RDIA incentives did reduce somewhat the advantage of eastern Canada.

Poor provinces also pointed out that they could not receive ADA industries, because the effectiveness of the program in these provinces could not be as great as in central Canada. The basic flaw was that the universal and uniform assumption underlying the ADA-ADIA programs could not, in fact, be met uniformly. Once again the old legal fiction of equally-endowed provinces was further challenged by reality. In a study of the effectiveness of ADA in New Brunswick prepared for that body by H. Larsen of the University of New Brunswick, the author observed "the ADA programme operates on the assumption that capital constitutes the only significant activity retarding and development retarding factor."[21] That might be true for the ADA designated cities of Southern Ontario or Quebec which had a skilled, mobile labour force, entrepreneurial talent, and good infrastructure. It was not the case in poor provinces. In New Brunswick alone,

> . . . capital is not the only constraint on economic growth . . . the mentality or atmosphere within the economy has not been sufficiently growth permissive . . . there has been a general shortage of entre-preneurship, quantitatively as well as qualitatively. The formation of attractive and efficient urban centres has lagged . . . the public sector's, general programmes, development programmes, and welfare program-mes have been designed and allocated with little concern for the needed structural and special changes.[22]

Ottawa eventually did improve upon its "passive investment inducing program"[23] through the ADIA replacement for ADA and later the RDIA successor for ADIA. In each step there was, as with Manpower and rural programs the narrowing and extension of the federal commitment to the special deficiencies of poor regions which had been untreated by a uni-form level of attention to all of Canada. The RDIA legislation improved upon ADIA to provide the infrastructure required in these regions for industrial growth—sewers, roads, schools, conservation and water supply projects, and power facilities.[24] While upgrading ancillary services and the size of industrial incentives, the RDIA still did not alter the passive attitude of the federal government to private industrial investment in the region with the result that the seasonal, primary resource and low skilled structure of the Atlantic economy was unchanged. With this greater in-trusion into both the private and provincial realms by the federal govern-ment, it was expected, however, that collaboration would consequently be improved with the recipients of the new federal incentive programs.

4. GOVERNMENT VIEWS CONCERNING CONSULTATION OVER INDUSTRIAL INCENTIVES

From the earliest days of the ADA legislation provinces had expected that they would be consulted about incentives to industry. Their willingness to devise more extensive industrial policy than the federal departments made them predisposed in general to demand a joint role with Ottawa. As their specific experience with even the limited federal incentives grew, provinces protested against federal unilateral action. They found that not only did the program fail to produce uniform results but that there were "spillover effects" from the federal location of industries. The task of supplying schools, water supply, roads, power, labour training, or housing to service the new industry was presented to the province and its municipalities often without prior warning or time to alter long term plans.

Federal policy upset provincial plans in more than one way. Ontario, for instance, discovered that its Muskoka region which the province had itself finally succeeded in shrinking to an appropriate industrial labour-resource mix and equipping for a new role as a recreation area, was designated for federal industrial incentives and, correspondingly, for an inflow of labour and services. Hence Ottawa wished to encourage industries that the province felt were increasingly less competitive, in a region more usefully productive in Ontario as a tourist resort. This type of conflict was repeated with variations in Quebec, where the province's decentralizing of industry, undertaken partly to preserve a culture, added complications; in the Maritimes, where local interests wanted additional growth centres designated; and in the West, where a preponderance of natural resources necessitated primary, not secondary, industry. In all these situations "consultation" consisted of a slightly earlier federal release of new policies to the provinces than to the press. As a result of their own improving competence as economic managers and the detrimental effects of ADA, provinces from 1965 on demanded a participation in the operation and extension of federal industrial incentives.

Once again Ottawa's response to this issue could be read in two ways. Pearson, advised closely by Kent, had taken office in 1963 with a rather simple understanding of the necessity of federal-provincial consultation. Hence during his proclaimed first "Sixty Days" of decision, during which "more constructive things will be done . . . than in any similar period in Canadian history,"[25] only four major pieces of legislation actually passed the House. A national development corporation, a national scholarship plan, a municipal loan board, a national contributory pension scheme and a national medicare plan failed largely because "the Liberal strategists had not given enough consideration to the fact that for constitutional reasons none of these pledges could be discharged without the support of the provincial governments."[26] This unrealistically centralized approach could be seen in the previously noted attitude of Drury toward the new ADA "there is no need for joint federal-provincial programmes."[27]

ADA will be co-ordinating rather than executive . . . it will not interfere with provincial action to the same end.[28]

However, at other times federal speakers alluded to the inevitable need for consultation whatever the scope of ADA.

. . . [the Agency] will also work closely with provincial governments and regional bodies.[29]

. . . the Area Development Agency will work with other agencies, federal and provincial in encouraging sound area or regional development.[30]

[The Agency] will consult extensively with the appropriate authorities in each province to ascertain provincial thoughts, plans and activities respecting area or regional development.[31]

For the most part and for most provinces the federal practice of non-consultation prevailed.[32] This was best demonstrated when provinces called together to "discuss" a replacement for ADA in May 1965, found that the meeting was held largely for the sake of information and protocol. One provincial official reported:

On the one hand it was not a meeting to discuss preliminary details prior to the determination of a programme; on the other hand, the Provinces were clearly not being called upon to discuss the policy or the broad conception. It was clear from the beginning that no changes or adjustment in the policy was [sic] contemplated and that the Federal officials were anxious to establish the policy immediately.[33]

When an official from another province repeatedly asked whether the conference was called for consultation or information, a senior federal adviser replied, "the Federal Government in providing an opportunity for the expression of provincial views cannot be expected to regard such consultation as a substitute for carrying out its responsibilities in fields of federal concern."

This narrow definition of consultation stemmed from a basic reluctance to accept provincial viewpoints about industrial expansion or to extend industrial incentives into a joint planning experience. Ottawa claimed its task was uniquely national, but to some extent this was a rationalization of its growing uneasiness over the unexpected split produced by ADA policies between rich and poor provinces. Since co-ordination of policy would have been the next logical step to follow intergovernmental consultation, Ottawa reduced the significance of consultation in order firmly to discourage expectations of co-ordinated federal-provincial industrial policy, which would have been unattainable to the extent that provinces—wisely or not—were usually in competition for the attention of similar industries.

This limited form of consultation was continued under the ADIA and RDIA programmes. In 1968, the ADIA was removed from the Department of Industry and placed under the Department of Forestry and Rural Development headed by Marchand and Kent. Subsequently, the new RDIA of 1970 was to be administered by the Department of Regional Economic Expansion, once again under Marchand and Kent. The relocation signified a further conversion of the industrial incentive as a tool to combat persistent, not cyclical, areas of economic stagnation. DREE did not, however, reduce the lack of harmony with provincial planning. Federal programs, rather than reinforcing provincial incentives, went their own way, occasionally competing with provincial plans. In Nova Scotia, the provincial Industrial Estates Limited was compelled to alter its own form of incentives to fit those of ADIA and RDIA.[34] Where IEL wished to diversify the provincial economy by attracting new secondary industry, DREE preferred the easier task of expanding resource industries as well as the predominant food and beverage industry base. In the poor provinces, where almost all of DREE's money was concentrated in industrial incentives and infrastructure, there was a marked absence of provisions for a provincial contribution in these fields (which either fell within or significantly affected the provincial jurisdiction).[35]

5. CO-ORDINATION OF FEDERAL INCENTIVES FOR INDUSTRIAL GROWTH

When first announced, we may recall, ADA was primarily seen as a new effort to co-ordinate various federal incentive programs—tax holidays, winter-time work projects, public works—for industrial projects in economically depressed areas.[36] For the most part it did achieve a close working relationship with the Department of Labour whose statistical input was essential for the operation of the program's criteria. Less success was achieved with the proposed close relationship with the Department of Trade and Commerce which considered Industry a superfluous creation and resented the loss of its own fast-growing, industrial division and personnel to the new department. Eventually in 1970 the two departments were combined into Industry, Trade and Commerce.

106

Relations between ADA and other federal departments were uneven as well. Some bodies did not have the narrow perspective of ADA and could not or would not alter priorities to fit specific industrial development in designated areas. Agriculture and Rural Development officials were disappointed that ADA was not to become a complementary "urban ARDA." One fundamental problem was that ARDA and the Adult Occupational Training Act were concerned with labour mobility, often on an interprovincial basis if necessary, while ADA and ADIA talked of bringing jobs to people or, at the most, intraprovincial mobility.[37] Intragovernmental co-ordination and planning were also hindered by the fact that a large part of the ADA-ADIA programs rested upon the initiative of the private, not public sector—both to apply for and accept grants. Since ADA and ADIA were primarily a welfare service to businessmen, governmental co-ordination was only of secondary interest to them, and most other federal programs could not be matched to theirs.

The greatest internal opposition to ADA, however, came from Treasury Board and Finance, which disliked the uncertainty of the size of the tax holidays granted and their effect upon the federal revenue budget, and were dubious about the soundness of firms that were located under the scheme. ADA was indeed a potentially heavy drain on tax revenues, because the big industries in Quebec and Ontario which used it predominantly *had* profits to which the tax holidays could be applied. Finance was not willing to make the abrupt change in 1965 to the new ADIA program, which largely excluded central Canada, without much better facilities to measure the economic implications of such a move. As welfare and deficiency programs for poor regions began to mushroom, moreover, the Department of Finance became all the more anxious to preserve a balance between economic efficiency and social welfare expenditures throughout Canada. While it disliked the proposed omission of much of central Canada under ADIA, the inclusion of grants under this successor to ADA at least made the cost of the program more easily measured than tax holidays had been. But the heavy concentration of the incentive program in poor regions under RDIA since 1969, once more raised questions for Treasury Board and Finance about the efficiency and balance respectively of government expenditures.[38]

The use of industrial location and development policy as a means to reduce disparities, whether in unemployment or the rate of economic growth, had thus been fraught with disputes over the ends and means involved. More than did policies for training, infrastructure, or rural adjustment, incentives seemed to strike at the economic distinctiveness of the regions of the federation. In fact, any attempt to alleviate disparities, be they differences in finance, services, skills, rural adjustment, or

107

economic structure, could be claimed to constitute abridgements upon the freedom granted in the constitution for provinces to determine their own political diversity. The threat felt by rich provinces from industrial incentive policies of Ottawa did not stem simply from the fact that more money was "lost" from the rich to the poor than under other policies for disparities. Essentially it was the central infringement upon the rate of potential economic growth which these diversions of industries constituted. It was this unknown factor of opportunities lost (which could not be measured as one could equalization transfers) which increasingly upset the rich provinces, as Ottawa probed into encouraging the mobility of industry as an alternative to the mobility of labour.

Ottawa's first industrial policy, ADA, did not envisage this larger question, and the difficulties met by the program were largely derived from the myopic failure to see the wider consequences of its activities. Subsequent policy (ADIA, RDIA) while grander, had still not examined the impact upon national prosperity of aid to depressed regions (which became a concern of the federal Department of Finance as well as the provinces). It was this "incremental"[39] response to disparities in finance, services, and economic growth which really constituted the yielding of the federal system to the relentless logic of regional disparities. Thus the federal government by its industrial policies was actually extending central control over both rich and poor provinces. This control consisted, therefore, of an increasing capacity to direct the relative progress of Canada's diverse regional economies. During the 1960s few saw this greater significance of federal activity in a variety of fields. One effort, however, to achieve a broader grasp of developmental policies is described in the following chapter: the creation of an Atlantic Development Board, to facilitate a comprehensive approach to regional disparities in one part of the country, at least.

Chapter Seven

The Bottomless Pocket:
Spending for Growth without Design

The federal interest in economic growth in the 1960s began eventually to pursue the major elements responsible for the more limited potential in some regions with the same relentless fervour as, earlier, provinces had sought the ever finer reduction of aspects of revenue differentials between regions. Although the Atlantic provinces were recipients of ARDA, TVTA, and ADA expenditures they had a special need for more complete diagnosis of the sources of potential growth in each sector of their economy. Other regions, being more prosperous, could avoid attempts at forced growth because of the general spread of wealth within them which prosperity usually encouraged. As this was not the case in stagnant regions, federal legislation was passed in 1962 in a deliberate effort to ensure the comprehensiveness of federal policy in regard to the Atlantic provinces.

The Atlantic Development Board (ADB) was thus established in 1962 to examine (and later to fund) means by which the production of the region might be advanced.[1] The ADB as it eventually functioned was not a radically different innovation; federal capital assistance to regions had been a feature of past legislation and was in the tradition of the Prairie Farm Rehabilitation Act. Activity by the ADB, which selected and partially paid for infrastructure projects, represented the provision of specific expenditures by the federal government for the Atlantic region rather than an intergovernmental transfer of revenues (such as the Atlantic Provinces Adjustment Grants). Like ADA, it evolved as a body which required or encouraged little joint participation by provincial governments. Unlike the earlier ARDA and TVTA agreements which depended upon provincial initiative, the ADA and ADB legislation regarded the provinces largely as recipients of their services. The legislation creating the ADB also gave it a planning potential, however, which could have made a significant contribution to provincial and regional planning consciousness in terms of new procedures, if not actual economic development, through structural change. It did not realize that potential. Hence this chapter essentially examines why the board failed to reach the goals which the provinces hoped to see it achieve.[2]

1. THE REAWAKENING OF THE ATLANTIC PROVINCES

The Atlantic Development Board, as established in the last months of the Diefenbaker government, drew upon several sources for its inspiration. One of significance was the Maritime's changing attitude towards their own economic situation, communicated directly to Diefenbaker's Cabinet by H. J. Flemming, the minister of National Revenue, who sponsored the ADB and had been premier of New Brunswick. Flemming's election as premier in 1952, and that of Robert Stanfield in 1956 in Nova Scotia, had reflected a new interest in provincial self-help and self-awareness, supplementing the traditional concession-begging attitude of the Atlantic provinces at Ottawa. This new awakening could be seen in the Maritime performances at the 1955 and 1957 federal-provincial conferences where they showed a readiness to come to grips with hard economic facts, talked less about what was their due, and acknowledged that Maritime problems had to be seen within the national business cycle. They offered sensible recommendations for a division of federal and provincial powers in areas of chronic depression. Two of their requests at the time were for a federal capital projects fund for the region, and specific help in hydro-electric power development, both of which constituted the foundation for economic revival and not just temporary aid.

An important directing force in the provinces' approach came from Professor W. Y. Smith, who initiated, stimulated, and tied together various centres of economic thought in the Maritime region during the fifties and sixties. Smith served as New Brunswick's first economic adviser (to Flemming) when economists in the province's civil service were few in number. He also chaired the Department of Economics at the University of New Brunswick, in the capital, and developed a specialty of regional studies. His courses were doubly useful: both for the academic economist who found consultative positions with Maritime governments and for the provincial civil servants who could take advantage of summer and night courses to understand better the nature of economic development. Smith also served as consultant to Nova Scotia's government, and there established the concept of "Voluntary Economic Planning"—the assembly of a provincial plan from studies of various business groups—which required the formation of a semi-public Voluntary Planning Board (VEP) under a newly expanded Department of Finance and Economics (1962). In New Brunswick, the government enlarged Smith's position to an Office of the Economic Adviser (OEA) in 1962, which considerably improved New Brunswick's statistical capacity and contentiousness in federal-provincial relations. Smith also trained the personnel of the privately-financed Atlantic Provinces Economic Council (APEC) and served himself at one time as its chairman.

The APEC represented another earlier aspect of the Atlantic region's reawakening. In addition to the improvement of leadership, organization and advice within Nova Scotia and New Brunswick, there developed a greater regional consciousness. The Atlantic Provinces Economic Council, the Atlantic Premiers' Conferences, the Atlantic Provinces Research Board and the hiring of impressive, expert economists from Britain[3] were all indicators of a desire to improve the knowledge of the region and its growth needs, and to be able to impress its demands upon Ottawa rather than receive federal alms.

Provincial submissions eventually began to have an impact. By the early sixties Ottawa had given New Brunswick aid for power development. Moreover, the entire region had received Atlantic Provinces Adjustment Grants, the federal Conservatives had promised (in Moncton in 1957) a large capital grants program and the provinces had themselves established the beginnings of industrial development assistance (New Brunswick Development Corporation, the Nova Scotia Industrial Estates Limited).

Further pressure for an Atlantic capital funds program came from the federal Royal Commission on Canada's Economic Prospects, the Gordon Commission of 1957. Its impact was not immediate because the government of the day under Diefenbaker did not feel inclined to accept the report of a commission appointed earlier by his arch-rivals, the Liberals. When the Liberals regained office in 1963 action was quick to come, however, because their minister of Finance was Walter Gordon himself. In his Report he had prescribed what was eventually to become the lasting form of the ADB:

> There is then a need in the Atlantic provinces for considerable expenditure of capital on basic public facilities designed to encourage development of the resources of the region. . . . The cost involved in providing these needed services, however, would seem to be beyond the financial competence of the provincial governments concerned.

111

[W]e suggest that the federal government agree to contribute a substantial sum for capital projects in the area. . . . The expenditure of federal funds in this way should of course be made and supervised by an appropriate agency of the federal government . . . we suggest that the federal government establish a capital projects committee for the Atlantic provinces or some other appropriate agency.[4]

2. THE ROLE OF THE ATLANTIC DEVELOPMENT BOARD AS SEEN FROM OTTAWA

The initial Conservative ADB legislation introduced by Flemming in late 1962, and the subsequent Liberal amendments when they came to power in 1963, reflected a difference in approach to the still unfathomed problems of Atlantic regional growth. Flemming's proposals were probably the more exciting because they left with the ADB the task of working the mystery of growth into actual policy proposals to the Cabinet. The approach in 1963 of the newly-elected Liberal regime was a more traditional one of a board with money to spend and few criteria for direction or assessment. By contrast the board created by Flemming was to advise the federal Cabinet on measures and projects proposed by the private sector, provinces, or by commissioned research which would warrant federal funds not available from other sources, for the "development" of the Atlantic provinces. Flemming's legislation, though cautious, reflected the desire that government acquire a greater facility in handling regional problems based on well-founded expert advice. Government officials in 1962 did not really know how to ensure development and lacked a systematic structure of enquiry. Neither the provincial nor federal administration had any useful experience in co-ordinating their departments' activities into a set of objectives, priorities, and strategies.

The money eventually supplied by the Liberals did not encourage a reform in the process and structure of government which federal ARDA officials attempted to impart to their own expenditures. What was missing at both levels of government were economists with an understanding of how the integration of long-run capital projects and existing institutions would secure development of the Atlantic region. Hence the absence of countervailing forces to the politician ensured that treatment of expenditures would be largely *ad hoc* and unco-ordinated—particularly during Diefenbaker's and Pearson's crisis-prone administrations.

In this context, Flemming's ADB legislation, which did not have its own project fund (and the Liberals attacked this omission), might have been the more likely to attain a better planning capacity within government, for its function was to be primarily one of critical assessment for the

Cabinet of development proposals.[5] This was particularly necessary if, as proposed, ADB was to explore the complex primary and secondary industry sectors and proposals for their development. It might be hoped that the ADB indeed had as its support the "whole resources of Canada" that Flemming rather glibly claimed, as well as the attentive ear of Cabinet, for he would have been required to secure departmental co-operation largely through reasoning, not financial persuasion.

Flemming's ADB suffered from a remoteness from government (as a body of private citizens appointed by the Cabinet without daily relations within the civil service or the party) and a lack of financial "persuasiveness." Hence the task of securing co-ordination would have been difficult in the best of times for the minister in charge of it. In the fragmented Diefenbaker Cabinet, ADB was particularly weak. Moreover, there was no provision for its proposals to emerge out of joint committees or departmental approval prior to reaching the Cabinet. The minister responsible for ADB was not its chairman and generally he had to receive suggestions rather than initiate them himself—although the remoteness of a quasi-political body of experts might have enabled them to search for medium or long-term recommendations. The board, however, was small; it was federally appointed, staffed by federal officials and located in Ottawa.

The revision by the incoming Liberal government of the board's operation six months after its creation while perhaps more practical, lost to the government the benefit of attempting a comprehensive analysis of where federal policy should move in this region. It bore very much the personal touch of J. W. Pickersgill (a Newfoundland M.P.), and his distaste, while in the Opposition, of the Conservative approach to ADB. Pickersgill had grown up as Mackenzie King's closest adviser, and during that period absorbed King's strong sense of partisanship. His experience with and within government (as civil servant and later politician) spanned four decades; the strong influences of the past never left him sufficiently free to respond to and judge problems in terms of the present or future. His astute knowledge of parliamentary tactics, his ability to manipulate the bureaucracy and his feeling for the political "game" made him an essential Cabinet colleague to Pearson. Characteristically, he saw the role of both government and bureaucracy as dispensing the favours and values of the Liberal party and there was never any doubt in his mind that it was "*the* government party."[6] Pickersgill's own model for the ADB was drawn from the Gordon report and mixed with a certain political acumen demonstrated by the late C. D. Howe in the St. Laurent government. Howe, who was then minister of Trade and Commerce had taught two useful facts to Pickersgill: that visible federal expenditures throughout the provinces could be profitably labelled as Liberal party expenditures, with obvious implications for the voter at election time, and that a department or agency with money to spend had power in Cabinet and the bureaucracy. (Following these criteria, Trade and Commerce indeed had been the most powerful peacetime department.)

The ADB was, accordingly, Pickersgill and "Pickersgillian."[7] It was moved from its arms-length quest for broadly appropriate government policy and placed squarely inside the government under Pickersgill as secretary of state, and with a $100 million budget to spend. So personal was ADB to Pickersgill that he took it with him to the Department of Transport when he became its minister. The logical relationship between Transport and Atlantic development was tenuous to say the least. When Pickersgill eventually left the Cabinet and House in 1967, ADB was first placed under Sauvé and then Marchand in Forestry and Rural Development. The board was one of the agencies moved into the new Department of Regional Economic Expansion and was terminated in 1969. It was replaced by only an advisory board of Atlantic notables with no executive function.

In light of the independence of departments each with their own priorities, Pickersgill did not wish to place the success of ADB upon the gamble that these departments would take up its recommendations. Flemming had felt the ADB could, "be responsible for presenting its recommendations to the government and co-ordinating the passage of projects approved through the federal departments which would be concerned with them."[8] Further, he had thought the board, in addition to having a passive role of conveying recommendations of others "should also have an active role in the sense of initiating studies and making recommendations."[9] Pickersgill, with his long political experience at Ottawa realized that no satisfactory machinery existed, and so avoided jeopardizing ADB's life by a difficult and vague role of co-ordination. Besides he considerably extended the concept of "active." Having now its own fund, the board could engage in projects without being at the mercy of other departments; and being a board with a "gapfiller" role there would be a minimum of political conflict with existing or proposed federal policy among departments. Hence the ADB during the Liberal regime was executive not advisory. Its spending function also made it political, for it provided its own visible indication of its choices and activities, whereas under Flemming's arrangement the departments would have received the rewards for action.

Pickersgill also had a freedom to be flexible because his ADB did not take upon itself the massive and complex task which had earlier faced Flemming of dealing with primary and secondary industry development.

The new Department of Industry (containing ADA), created by the Liberals was to look to development in these sectors. Instead the ADB concentrated efforts more narrowly upon infrastructure, on power needs, fresh water supplies, sewerage, roads, and bridges projects, which at that time would not be detrimental or prejudicial to the developments in other sectors.[10] Indeed, the board's function as a "gapfiller"—closing chinks left by unco-ordinated federal policies—was a necessity because of a lack of integration among the federal programs affecting the region. "Gapfilling" as opposed to co-ordination did not put the onus on the board to work with other departments. Nevertheless until the arrival of DREE and vigorous attempts at co-ordination, this procedure was costly and occasionally contradictory. Without criteria for expenditure—except for a few negative restrictions which prevented the favouring of one province—ADB could operate over a vast number of projects, with the result that the $100 million fund was exhausted within the first three years. Thus ADB operations inevitably clashed with ADA's refusal to put funds into growth centres, while relations with ARDA were only harmonious by coincidence, not design. In any case with a few limitations, ADB operated as Pickersgill wished. He did, however, establish in advance explicit ratios for dividing the fund between the provinces, to avoid accusations of interprovincial partisanship.

Clearly Pickersgill's main interest in ADB was as a board to spend funds in the Atlantic region, for he made very little mention of additional provisions in the legislation to design criteria and a framework for spending. "Gapfilling" evidently pervaded attitudes as much as policies. The board was also empowered "to prepare in consultation with the Economic Council of Canada an overall co-ordinated plan for the promotion of the economic growth of the Atlantic region." Project spending, however, was not conditional upon this and such was Pickersgill's lack of enthusiasm that a planning division was only finally created two years after ADB had already been in operation. His particular choice of a director produced an official who, by his careful and methodical nature, would not deliver a plan until extensive studies on the potential of all sectors and the inter-relation of each had been completed and assembled into a document of reasonable goals and strategies. Some even claimed that the planners embarked on a "research spree" instead of a research program directed towards the development of planning objectives and policy priorities to achieve these. In fact, no framework, objectives, or strategies were generated by this careful process, not even by 1969 when the board was disbanded. The ADB never pressed the planners for a decision, and so its spending went on in an unfettered empirical fashion.

That a planning division was appointed at all was a sign of pressures upon Pickersgill who, to get access to funds for ADB in the first place, had evidently agreed in principle to a planning group.[11] There was, however, no indication that ADB expenditures without this planning were foolish or harmful. The size of expenditures without a framework for policy decisions made the federal civil servants, and especially Finance and Treasury Board, increasingly uneasy—particularly when the initial fund was exhausted so rapidly. Pickersgill's motivation was apparently the political rewards of spending; Finance and most civil servants (even in ADA) had a preference for research. Uncontrolled expenditures and the delay in selecting planning staff arose ultimately from a shortage of skilled economists knowledgeable in the planning process as well as a lack of respect by politicians and old-time officials for planning and program integration. It is interesting to note that the pressure for planning came from officials with previous planning experience in Saskatchewan. One was the director of ADB's planning branch and two other former Saskatchewan officials held senior federal Finance posts where they were also ideally located to apply pressure.[12]

Potentially the ADB could have brought a new or at least better organized direction to federal activities in the Atlantic region. Not only could reforms have been brought to the process of devising and harmonizing policy at Ottawa, but a different approach to the structure of the provincial economies might also have reduced the need to rely, as did ADA, on change through private industrial activity. A change to the process or structure was avoided, thanks largely to the dominating personality of Pickersgill and his aversion to innovation in the highly structured government system at Ottawa. Furthermore, ADA frustrated rather than improved relations with the provinces.

3. THE ROLE OF THE ATLANTIC DEVELOPMENT BOARD AS SEEN FROM THE PROVINCES

Ottawa's largely unexciting and intensely pragmatic response to the Atlantic disparities failed also to open new paths in federal-provincial relations. There was very little mention of the role of the provinces either in the House debates or in the ADB legislation. Given the lack of inclination and capacity to plan at the federal level, and the *ad hoc* nature of federal expenditures in the past (despite the more systematic reforms made under ARDA and TVTA), there was no necessary presumption that ADB should be a joint federal-provincial endeavour. The lack of equivalent capacity at the provincial level, despite encouraging signs of change, made (as ARDA officials had also discovered), the possibility of joint planning difficult. Interestingly enough the ADB was required in its legislation to consult with the Economic Council but no reference was made to consultation with the provinces except for a provision for the joint administration of projects. In fact, under the Conservatives' legislation provinces had to make submissions to the board which placed them in the embarrassing position of being judged by little more than selected local notables.

A gapfilling board, however, did not need prolonged consultation nor for success much originality of thought. And Pickersgill primarily wished to spend, not be confined by extensive intra- or intergovernmental negotiations. Provinces were, indeed, consulted and informed by the projects division of ADB and they frequently shared in the financing of ADB programs; but there was no provision for joint selection or assessment of projects.[13] As for ADB's planning division it had closer, yet more difficult relations with the provinces.

There was little that was innovative in the board's expenditures. Of course it could be stated that it represented Ottawa's first exclusively regional approach to economic disparities using both projects and extensive planning, but this was deceptive because these were not designed to generate a regional response from the Atlantic provinces, nor did they make much contribution to improving the capacity of the individual provincial administration. Pickersgill's spending in each province was guided by fixed ratios. This did not require provinces to think critically of their comparative position within a region if they could confidently expect a *quid pro quo* for federal activity in a neighbouring province. They responded to ADB initiatives but did not devise them. In one case, Nova Scotia was offered $12 million to develop electric power for which the province, at the time well-supplied with power, had no use. Because ADB refused to allow the funds to be diverted by the province to other more pressing needs, Nova Scotia was obliged to forego the offer for eighteen months until thermal electric projects were devised to use up the money.[14]

Ottawa was not alone in its lack of enthusiasm for a regional economic approach. Even as ADB was being formed, the research capabilities of each province in the Maritimes were being extended. Consequently, regional bodies were gradually eclipsed by individual provincial agencies. The intergovernmental Atlantic Provinces Research Board was disbanded, leaving only the privately-sponsored Atlantic Provinces Economic Council which gradually lost its uniqueness and visibility among increasingly numerous federal and provincial groups. When Prince Edward Island established a Treasury Board, New Brunswick enlarged the Office of the Economic Adviser and created a Development Policy Secretariat. Nova Scotia set up its Voluntary Economic Planning Board.

The result was that each province was able to generate better statistics, develop a better idea of objectives and be better equipped to face Ottawa individually. New Brunswick established a department of Economic Growth and instituted an Equal Opportunity Program throughout the province, reducing inequalities of education and municipal property assessments. Nova Scotia turned to a consideration of its own needs through VEP and Newfoundland continued to be an aloof empire ruled by Premier Joey Smallwood making direct pilgrimages to Ottawa and having no contact with other Atlantic premiers.[15] Thus even if they so wished, federal officials would have found that the Atlantic provinces were not in a mood to be treated as a single, coherent region.

On the whole, policies to reduce regional disparities had to adjust not only the structure of a region's economy but also the productivity of its inputs. This would include both the skills and techniques of the private sector and, equally, the efficiency and effectiveness of public activity. It has been suggested that ADB's programs could not, as infrastructure and gapfilling projects, contribute much to the reform of the incremental process of provincial policy-making. The ADB activity did not (and perhaps could not) develop a regional consciousness.[16] And it failed to direct the development of provincial capacity for self help. Lacking initially a planning division and constantly lacking a plan, the ADB had no decisive objectives or strategy to impart to provincial officials except for a narrow and immediate commitment to infrastructure. Federal expenditures under ADB, unlike ARDA and FRED, did not deliberately encourage structural or methodological changes within the provinces except indirectly through provincial frustration with the lack of co-ordination or absence of any evident overall rationale in federal programs. The APEC accused ADB of having tactics but no set of goals towards which they might be directed and, lacking a planning process, unlikely to produce these goals.[17] The ADB planners intended to establish goals once the tedious sector studies had been completed, but clearly expenditures could not be withheld until that eventuality.

Nova Scotia had little success in trying to relate ADB planning to its own Voluntary Economic Planning office. VEP could not co-operate with ADB: the senior officials from different environments and backgrounds clashed and VEP did not feel that Nova Scotia needed the assistance of ADB's planning activity. Upon this rejection, ADB turned to the provincial department of Trade and Industry to act as a liaison with individual departments; its efforts with these officials to develop relevant statistics were productive. When VEP realized that ADB was working within the Nova Scotia government, it sought to be included on departmental joint meetings. Trade and Industry, as liaison, argued that permission would have to be received from the individual departments involved. But these departments were reluctant to admit VEP to their confidential negotiations because it was only a semi-official body. VEP's consequent irritation was transmitted to the minister responsible for it—who was also premier. Hence its annoyance with provincial departments was converted into a protest against ADB activities, and complaints of lack of federal co-operation became the official Nova Scotian line although harmonious relations were in fact the case—except for VEP's experience.[18] Trade and Industry, however, lacked a sufficiently strong or senior voice in Cabinet to affect the official provincial stand.

Nova Scotia's planning experience with its own VEP was little better. VEP had been a government response to a desire to plan but unwillingness to dictate. Hence the private sector had been asked to develop sectoral plans which were put into an overall plan for the province. But without any objectives or constraints, and without a secretariat of well-informed economists who could have discreetly directed matters— although not seeming to—the sector studies and plan became an undisciplined collection of private sector *desiderata*, of individual targets arranged by businessmen without a framework or process by which they could be achieved. There was little effort at co-ordinating the targets of various business groups; the VEP director was an engineer, not an economist; he lacked senior staff and knew little of the economic and administrative aspects of planning. Because the VEP again was not a body within government, its plan, which could not readily be implemented, could be ignored—and this is just what occurred.

In short, neither the federal nor provincial planning attempts provided a framework or rationale for policy decisions. This was not an overwhelming deterrent to provincial politicians, who continued to accept ADB projects, but it was evidently a disturbing situation for provincial (and for federal) officials. To the extent that ADB was a gapfiller, it might be asked whether these gaps were a consequence of deficient federal or provincial programs. Most of the ADB activity in the Atlantic provinces was the equivalent of provincial activity in the other Canadian provinces. Thus the ADB role was really more an intrusion into provincial fields to supplement federal activity than a filling of chinks in truly federal programs. Provincial politicians made little mention of this fact, although senior officials in New Brunswick and Prince Edward Island became so concerned with the lack of co-ordination in such an approach to projects, as well as with the lack of consultation, that they made serious though abortive efforts to develop a regional organization to counterbalance ADB's effects in the area, and its influence on other expenditures by Ottawa. But petitions made to federal officials about the lack of consultation or ADB's direct dealing with provincial departments met with little success.[19]

While the ADB activity did not directly encourage improved provincial structural or procedural changes, it did serve by this very failure to increase the province's frustrations with being treated as passive recipients of unrelated federal policies and indirectly led to reforms within their governments. New Brunswick's departments were poorly prepared to respond both to the unco-ordinated approaches of numerous federal agencies, like ADB, and the greater rationale in shared-cost programs being demanded by its Treasury Board. The board attempted to make sense of budgetary formulations and cut across departmental lines to co-ordinate mutually reinforcing policy. The Office of the Economic Adviser also provided an increasingly competent statistical service to departments and it examined the largely ignored aspects of federal-provincial relations to help ministries to think ahead and survive in relations with Ottawa. Eventually, too, it was able to offer departments assistance with stalemates in their negotiations with Ottawa. To this end the Development Policy Secretariat was established to take a long term approach to provincial economic and social policy. While it would be wrong to consider that these structural changes alone improved the quality of provincial services and negotiations, they did reflect the desire for at least greater competence in dealings with Ottawa.

A similar concern was expressed by Premier Smith of Nova Scotia. Experience with regional policies of federal departments, federal fiscal and monetary policy, and particularly the activity of ADA and ADB, convinced the premier that federal policies were being imposed with little consideration of the special problems of the Atlantic region or the particular requests of the province of Nova Scotia. Realizing that as VEP was outside government it could not be an effective planning body, Smith expanded the role of a provincial planning group set up earlier by ARDA —the Program Development Agency (PDA)—which had been disbanded in 1969 after DREE terminated the federal share of funds for such a joint body. The premier convinced two senior federal ARDA officials who could not continue to function under Kent, to come to Nova Scotia and revive PDA, thus better equipping the province to make specific demands upon Ottawa in accordance with provincial planning. Consequently, L. E. Poetschke and T. Duncan gathered the PDA staff and redirected its operations under a more comprehensive Secretariat to a Cabinet Committee on Planning and Programs. Its extensive operations, including the formation of an urban plan for the Halifax-Dartmouth district, touched all Nova Scotian departments, but it, too, was disbanded in 1971 when a new Liberal premier and party took office.[20]

Prince Edward Island's response to ADB and similar programs was, like Nova Scotia's, a manipulation of the FRED program to improve provincial capacity. The initiative was almost solely that of the new premier, Alex Campbell, elected in 1966, amidst little federal interest and only suspicious support from his own rural Cabinet ministers. The ADB was not a creative tool within the island province, because its activities there of pursuing rural electrification and almost unneeded road improvements had been selected to "match" activity in other provinces. Campbell rejected this approach as inadequate, and in 1966 initiated planning for long-term development. Using federal ARDA funds he "imported" a director and staff from other provinces and established them in an Economic Improvement Corporation. The corporation, under the premier, eventually created a plan which received support as an official federal FRED project. The consequence was, once again, a province that felt better able to conduct matters of regional development to the benefit of its own priorities and preferences.

There was, therefore, a period during the late sixties when, in response to the current style of federal relations, the Atlantic provinces individually sought to improve their own ability to act upon regional disparities. The failure of ADB to generate a regional plan or actively to involve the provinces hastened their efforts to better the situation themselves. DREE took over ADB in 1969 and ended its planning exercise as being inconsistent with the secrecy and flexibility required by the department.[21] The board became a quasi-public advisory council. Only the infrastructure projects were continued under a "special areas" program.

Consultation was more urgently required with DREE, however, because it did not operate on the basis that each province must be treated similarly, and because its decisions were more secretive, with correspondingly less public or provincial scrutiny of its objectives. Ideally Ottawa wanted to move towards a more efficient location of transportation, power, and industries within the entire region. Hence different facilities in each province were financed by Ottawa.[22] A tension still existed, however, because provinces could not see these discretionary policies within an overall, long-term plan for the region. It appeared to these provinces that DREE policies would not, in fact, greatly alter the complexion of the Atlantic economy.[23] Moreover, these differences of opinion were occurring as DREE was altering its concept of intergovernmental consultation. Kent showed no willingness to recognize or encourage provincial planning and for this reason ADB as a joint, consultative body had been terminated. Indeed, DREE considered its activity to be the administration of federal policies within regions of Canada rather than support to provincial governments.[24] Thus, lacking confidence and intimacy in their relations with Ottawa, the Atlantic provinces defensively continued to demand equivalent services from DREE.

In general, the Atlantic experience with development policies during most of the 1960s was one largely of unrelated activities at both levels of government. To a significant degree, ADB was responsible for this situation. Because the board's activities were mainly confined to individual public works projects they did not develop at Ottawa the co-ordination of policy and, in the provinces, the improvements in economic structure and planning which were both achieved to some degree by ARDA and which ADB could have been well suited to provide. Federal "style" as set by Pickersgill accounted somewhat for the limited horizons of the board and the shaping of its policies which placed ADB outside of the ebb and flow of more novel activities elsewhere. More significantly, it was rendered impotent by the absence of goals established to improve the self-sufficiency of provinces or the harmonization of federal policies. As well there was an absence of a hierarchical decision-making structure in the Pearson Cabinet. Finally, the Atlantic Development Board did not participate in the "pecking order" of departments and avoided situations where it had to impose its wishes on others.

This "other-wordliness" of the board—or the fact that it still used approaches of the pre-1960 period—eventually became its downfall. Its highly independent spending decisions and the elusiveness of its promised planning rationale could not survive the growing discipline of federal budgetary groups which, as the next chapter illustrates, gradually pervaded most departmental activities by the 1970s.

Chapter Eight

The Power of the Purse: Budgetary Control of Regional Policies

As much as disparities themselves, policies to alleviate them were brought under closer scrutiny and supervision during the 1960s. Over the decade, budgetary groups in all Canadian governments began to impose a discipline on regional development objectives and expenditures motivated by the alarming and costly proliferation of these programs. Thus reforms of a structural nature came to embrace more than just the technological and skill inputs of a region's economy and included an examination of the procedure of policy making and policy implementation.

Until the 1960s, programs had tended to be conceived and administered both at Ottawa and provincial capitals by individual departments alone, producing an overall policy and budget framework of government that was consequently the result of a largely incremental and aggregative process. During the 1960s, however, these procedures were made more articulate, centralized, and distributive through the gradual ascendency of a government's finance department, the Treasury Board of Cabinet and newly-emerging bodies for co-ordination of policies and planning usually attached to the first minister's office or the Cabinet. As the perspectives of these non-program bodies were established, matured, and won political support, the programs of individual departments were subjected to higher and broader degrees of abstraction. It also transpired that the interests of these various bodies and the department concerned often failed to agree over the methods and aims of specific programs. The general patterns and the importance of these "extra-departmental" forces (i.e., those not primarily responsible for conceiving and operating a specific program) for the evolution of regional policies will be established in the next three chapters. For ease of analysis a somewhat artificial division—in the Canadian setting—has been made between bodies establishing budgetary and personnel policy as well as assessing policy on the one hand and, on the other, those entrusted with the formulation of comprehensive development policy and co-ordination of programs (dealt with in chapters 8, and 9–10 respectively).

1. THE TRADITIONAL FORMS OF BUDGETARY CONTROL IN CANADIAN GOVERNMENTS

An earlier chapter touched upon the most prominent features of finance departments at both levels prior to 1960.[1] Their roles often lacked distinction or pervasiveness. Frequently they were passive and responded only to the need to find revenues for the spending of other departments whose expenditures, in turn, had been approved by *ad hoc* political bargaining in the Cabinet rather than as an integral part of an overall economic framework for government activity. Finance departments were rarely a countervailing force of economic expertise to the narrow interests of departments but were largely an accounting and financial management operation. In fact, so rudimentary were the provincial departments of finance that very often the premier was also the minister of finance, administering revenues to departments from his own back pocket. British Columbia until 1971 was long representative of this practice; the premier in effect controlled the rate of departmental expenditures himself. Because he combined the pinnacles of political and economic power, few departmental changes could be made without his approval, thereby excessively centralizing decision making. The Treasury Board of British Columbia's Cabinet under Bennett consisted of the premier, deputy minister of Finance, and only two other ministers who sat in judgement upon all the expenditures and management of government services, however small. There was reportedly no planning or priority-setting process outside the premier's mind, no secretariat to the Treasury Board existed, and there was no use of the more sophisticated and modern techniques of program development and evaluation. Premier Bennett's budgetary control was highly personal and pragmatic, reinforced by the success of his past financial gambles, corrected by his famous "second looks" and made possible by a buoyant and rapidly expanding provincial economy.[2]

At Ottawa in the years prior to 1960, the Department of Finance was not even the most senior department or the most active economic advisory agency. During St. Laurent's period of office, the Trade and Commerce department under C. D. Howe supplied much of the economic policy (on resource and industrial development) for the federal Liberal Cabinet. This function was not matched by any great macroeconomic research in the Department of Finance.[3] Indeed the Glassco Commission of 1962 found that economic research and economic intelligence was "conducted by only a handful of professional economists,"[4] located not in Finance but in the Department of Trade and Commerce and the Department of Agriculture. In consequence, the commission recommended that "the Department of Finance should become more positively oriented to its responsibility for the forumulation of a comprehensive economic policy."[5] But Finance had operated primarily as a revenue-raising department, casting generally negative comments upon proposals for expenditures. It lacked sufficient expertise or political power to bring programs under a systematic review process. Instead, there were few prior checks on a department's policy proposals to Cabinet, and those that did exist were often *ex post facto* or exercised over the smaller and politically weaker departments.[6]

2. Changes to the Roles of Central Budgetary Groups

During the 1960s the method of financing and organizing government expenditures was broadly altered, and extended considerably to a point where it had profound consequences upon federal-provincial relations in general and policies for regional economic growth in particular. While each government had different experiences, the similarity of problems facing budgetary authorities produced certain like responses to government expenditure policy which can be best illustrated by the federal example. (Provincial internal reforms, while less immediate and of varying scope, will be discussed later in the chapter in the context of intergovernmental relations.) Two main developments at Ottawa introduced the assertion of central budgetary control: more competent staff and a positive approach to budgetary and economic management.

Just as the finance portfolio was divorced from the premiership during the 1960s in the provinces so, also, did similar staff extensions take place at the federal level within the Department of Finance, reflecting a need to improve the economic research capability of the department in light of the unexpectedly sluggish recovery of the economy from the 1957 recession. The recruitment of economists and other qualified staff was a prerequisite for taking a more influential role. Their growing prominence in government was also required over the decade to cope with the proliferation of programs, such as ARDA, FRED, and ADA, designed to allocate considerable federal funds to regional disparities; whether for fiscal, service, or economic reasons these policies drained Ottawa's coffers at an alarming and evidently uncontrollable rate. There was, consequently, a need for economists who could watch the direction not only of the national economy but also of regional economies. While there had been economists in government since the Second World War, the designation covered a wide variety of roles, very few of which had to do with fundamental economic analysis.[7] Even the limited number of economists in the Finance department had been primarily interested in macroeconomic policy of a Keynesian sort, using fiscal policy to stabilize a national level of prosperity. Change was needed in the 1960s, because fiscal policy was too limited, stabilization policy too cautious, and measures of aggregative performance too sweeping in concept. Subsequently denounced as "simple-minded Keynesians"[8] the earlier government economists were not equipped to consider different regional potentials, to perform microeconomic analyses, to give planning advice, or even to formulate a planning process.

What was in short supply, therefore, was not economists as such but those with an ability to create systematic development plans for economic growth in all parts of Canada. This required not only a talent to demand, compile, and assess the relevant statistics but also an understanding of the causes of economic stagnation.[9] In chronically poor provinces it necessitated, besides, a venture into the techniques of public information, participation and modernization, which were largely untried until the *animation sociale* experiments under BAEQ in Quebec. Moreover, the new economist had to possess one further talent—a capacity to make their proposals palatable to politicians who tended to be traditionally suspicious of experts. Given these complex requirements for economists at both levels of government, the response was far from uniform.

The change in the role of Finance and Treasury Board in the federal government during the sixties was not so much one of gradual evolution as a transformation brought about by tensions between personalities and personnel. When Walter Gordon became the new Liberal government's Finance minister in 1963, he reflected the popular frustration and impatience with the Conservatives' tenure of office and missed opportunities for economic growth. Caught up in the enthusiasm of the initial months, Gordon wished to make his first Budget reflect new and innovative thinking about economic potential. He had no patience with the short-run, cautious, almost pre-Keynesian approach of his predecessors, George Nowlan and Donald Fleming, or with the belief that government could simply spend its way out of crisis. Initially, however, the staff of the Department of Finance was unable to meet Gordon's challenges. While they were more than capable, at least one senior civil servant, the deputy minister, Kenneth Taylor, had been exhausted by twenty-five years' service and by strain under the Conservative government, and his staff's morale was low.[10] The department was understaffed and lacked much of the talent it had shown during the previous Liberal regime, when in many respects it had run the government although in a good, chartered accountant fashion. During the Conservative regime, Finance could not guide expenditures in the presence of Cabinet divisions, ministerial factions, and little support from Diefenbaker.[11] Fleming and his department had had to spend excessive effort merely defending their policies rather than refining their techniques.

The difference under the incoming Liberals was one largely of time, perspectives, and breadth. Walter Gordon found that while he impatiently talked of long-run adjustments to the potential in the Canadian economy (reinforced by his Royal Commission experience) his staff were more concerned about the next six months of the dollar crisis. Finance officials had picked up the day-to-day equilibrating and defensive habits of their Conservative ministers and had not adjusted to the longer-term perspective of their new minister. Accordingly Gordon felt that he would have to rely upon outside advisers to capture the right spirit of change for his new Budget. The Finance staff, alienated by this move, were further dismayed by his apparent unwillingness to listen to their advice, based upon experience, regarding the unworkability of his proposals.

A man of Gordon's nature in the government was not unique; James Coyne, the governor of the Bank of Canada in a slightly earlier feud with his Conservative masters had touched upon the same issue. While he saw the necessity of securing the country's financial stability, he also realized the problem would be unsolved until the economy was cured in a longer term sense. And even though Gordon ultimately became a political victim of his own impatience, he and his successors were supported by other Liberal ministers and advisers who held similar views. In a sense, then, Finance and Treasury Board were propelled into new activity by certain strong advisers and politicians—many of whom were professional economists themselves. Gradually there developed strong centres of support elsewhere in the bureaucracy, focussed on new deputy ministers such as Tom Kent (Manpower), Simon Reisman (Treasury Board), A. W. Johnson (Finance), and Gordon Robertson (Privy Council).

These new "political" economists brought a different perspective to bear upon the extent of the federal government's legislation and the uniformity of its impact. Their aim was to re-establish the economic power of the central regime through intra- and intergovernmental reforms. They did not share the civil servant's fondness for uniform and rigid policies (which made for ease of administration), and they were quite prepared to replace general national policies for current spending with specific regional surgery on a long-term basis. In intergovernmental matters they were willing to initiate without being intimidated by the federal constitution. If providing greater social security for the individual required the violation of constitutional jurisdiction—as many felt the Canada Pension Plan and Medicare did—this was not necessarily an inhibiting factor for the Liberal advisers to Pearson. (In fact these two programs were designed by Kent and not by the federal Health and Welfare or Finance officials). With this new personnel, the federal Liberals undertook to reform simultaneously the nature of budgetary management and economic planning in order to develop a positive pursuit of balanced economic growth by government.

The expansion of Finance staff for economic research and economic intelligence, in order to provide comprehensive and regulated plans for developing national and regional economic potentials, was closely accompanied by reforms in the type of analytical support provided to the Treasury Board of Cabinet for its process of allocating scarce resources among competing departmental proposals. In fact, the budgetary-economic reforms of the sixties had their first impact upon program departments through the analysts and accountants of the Treasury Board staff, rather than through Finance economists. The latter were groping with macro-economic problems of the overall functions and priorities of government which, to be adopted, required full Cabinet acceptance of the necessity to establish, rank, and implement these broad goals on a systematic and total basis. The victory of this "rational" approach over the long tradition of incremental policy formation was only beginning to be apparent—and only at Ottawa—by the late 1960s.[12] In the meantime, Treasury Boards pressed on with reforms which could be implemented at the departmental level without first forcing the Cabinet to decisions on the broader issues. Financial and personnel reform to execute given federal policy guidelines was a technical and managerial change of *means*.[13] Further sophistication in development of economic policy required a progressive articulation of and commitment to *ends*.

Successive federal Treasury Boards traditionally had taken a negative attitude towards departmental expenditure requests.[14] They felt their job to be one of cutting the size of program applications as much as possible. Their interest was primarily in the cost of inputs and their criteria for approval tended to be based upon linear projections of earlier departmental spendings. Until well into the 1960s (as, in fact, several royal commissions had complained) Treasury Boards were interested in the costs and process of budgetary allocations to a program, not the objectives of its policy. Budgeting procedure had made few requests for alternative means of achieving priorities and what assessments there were of the output of programs occurred *ex post facto*. In short, budgeting was retrospective and unsystematic. It financed existing commitments, concentrating upon the means of doing so (or inputs) and raised few questions about final results or progress towards them. Creative departmental budgeting was further broken down by the interjection of Comptroller of Treasury suballotments for controlling the release of funds to departments.

It was in this environment that most of the earlier regional disparities programs like TVTA, ARDA, and ADA had been established—and had thrived. In these three programs, it will be recalled, little was said about their specific objectives and much emphasis was placed upon the *process* of decision making, such as provincial initiative and community action. ADA, for instance, was greatly concerned about the neutrality, automaticity, and objectiveness of designating regions though remaining vague about the aims or consequences of its activity. Similarly TVTA and ARDA greatly increased training capacity and numbers of rural projects without demonstrating clearly why this was being done, other than out of a general concern for the welfare of program recipients. This relaxed departmental attitude had not been greatly challenged by the central resource allocation staffs of Treasury Board and Finance. In fact, in the early sixties Donald Fleming's concern for balanced budgets typified the interest in the neatness of process and vagueness about objectives. Program directors were also their own assessors and they, like Treasury Board and the Cabinet, had only the most rudimentary notion of cost effectiveness or efficiency[15] apart from a subjective "feel" for political or social effectiveness.

Innovations in financial management during the mid-sixties progressively set aside these earlier budgetary practices with significant consequences for the relationship of a department's policies to its funds from Treasury Board. One reform was the introduction of the business economist's "systems analysis." This required a long-term definition of policy objectives, within which alternative programs were designed and systematically tested for their performance in achieving these objectives in terms of cost effectiveness and efficiency calculated through the quantification of means and ends and the use of cost-benefit analysis. This reform, which had been urged by the Glassco Commission in 1962, was a form of "performance budgeting" incorporated and extended to more ultimate objectives. It offered not only the display of a program budget on a different form, but also a new method of continual analysis of the program's performance. It is more commonly known today as PPBS, the planning-programming-budgeting system of resource allocation.

PPBS was fundamentally a budgeting management technique that financed programs on the basis of their projected outputs as well as the cost of inputs. It aimed at achieving a budgetary allocation of resources for some definite objective; hence its *sine qua non* was the outcome of policy making, not the process. A "good" program therefore was not simply one which underwent a rigorous process of coding and costing inputs or of consultation but one which demonstrated the best cost effectiveness or cost efficiency of various alternative means (or combination of inputs) for achieving a policy objective. In the endeavour to attain budgeting by objective, several recurring features of the PPB system developed. Emphasis was placed on the collection of data about a program's inputs and outputs; selection among alternative programs and assessment of program performance tended to be done by a central group rather than as a bottom-up procedure; and, the formation of the budget became a distributive rather than aggregative process.

The adoption of the PPBS technique by Treasury Board staffs led frequently to conflict and deadlock with departments and their traditional methods of formulating and operating programs. In some cases the strains were so serious as to cause Cabinet guidelines to be met by much delayed departmental programs because of a Treasury Board staff stalemate with program departments. Departments did not distinguish between five-year program planning and yearly program budgeting. When departments continued to devise policy proposals on a narrow, subjective, and input-oriented basis, the budgetary planners refused to authorize funds for programs that could not be fitted into a quantitative, objective and distributive "format." Departments found their efforts exasperated by the cult of the technician, who was removed from actual program experience, who demanded endless quantitative information, operated in central secrecy, insisted upon a rigid and often artificial program format, preferred "hard" measurable services to more esoteric, social improvement ("soft") programs, and sought impersonally to join departmental activities and traditions into broader co-ordinated relationships.[16] One provincial official observed that PPBS and Treasury Board were "choking" the system. Because departments had not been used to thinking in terms of alternatives they were unfamiliar with this form of decision making; without alternatives they were unable to assess the results of programs. Consequently, the new central planners often felt departments could not be trusted to plan critically. Frequently the only compromise was that departments "displayed" their budget on a PPBS format without coming closer to a cybernetic process in thinking or assessment.

At Ottawa the reorganization of Treasury Board and Finance which put each under its own minister in 1966, as well as the increasing political support since Gordon's time for the strong role of the central budgetary and economic departments, explained the evident success of the modernization of the budget-making process and the role of economic forecasting. Treasury Board had considerable success in converting programs such as TVTA, ARDA, and ADA to the new "second generation" series which included OTA, FRED, and ADIA respectively. These new programs reflected the influence of PPBS in that they pursued more clearly-defined objectives, the technician was placed in greater control, formats were more rigorously defined, decision making was removed from peripheral bodies, and inputs and outputs were primarily quantitative. Not only were programs less able to command funds according to political prestige or traditional rates of growth but some as well, such as ADB, TVTA, and FRED, suffered the new experience of an abrupt demise. In fact, the Treasury Board was able to hold even the largest departments, such as Defence, to an anti-inflation, low-growth budget in the late sixties. In regional development its greatest success, apart from expenditure control, was in program management through the creation of DREE to co-ordinate and administer upon a PPBS format the scattered federal programs for disparities. (This will be examined in chapter 12.)

Unlike Treasury Board, whose interest in regional development programs was to secure efficiency and effectiveness in the execution of Cabinet policy objectives, the Department of Finance was concerned directly with the priorities attached to such objectives. Its confrontation of program departments was more from a policy-priority viewpoint than actual management. Finance had been accustomed to policies for national growth being directed by federal departments, but from 1963 on—first in ARDA, then ADA, and later in FRED and ADB—it found increasingly that individual departments were devising programs that concentrated federal funds and in some cases also decision making at a regional level. This led to a concern for the achievement of efficiency and productivity in Canadian industry, particularly in light of the country's heavy dependence upon external trade. Hence Finance officials found themselves obliged to develop a new role as defender of a balance between economic proposals for maximizing "welfare" (regional aid) and those for "efficiency" (national productivity). To this end they challenged the artificial, disproportionate diversion of funds under ARDA, ADA, and later DREE to underpin regions of low productivity and slow growth and strove to achieve a balance between these and other federal policies for fast-growing regions in which Canada's prosperity was generated. Finance felt compelled to compensate for DREE's disproportionate expenditures in the poor provinces by refusing to yield to pressure for complementary discretionary monetary policy which would only have heightened federal discrimination against rich regions. Finance did remove capital cost allowances in 1969 from industries in some urban centres, but this was more a means of curbing the source of inflation than a redistribution of economic potential.[17]

The uneasiness of the Department of Finance with regional development policies, while evident during the days of ARDA, ADA, and FRED, was particularly heightened by the activities of DREE in the late sixties. Because of the manner in which it defined its objectives, DREE's relations with Finance were less harmonious than those with Treasury Board, whose concern was confined to the administration of policy. Relations were exacerbated generally by Kent's secrecy and his unwillingness to see Finance as a policy-supervising body; he felt his commitment to be a political one to Prime Minister Trudeau rather than a financial one to economic planners.[18] The conflict of departments was, however, not merely restricted to personalities.

Finance expected DREE to produce a rationale for such large regional growth expenditures within a national economic setting. Aid to regional infrastructure or fiscal needs had some finite limits, but DREE's declared provision of jobs as a goal was tied to a problem larger than regional disparities. Low-skilled labour generally tended to fall out of work earliest and remain out longest during a cyclical economic slump. Thus provision of jobs was more than a device for reducing disparities and constituted a continuing employment-stabilizing payment which many felt should be available nationally.

The dispute between Finance and DREE centred about the latter's industrial incentives policies which, while similar to those policies of ADA or ADIA, were considerably more generous and flexible. Finance felt, as had the rich provinces with ADA, that regional development policies—particularly in a period of slack growth—should be viewed in light of the potential growth which was being diverted from the most productive regions. Accordingly Finance applied pressure against DREE's decisions to encourage a redirected concentration of federal funds in one region of Canada, when all had similar problems of varying intensities.[19]

Finance's pressure achieved some success with the announcement by DREE in 1970 that the Montreal-Cornwall corridor would be eligible for industrial incentives. This was a most uncharacteristic action of DREE which suggested strongly that it was an imposed decision. When established in 1968, the department was to develop a long-term policy of concentrating strictly upon chronically poor regions. With this heavily-industrialized corridor now included, DREE increased its coverage from a third to one half of Canada's population, and because this new region was designated for short-term alleviation of cyclical under-investment for three years, the application of DREE policy served here as a short-run tool for the adjustment of the labour market.

Before a Commons committee, DREE's minister, Jean Marchand, demonstrated his lack of enthusiasm for the new program. Rather lamely he asserted that Montreal was a "regional problem"[20] which begged rather than answered the question as to DREE's initially-declared commitment to regional poverty. Furthermore, although the incentives for the new corridor were then added to the existing incentives for industries locating in the Atlantic provinces to prevent undue discrimination between old and new regions, this was only a token gesture for only three times had Atlantic industry qualified for the maximum possible loan under the existing incentives.[21] The new corridor was, in fact, the most magnetic of all DREE's designated regions. Evidently Marchand was not the originator of the designation of the Montreal-Cornwall region. Curiously, he observed in committee that he had to "fight like hell" (apparently in Cabinet) to ensure even that the new Montreal incentives would be added to the Atlantic rates, "because I did not want to destroy the balance."[22] Finance evidently had a different view of this equilibrium and succeeded in reducing somewhat the freedom of Marchand to determine its nature.

The above case also suggests that Finance and Treasury Board in the issue of regional development conflicted over the role of the department they had jointly created for this purpose. Finance's interest in counter-cyclical activity occasionally thwarted the efforts at long-term consistency of policy attempted by DREE with Treasury Board support. As Bruce Doern has pointed out,[23] only very recently did the federal Treasury Board officials acknowledge the unavoidable continued presence of improvised and *ad hoc* policy making alongside the PPBS process that aimed to produce a highly integrated approach to policy and program execution. In terms of DREE's relations with provinces, however, Finance and Treasury Board rarely disagreed with each other.

3. Closer Financial and Economic Control in an Intergovernmental Setting

It was not solely the internal management technique of PPBS that sparked the move among senior federal officials to refashion federal-provincial programs. At stake was the balance between the forces of unity and diversity. Central Finance officials became alarmed during the 1960s with the way in which politicians spent federal money. Officials commonly expressed this as a dislike of their role as "banker"—through the largely passive extension of federal funds by politicians for programs designed and administered by the provinces. They wanted a right to extend central decision making not only over federal departments but federal-provincial relations generally.

Apart from anxiety over uncontrollable costs in joint programs, federal officials felt that the situation became more alarming as the impact of the Quebec crisis upon Ottawa resulted in what were seen as progressive political "sellouts" of federal social and economic authority to Quebec. The dispute over the role of Canada Manpower Centres in that province, the federal acceptance of a Quebec Pension Plan, the size of the FRED project in Gaspé, the offer of aid to Quebec universities with but few provisions attached, and the federal transfer of full control of joint welfare programs to the province, all convinced senior federal officials that not only would the provinces's special status soon become one of associate statehood but also that Finance staff could not carry out truly national fiscal and economic policy under such circumstances.

Finance officials considered also that federal *ad hoc* policies elsewhere, such as aid to dairy and wheat produce, coal subventions, subsidized Maritime freight rates, and grants in aid of fishermen, constituted a *de facto* form of regional policy without design. Likewise, further tax abatements or periodic, isolated adjustments to the equalization agreement formed a similar type of incremental federal policy which required unravelling and a place within national objectives, if valid. The programs of ARDA, ADA, ADB, and TVTA were also regarded as contributing to jurisdictional confusions not to mention uncontrollable expenditures. Absent from all of this was a pervading sense of the objectives of a federal government. In a sense, the central regime felt manipulated by the regions rather than conversely.

Indeed one may distinguish from 1965 on, a very definite attempt to break with this condition led by senior Finance and Treasury Board officials. It extended across the full range of government services, from the second generation of rural development programs, the cancellation of the improvised capital projects of federal departments, such as wharf building, and the confrontation of Quebec in the Constitutional Conferences over the extent of its special status, to the clarification of fiscal relations through new opting out,[24] equalization, and tax sharing formulae. The initiative for this tougher approach to the provinces came not from Prime Minister Pearson or even a significant number of ministers but from officials and political advisers such as A. W. Johnson, Simon Reisman, and Tom Kent, and was very much a reaction to political incrementalism and opportunism from those concerned with the loss of initiative from the federal level to the provinces. It was eventually championed at the political level by Pearson's successor, Pierre Trudeau, and a much stronger Prime Minister's Office.

The consequence of these reforms for program departments operating with other governments was twofold. First, they progressively lost exclusive control of their own policy and were subject to other federal objectives—in the matter of management and economics—beyond those of closer and harmonious relations with their provincial counterparts. It will be recalled that this was the experience of provincial officials with the abrupt introduction of OTA by Ottawa. This was felt equally when DREE took over existing federal programs.

Second, the activity of federal Finance and Treasury Board officials in every aspect of federal-provincial relations demanded a new approach from the provinces. By its various "hard line" policies Ottawa had now challenged the past practice that in joint programs the federal government should not seek to direct provincial expenditure decisions. Partly as a response to this, and as a result of growing internal dissatisfaction (as at Ottawa) with the lack of co-ordination among programs, the provincial budgetary officials also attempted to achieve a more coherent provincial point of view at federal-provincial conferences. However, the success of central control in the provinces was not as uniform as in Ottawa, and the varying degrees of budgetary discipline affected the extent to which provincial program departments had the flexibility to yield to the new federal approach to intergovernmental relations in order to keep programs intact.

At the provincial level, the forces for changing the outlook and influence of the treasury departments varied considerably. In Quebec, for instance, although departments undertook a frantic campaign of social modernization this was unmatched by an institutional or conceptual change within the processes of government. The result was that expenditures were not managed by any central agency. The province literally spent itself into exhaustion and bankruptcy by 1966.[25] During that time the Finance department continued to exhibit a largely unreformed role that was primarily balance-sheet and revenue-raising in nature rather than one which could regulate the flow of political decisions in accordance with fiscal capabilities.

Saskatchewan, at another extreme, had developed a modern budgetary control technique ever since the Second World War. Under the CCF party in 1945 an Economic Advisory and Planning Board had been established, composed of ministers and professional economists to advise on the management of various public enterprises and program planning. As well, a Budget Bureau and Cabinet Secretariat were set up to help ministers make program and spending decisions. During this time the province acquired the technique of designing and living within budgets. But although all this impressive machinery had been created and set into operation, a 1965 Royal Commission on Government Organization was still able to comment that, "Your Commissioners have been surprised and disturbed by the lack of planning of programmes within the Government of Saskatchewan. Much of the difficulty experienced by departmental management in developing workable plans has stemmed from the failure of the budgetary process to match expenditures with objectives."[26] Departments had been able to preserve their independence to the extent that high level co-ordination was unable to penetrate to lower program echelons. Provincial budgets remained aggregative and policy was primarily formulated at the departmental level upon whatever criteria seemed appropriate.

Alberta typified the wealthy province in its aversion to the need for more pervasive budgetary control or more comprehensive definition of economic goals and priorities. Prosperity since the Depression had converted any vestiges of the Social Credit collectivist economic philosophy there largely to a past memory. Social Credit became more a label for pragmatic, capitalist, conservatism than anything else. The Treasury Board, created in 1926, was not even convened from 1948 to 1965. The Department of Economic Affairs, established in 1930, was abandoned in 1952 and had not, in fact, contained economists; its activities were confined largely to secretariat work for the Cabinet and registration of corporations. This department was replaced by Industry and Development, later called Industry and Labour, and then renamed Industry and Tourism—titular changes that reflected the increasing transformation of Albertan government to free enterprise. The shift in functions to peripheral (industrial incentives) economic activity was a result of the unprecedented prosperity in natural resource development.[27]

With generous tax revenues from vast oil discoveries, the Albertan departments often failed to find enough ways to spend the budgetary surplus.[28] Not surprisingly, Alberta's budgets in this environment during the fifties and the first half of the sixties were aggregative rather than distributive and were composed largely by individual ministers asking the treasurer for funds on an empirical basis. As the economy slowed in the mid-sixties, the Cabinet somewhat nervously reactivated the Treasury Board and created a Budget Bureau to serve the board and eventually provide policy recommendations for expenditures, once its economists (the first ever in Treasury) had acquired expertise and a system.

The Alberta Cabinet was eager for a solution but uncertain of its nature. It failed to provide the new Budget Bureau with terms of reference but passed this question on to the bureau to settle for itself. The bureau, in fact, was pressed for expenditure recommendations almost three years before it felt itself competent and large enough to plan. Most of the bureau's recommendations were nevertheless accepted by the Cabinet, which, according to officials, was unable to develop a critical political response to what properly were only a series of budgetary proposals and priorities. Indeed, it accorded to the provincial treasurer a full veto power over departmental estimates for what it was hoped would be only a temporary period of restraint. Thus the guidelines prepared by the bureau were translated directly into policy and became the upper limit of expenditures for departments. The Cabinet, unused to living within a budget, preferred to leave the rationalization of its incremental approach to the Budget Bureau as well as to the executive assistants attached to the premier's office. Unavoidably these officials became the focus of the wrath of individual ministers and the suspicions of other officials who had to make the reductions ordered by the Cabinet.

In other provinces central budgetary personnel experienced greater or lesser degrees of influence.[29] Ontario achieved reforms in its Treasury Board and finance staff similar to those at Ottawa.[30] In the Maritime provinces the Treasury Board staffs were a new addition to government. (Nova Scotia and Prince Edward Island only established their staff in 1970.) They possessed insufficient power to exercise influence over the largest and most political departments because their respective cabinets evaded supporting the staff reform of the budgetary process by issuing political instructions to each department.

One objective of reforms in Finance and Treasury Board staffs was to weaken the vertical accountability of similar federal and provincial program departments to each other, within their self-created empires, and to establish or reinforce horizontal or lateral relationships within their respective governments.[31] The goal was not uniformly achieved in all governments by 1971 because of the absence of political support in some cases or late starts in others. This created a situation where the timing and pace of reforms at two levels of government were not concurrent, thereby giving the federal officials, as the more advanced reformers, the initiative and advantage.

To the extent that the federal programs subsequently came under a broader degree of co-ordination, and were subjected to a new technique of budgeting control, the provincial component was correspondingly reduced as a source of influence upon them. It was because of restrictions thus placed upon federal bargaining, that provinces became much more the recipients of decisions about program constraints or redirection, rather than continuing partners in the process. Thus, while the reforms in management and economic outlook produced a more concerted and generous effort towards remedying the deficiencies in economic growth, in some instances the requisite program design was removed from the source closest to case load and need by the federal unilateral action. This yielded mixed blessings. On the one hand, in the eyes of operating officials, it made programs more impersonal while, on the other hand, in the eyes of economists, it cast regional programs into a more proper macroeconomic context.

This broadening of the context for program evaluation was a result of the economists' "performance" approach to joint endeavours. But it was also a consequence of a greater interest during the 1960s in overall political and social planning of the public sector's activities, a matter to be next considered.

Chapter Nine

Provincial Planning and Co-ordination of Developmental Policy

During the 1960s centralized and systematic efforts were made in some provincial governments to improve upon plans and programs scattered among various departments. Regional development policies were a major focus of such undertakings. Much of the activity in poor provinces consisted of the reduction of duplications and complexities in policy and the creation of different political tools and forces to develop efficiency and effectiveness in the use of limited resources, in order to achieve the levels of prosperity attained in rich provinces by the haphazard and feverish activity of private industries exploiting natural resources. Comprehensive planning differed from existing departmental planning not only in its breadth—frequently a multifunctional approach to problems—but also in the technique that the new group of planners brought to the public service.[1]

One of the greatest difficulties encountered in planning for regional economic growth in the poor provinces was not misplaced expectations about the results of planning but, rather, inappropriate structures and processes with which the plan implementation groups had to operate. Both planning and co-ordination of policy called for a systematic sequence of inputs and outputs to proceed to effective and efficient results. Comprehensive planning required the integration of departmental activities into supra-departmental objectives. The planners discovered, as had Treasury Board and Finance in budgetary and economic matters, that departments were not immediately receptive to new and untried approaches from an outside group.

As a general introduction to the specific studies of provincial development planning which follow, it should be observed that in Canada coordination and planning of policy was undertaken by advisory groups with very different origins, goals, and jurisdictions. Because of an insufficient demarcation of authority, their directives to operating departments responsible for greater policy detail or program administration were often contradictory. Planners, whether private or civil service in nature, or quasi-political and attached to a semi-official body, Cabinet, or the premier's office, attempted to direct the implementation of policy within or among departments, although, strictly-speaking, qualified only to plan the general parameters. This was the case specifically in Quebec, Prince Edward Island, and Nova Scotia. In other situations, groups equipped to provide a management or expenditure control service for departments, such as Treasury Board staff, became involved in deciding priorities or actual administrative details (as in Manitoba, Alberta, and Ontario). Finally, departments or agencies within governments which had been entrusted with broad development functions, rather than narrow outlooks, in some instances degenerated into duplicating specific programs provided by other departments (as in Prince Edward Island and Nova Scotia). In view of these various means of establishing provincial regional development objectives, an examination of provincial attempts to achieve clarity in those aims helps one appreciate the malleability of the process and the structure of policy making involved.

1. Specific Provincial Experiences with Policy Planning and Co-ordination

(a) Quebec. The first experiment with comprehensive provincial planning began in Quebec with the election of Jean Lesage and his Liberal party in 1960. His victory brought an end to the reactionary, corrupt, and autocratic regime of the Union Nationale under Maurice Duplessis, whose underspending (on education, roads, and health) had allowed the province to slip further behind in social capital and standards of living, as compared to its very prosperous neighbour, Ontario.[2] Even within the province, the contrast between English and French-speaking elements in business activity was clearly evident. A modern, efficient, Anglophone system stood apart from an archaic, isolated, small-scale, family, Francophone system. Accordingly, comprehensive planning was seen by the new Liberal regime as a means of catching up with the "English way" of business and of entering into the national and continental competition for investment, skills, and jobs.

Most important, however, planning was seen as a means of retrieving from the Anglophone his dominance of the provincial economy. Planning would provide more extensive and competent control by the French Canadian (through government) of the direction and process of economic modernization, in accordance with the proclaimed desire to be *maitre chez nous*. Planning thus became an emotionally-charged process in Quebec, because it was regarded as a means to control and protect the province's unique cultural, social, and political life. As such, establishing the economic means for change often took a lower priority to the building of research machinery, and generally there was little clear articulation of the means by which planning could achieve a transformation. Speeches of the early sixties were replete with aspirations for the Quebec government alone to direct the destiny of its people, although it was believed confidently that Canadians, through the federal government, and foreign investors would continue to finance the experiment.

That the endeavour eventually failed was not because of the insincerity of politicians or the complexities of the federal system but because of a lack of machinery and education receptive to the modernization of the provincial economy by government. Comprehensive development was impeded by the inertia of departmental and local interests in the Quebec political system. Moreover, the province was required to construct its own form of planning in the absence of North American experience. For advice and a possible planning model, Quebec turned overseas to the only country with a workable and accessible plan—to France.

Much of the work of transposing Rueff's planning in France to Quebec was performed by the deputy minister of Industry, René Tremblay.[3] Despite his warnings that Quebec's economy was different, the French technique appealed to visionary French Canadians who with their Gallic counterparts shared the grand perspective of planning. They deemed Montreal to be an Anglophone enclave within the province and saw governmental direction of growth as a means of extending to regional industry the influence—from Quebec City—of the Francophone. The Gaspé study (BAEQ) reflected elements of this attitude. In France, however, regionalization of policy was made possible because a strong central planning body was matched by regional mechanisms. Quebec established similar machinery, a Conseil d'Orientation économique du Québec (COEQ) for planning and ten regional bodies, but these lacked both support and authority within the existing political system.

There were three attitudes toward planning in Quebec. Tremblay, within government, urged limited, practical spending to educate agents for change: teachers, managers, and civil servants. The COEQ, outside, was caught up in the grand planning and organizational style of France (without a comparable situation); and individual ministers, although eager for economic development, were prone to impressive *ad hoc* activities confined to their departments. Planning in the Quebec setting required the education of each group by the other: the politician had to be prepared to compromise his department's functions for the comprehensive goal and planners had to discover that the completion of a plan was not synonymous with its implementation. Without co-operation, the groups that provided objectives, priorities, policy, programs, money, and administration were not systematically related. Thus with no overall co-ordination, government, in its fullest sense, was a discontinuous sequence of events.

Because COEQ was a planning body outside the departmental structure, it particularly required a favourable ear within the system to achieve an impact with its proposals. The Council, created in 1961, had a board of prominent labour, industrial, and business figures, supplemented by its own staff and occasionally private planning advisers. It was entrusted with the preparation of a development plan for the province and the provision of economic advice to government.[4] The planning failure of COEQ can be traced largely to its isolation from contact with the governmental process.[5] The Council was in a difficult and ambiguous position as it was to be a planning body representative of public opinion without being either open to the public in its research and confidential recommendations to the premier or able to accept departmental representatives in other than an advisory capacity. Hence, it was suspected by both for its secrecy and lack of access. Because of this ambiguity and isolation, it was all the more important that there be some influence in government to prepare a favourable reception for the Council's plan and to make the process and requirements of implementing a plan clearly understandable.

Tremblay was probably the greatest potential ally of COEQ within government. He was well located as deputy minister of Industry and Commerce, and as an economic adviser to Lesage, who himself had little experience with development economics. Tremblay also had within his department Quebec's statistical bureau under the capable guidance of J. B. Bergevin, later the deputy minister of Agriculture and chairman of the Comité permanente d'aménagement des ressource (CPAR). Tremblay's influence was neutralized, however, in so far as co-ordinated planning was concerned, by the highly individualistic nature of departments run by powerful ministers and deputies over which the Cabinet and Treasury Board had little control. While intrigued by the vision of planning, ministers were unwilling to sacrifice their freedom of action to it and largely remained powers unto themselves.

The opportunity for Tremblay, his staff, and his minister, André Rousseau, to educate the Cabinet in interdepartmental co-operation was lost in the early years of Lesage's administration. In a snap election called in 1962, Rousseau was unexpectedly defeated, and Tremblay moved to Ottawa. Their replacements were men who were neither economists nor familiar with development planning; they withdrew from the role of advising Lesage on these matters. Tremblay's staff was left without a channel to the premier and his economists moved to jobs in private industry. Thus while Quebec undertook isolated economic development policies such as BAEQ or those for industrial expansion, the total approach to monetary, industrial, agricultural, resource, and municipal policies was not pursued.

When the COEQ issued its first plan, IA, it encountered the very problem of inappropriate structures which had worried Tremblay.[6] It abandoned the approach of a comprehensive development plan because of "poor co-ordination between programs of different departments and Quebec's economic structure which blends the characteristics of a developed economy with elements of a traditionally unsophisticated, sluggish economy."[7] The French style of planning was dead in Quebec because planners lacked fiscal and monetary "carrot and stick" inducements provided in France and they could not count upon voluntary responses to their projects.

The new director of COEQ, Roland Parenteau, in 1964 shifted the concentration of the Council to the problems within the bureaucratic system which had scuttled Plan IA. Planners had "delivered" the scheme only to find neither departmental or local structures and attitudes receptive. Parenteau was more pragmatic; he tried to plan for government activities actually in progress—those things well within the reach of policy directives such as the role of public investments in schools, welfare, and industry. Rather than attempt an overall plan, therefore, COEQ focused upon the operational efficiency of programs. One attempt, to decentralize the provincial decision-making process to ten economic regions as in the French plan, was unsuccessful because decentralization threatened to upset the traditional power structures of departments in Quebec City and also threatened to impose a new tier of regional authorities. Both government departments and their local clientele tended to reinforce each other in their resistance to change. A more general cause of the failure of Parenteau's approach was that COEQ had shifted from comprehensive to specific governmental activity still without being brought within government itself. Ironically, the very isolation which was appropriate for COEQ when it was providing an integrated set of policy guidelines and programs for Quebec's economy became wholly inappropriate when the COEQ became primarily a government planning board immersed in immediate problems.[8]

After a searching public analysis of its successes and failures in its

143

1966 Annual Report,[9] COEQ effectively recommended its own termination and suggested two separate replacement bodies for its dual functions of creating and implementing development plans. COEQ's replacements were proposed as an Office du Plan du Quebec (OPQ) and a Conseil de développement. More important of the two was to be OPQ, a planning body firmly located within the government hierarchy and buttressed by two essential support groups—one political, one private—a Commission Interministerielle du planification and a Conseil du planification.

These proposals were not finally acted upon until 1968, after the Union Nationale government that replaced the Lesage Liberals in 1966 had spent two years cautiously examining the secretive planning mechanism they had so roundly criticized while in opposition. In 1969 the Quebec regime made amends for having passed only the OPQ legislation in 1968 without instituting the Conseil de développement. The OPQ was converted to the Office de développement et de l'amenagement du Québec (ODAQ).

The changes during the four years, 1966–1970, were not simply titular refinements, however, but were, instead, the surface indications of a fierce struggle within the Quebec governmental system over the role and power of comprehensive planning. In the end, the development planners lost, as had the COEQ.

The intent of COEQ's original 1966 recommendations for a split in its planning and consultative roles was to anchor the proposed new Office du Plan (OPQ) firmly within the political system in Quebec City and provide it with a strong Commission Interministerielle (of deputy ministers) to engage in the unavoidable struggle with departments over the implementation of a comprehensive plan. Neither attempt succeeded; the Commission lost its prestige as deputy ministers sent subordinate members to meetings, and the Office du Plan became the Office de développement (ODAQ) with, once again, a combined consultative and planning role as well as responsibility for implementation. As had been feared by the directors of both COEQ and CPAR in their 1966 recommendations to Premier Johnson, such a diverse role sapped the strength of ODAQ. Its attention was diverted by the day-to-day problems of implementing both the BAEQ and RDIA legislation in the province. Daily crises of negotiations and inter-departmental differences arising from these agreements required *ad hoc* response and dampened an intellectual atmosphere conducive to long-term planning. As a result, ODAQ did not become the centre for co-ordinating policy design or implementation. Design fell somewhat by default to the individual departments which, while thrwarting the success of COEQ-ODAQ endeavours, had built up their own planning units and in a sense were better equipped to resist central planning.

Left on their own, Quebec's departments would have continued to develop in an unrelated fashion because of the failure of COEQ or Treasury Board to control the highly personal and non-systematic relationship between a minister, the premier and the treasurer. René Tremblay's interest in interdepartmental co-ordination was inherited by the Quebec Department of Federal-Provincial Relations, set up in 1960 and later called Intergovernmental Affairs. Its main concern was with the lack of cohesion among provincial departments when they negotiated with the federal government, which meant that Ottawa could play one department against another and succeed in getting favourable, isolated agreements that, collectively, jeopardized the development of the economy according to the province's goals.

Intergovernmental Affairs favoured the strengthening of those provincial groups that might achieve co-ordination through either program or budgetary planning. It was in a strategic position of influence because of its presence at all intergovernmental meetings and the political value of its overall vantage point. It hoped to encourage the modernization of the Department of Finance from its accountant's role of lending, borrowing, and bookkeeping to one of positive economic management, but Finance's activity during the Lesage administration continued still to help departments "spend their way into new policies." In fact, it was COEQ which undertook the exploratory inquiries into PPBS budgetary formats.

Intergovernmental Affairs went as far as trying to reorganize services to Quebec's Executive Council (Cabinet) by suggesting a Secretariat General to improve co-ordination, but the effort failed. Instead the department became involved in a struggle with the secretary of the Executive Council for primacy in the role of departmental co-ordination. The problem was the same as that encountered by René Tremblay earlier: while individual efforts at co-ordination met with limited success, they were too small and peripheral to constitute a major influence upon Cabinet thinking or to be tools for social change. The Cabinet failed to carry basically sound ideas for priorities and management into the implementation stage. In the absence of political support for co-ordination departments continued their highly individualistic operations.[10]

Neither the federal government nor any of the provinces ever attempted the comprehensiveness of Quebec's experiments with development planning. Others, however, did undertake less extensive planning, often beginning within the comprehensive *rural* approach of FRED. Nova Scotia, New Brunswick, Prince Edward Island, and Alberta all established planning groups that initially were a direct result of encouragement or funds from the federal ARDA staff. Manitoba and Nova Scotia also had their own earlier experiments with planning, which merit our attention next.

(b) Manitoba. At the beginning of the sixties Premier Duff Roblin, strove to bring his province out of a collective depression about development prospects, by establishing the Committee on Manitoba's Economic Future and the Manitoba Development Authority. The Committee's report, *Manitoba 1962-75,*[11] glowed with the visions of the fabulous potential that lay in the province, real or imagined. It revived the dream, which had been a lingering hope since the wheat boom, of an economy whose diversity and exploitation rivalled Ontario's. The report, and a subsequent Manitoba Economic Consultative Board, served as a communication bridge between public and private sector expectations. Roblin was not, however, practically committed to the idea of comprehensive planning and, accordingly, the Manitoba Development Authority (MDA) as a committee of Cabinet was entrusted with only a vague authority to promote and co-ordinate the economic development of the province. Certain aspects of the report were used in the negotiation and administration by the MDA of the FRED Interlake program. The Authority co-ordinated the industrial loan policy of the Manitoba Economic Development Corporation, the provincial financing of local education, the reform of municipal organizations, and attempted to achieve some provincial uniformity in responses to various shared-cost programs with Ottawa.

Roblin, as chairman of the Authority, ruled with a dictatorial hand. He was drawn repeatedly into the numerous interdepartmental feuds involving the MDA, which became commonplace as departments lost or had their traditional functions or decision-making powers merged in response to contemporary problems. With no operating responsibilities, the Authority's effectiveness depended upon the co-operation of other departments, but these were jealous of their jurisdictions. Departments did not permit the MDA to review their proposals to Cabinet. The absence of formal mechanisms, and consequently the need to strike individual bargains, actually reflected a concern of ministers in both Roblin's Cabinet and those of his successors that extensive official contracts would strengthen the bureaucracy with regard to the politicians.

Walter Weir, Roblin's successor as Conservative premier, inherited the Manitoba Development Authority but refused to sit as chairman, hoping to avoid feuds. Instead, he hired private consultants to analyze its structure. Their recommendations for replacing the MDA did not end the feuds any more than did Weir's remoteness. As premier he could not avoid the ultimate responsibility to adjudicate disputes. The new organization, which consisted of two Cabinet committees and three secretariats, did not alter the fact that the same MDA politicians and officials with the same problems and outlooks sat in these new structures.

When NDP premier, Edward Schreyer, assumed office in 1969, he inherited the committee feuds. He made himself the chairman of the Planning and Priorities Committee of Cabinet, served by a secretariat for continuing programs and a secretariat for planning. The minister of Finance was made the chairman of the Management Committee, whose role was essentially that of a Treasury Board backed by a management secretariat. While Schreyer thereby acknowledged the fact that the premier was inextricably involved in solving disputes by taking the chairmanship, this acceptance of *de jure* position in addition to a *de facto* primacy burdened him with the additional work of actually being chairman. This placed his secretariats in a position of having considerable influence on the overworked premier, so that his decisions on development might either have been his or those of secretariat officials. Schreyer anticipated the logical conclusion of this situation by experimenting with a partisan secretariat. Hand-picked officials were, moreover, a reflection of the socialist's belief that the administrative system must, in a sense, be "infiltrated."

Regional development policies were delayed and not co-ordinated somewhat because of the newness of Manitoba's committee-secretariat system and the premier's other responsibilities. The Cabinet committees and secretariats took considerable time to work out their respective jurisdictions; they tended to clash in their policy, framework, and priority directives to departments. Continuing difficulties centred about a stalemate between the Management Committee (Treasury Board) and the Priorities and Planning Committee, whereby the Treasury Board's concern with departmental conformity to the PPBS format prevented the flow of funds to departments, although the Priorities and Planning Committee had previously authorized the priority expenditure and departmental program. In short, by attempting to implement PPBS in one sweep the Treasury Board, effectively set its own priorities by delaying funds, although, strictly speaking, it was supposed to perform only a positive management service to departments empowered to carry out authorized development responsibilities.[12] In essence, then, the pre-audit system became in itself a priority-setting process. It served as a more brutal but less co-operative form of co-ordination.

(c) Nova Scotia. Like Quebec, Nova Scotia had turned to the European examples at the beginning of the sixties for a model for planning. Unlike the French Canadians, however, they were intimidated by the obvious need for fiscal and monetary tools as well as a definite assertion of government over the people which would have been required by the French example. As a result, they settled for voluntary planning. The form of the Voluntary Planning Board for Economic Development (VEP) was

similar to COEQ: private industrialists, businessmen, and labour leaders provided with government funds and a staff engaged in assembling an economic development plan for government. As mentioned earlier, these plans of 1966-7 were unsystematic and unrealistic and of little use to government.

The idea of a Cabinet Committee on Planning and Programs and a Secretariat under L. E. Poetschke was, it will be recalled, primarily a personal interest of Premier G. I. Smith who had replaced Robert Stanfield at the head of the Conservative government in 1968. He had become dismayed with Nova Scotia's stale and passive performance at federal-provincial conferences and the consequent necessity of having to drift with every whim of federal policy for the Atlantic region. Poetschke, in a brief to the Cabinet, prior to the establishment (in 1969) of either the Committee or Secretariat, observed that while the federal government had assumed many new regional responsibilities during the sixties, it had been unable to devise either new machinery or effective co-ordination, as bitter experiences with ADA and Manpower had seemed to verify.[13] He commented that federal and provincial departments were organized sectorally while virtually all important economic and social problems overlapped several sectors. Their methods prevented examination of the real causes of lack of income or poverty. Because there was no effective mechanism to formulate long-term and broad policy the Cabinet had to rely upon departmental advice. Agreements signed with the federal government promised co-ordination between these departmental programs but in practice this was absent. In conclusion, he observed that the provinces were led to believe that their problems were jurisdictional and hence solutions were sought in the transfers of power.

Poetschke thought that the province of Nova Scotia could deny this conclusion and challenge federal activity by a modernization of the approach to responsibilities. He wished to direct the planner's interests to a problem, opportunity, or area rather than to a limited traditional juris-diction. He particularly favoured programs for structural change to complement the construction projects undertaken in the province by various federal departments. He argued that public works constituted subsidies to an out-of-date economic, social, and political system in the Maritimes.[14] This, in fact, was essentially the conclusion of the Economic Council of Canada, that regional economic disparities arose more from a lack of skill and poor labour force participation than from a lack of infrastructure.[15] Larsen's ADA study (discussed in chapter 6) had found that economic subsystems were unable to respond to technological changes, consumer demands, or new administrative processes. Poetschke and his Secretariat stressed the improvement of procedures and methods rather than the extension of public works or passive industrial incentives as essential prerequisites to specific development projects. New machinery would enable assessment of long-term economic trends and the development of broad policy to affect major changes in the direction and integration of operating agencies to implement these programs.

Within the general framework of their development plan, the Secretariat devised a number of programs which were to encourage modernization in the public and private provision of services in order to attain the sophisticated level of behaviour found in the richer (and more competitive) provinces. A public housing program attempted to help builders and service agents qualify for federal National Housing Act loans as competently as those in other provinces. Special designed were established for pilot housing projects which would enable the building of units within the cost of Nova Scotians and yet eligible for the very inflexible terms offered uniformly across the country (despite varying needs) by the federal Housing authority.

Management diagnosis and training services were offered to firms in Nova Scotia to encourage the production of new goods, the development of new skills, and generally to provide more useful "spinoffs" than those of the largely unskilled, limited requirements of traditional primary resource exploitation. ADA and ADB activity had only produced improved infrastructure and industrial development, which by their nature had changed very little the industrial structure of the province or the capabilities of the labour force. In addition, the Planning Secretariat undertook to generate a new orientation in government to end highly fragmented departmental approaches to common problems, and "provide a broad framework that can serve as a common guide to decision making and action all along the line."[16] Their premature efforts at consolidation eventually in 1975 bore fruit in a regional metropolitan system for Halifax-Dartmouth as well as municipal consolidations throughout the province.

As a concession to departments, the Secretariat, however, undertook to ensure that immediate programs resulting from co-ordinated planning would not prejudice the selection by individual departments of future policies. Programs were designed to supplement federal activities in regions and sectors of the province which had been bypassed by DREE's concentration in public works. Generally they aimed to broaden the involvement in, and strengthen the mechanisms for planning.

In a sense, Poetschke had to gamble that the Nova Scotian departments would be receptive to this enlightenment and programs of "intangibles" (as administrative changes must have seemed when compared with public works). These new proposals did not favour the traditional approach, by which departments, either individually or in conjunction with unco-ord-inated departmental activity from Ottawa, spent their way into new policies. Instead a new and unnerving systems approach was tried, aimed at redirecting a department's interests to problems rather than to its catalogue of narrow regulations and programs. Departments had also to be willing to accept Secretariat collaboration—even in the administration of programs. What often seemed to departments to be a reinventing of the wheel by the Secretariat or the duplication of existing programs or bodies (for industries and housing) was really an effort by the Secretariat to redirect and monitor the process of policy execution. Poetschke emphasized that he was dissatisfied with the limited examples of so-called co-ordination in other provinces: "More studies, clearer goals, better articulated strategies and sharper programs are not likely to take us off the road to inflation and social chaos unless we build the machinery and make the commitment to an action process that relates to the real tasks and the real issues."[17] Departments, however, either did not accept or understand the Secretariat's argument that a new systematic approach required considerable collaboration and guidance. It lost sympathy with the very process it was attempting to develop.

The traditional and highly conservative Nova Scotian departments, which had even proved troublesome for modest modernization efforts in the ARDA and ADB programs, were unprepared at the staff level to take such abrupt and rapid changes. Moreover, the ministers were insufficiently enthusiastic to convey to their officials their support for the Cabinet Committee on Planning and Programs and its Secretariat's approach to co-ordination. Increasingly observers, from deputy ministers to the Opposition, felt that the Secretariat was operating beyond its mandate. It was accused of implementing its own programs (using the remaining funds of its predecessor, the Program Development Agency) rather than planning, and thereby imposing an extra and unnecessary layer of bureaucracy.[18]

The Secretariat was clearly impatient with traditional Nova Scotian methods. It bypassed both the provincial housing authority and Department of Trade and Industry in some projects. It let contracts and guarantees in the housing field which should have received prior clearance from Finance. It engaged in a running political battle with Kent and DREE and refused offers of funds from Ottawa—a novelty in Nova Scotia. The Secretariat itself was a politically-chosen body not bound by normal categories and pay scales of the civil service. Its members were selected largely from outside the province, which made the traditional civil servants all the more uneasy over the new ways of these "imported experts."

This situation developed both from an overzealous Secretariat and loose terms of reference. The most flexible term was defined as follows: ". . . the Committee will continue its effort to explore and identify problems and opportunities related to development; to evaluate results of development action; and, under the direction of the Executive Council [Cabinet] to test approaches to solutions or problems and development opportunities."[19]

These "tests" took the form of pilot projects largely directed by the Secretariat with insufficient consultation of those departments which would not think in a comprehensive vein. While the Committee, and then the Cabinet, had to approve these activities, the minister responsible for presenting the Secretariat proposals was clearly overworked by holding two major portfolios—Finance and Labour—and apparently was unable to give them close attention. The Committee and Cabinet evidently accepted his recommendations and only subsequently received notice of the breakdown in interdepartmental co-operation.

The end of this unique and refreshing gamble in Nova Scotia came with the election to office in 1970 of the Opposition under Gerald Regan who had been an outspoken critic of the Secretariat.[20] Within two months he dismissed the staff, without consulting them about the problems of programming, and proposed that their functions could be better performed within the departments. He stated that "the Secretariat had confused 'planning' and 'implementation' and had developed a number of programmes in widely diverse functional areas,"[21] and that it had been "introduced as an additional layer of bureaucracy or super agency rather than attacking the fundamental weakness within the existing structure."[22] A more basic reason for dismissal, however, was that it jeopardized relations with Ottawa (as will be discussed in chapter 10).

(d) Prince Edward Island. The decision to plan in PEI was carried through Cabinet in 1966 by the new young Liberal premier, Alex Campbell, who realized that the province was falling further behind the rest of Canada and that the FRED funds for planning would not be available indefinitely in light of the federal "hard line" with provincial governments. Moreover, he was convinced that even if FRED projects did not succeed in converting the Island's largely rural economy, they would, he hoped, improve decision making and bring greater efficiency to the civil service which was at least two and a half times larger per 1,000 citizens than elsewhere.[23]

Opposition in the legislature and Cabinet stemmed from a defensive concern that the *status quo* was being upset and a conviction that the development plan was being formulated in the wrong manner.[24] Provincial officials were distrustful of an imported planning group, the Economic

Improvement Corporation, supplied by FRED funds as in Nova Scotia, and they felt slighted and bypassed by the extreme secrecy of EIC's operations. To the EIC and the premier this seemed necessary; the Corporation was concerned lest rumours leaked out about the plan which would bring judgement on the process before the delicately balanced package could be fully assembled. Hence, to avoid hasty assessment of incomplete proposals, the EIC and premier wanted to maintain secrecy. The EIC reported directly to the premier and there was little provision for the contributions of local people or departmental opinions.

The concern over EIC's planning procedure, and the fear that it would mean a further submission to federal funds and values, became the central election issue in the province in 1970.[25] Campbell's re-election, while it ensured the plan would be implemented, did not enable the continued operation of EIC. In response to complaints during the campaign that the EIC was designing and implementing its scheme from its remote attachment to the premier's office (and under pressure from Ottawa), Campbell replaced the EIC with a Department of Development (DOD) to co-ordinate the implementation of the plan. Even this agency was to be temporary; as a concession to existing departments the premier agreed that the DOD would be phased out once the plan and programs were implemented. It was partially dismantled sooner than anticipated. An Office of Planning and Development, attached to a committee of Cabinet, carried out revision of the plan. The administrative functions that DOD had accumulated were returned to existing departments. Some DOD functions have been kept within that department, and it serves as the major operational liaison with DREE.

Thus the Island's plan, though comprehensive, had progressively to be operated closer to the provincial department structure with its largely unchanged outlook. Eventually this might have been desirable; but departments among such a small population (100,000) have often tended to be very municipal in their operations, their ministers personally handling complaints and problems without extricating themselves for a better understanding of overall direction. Planning in this island province, while it has generated some definite programs, is still too fragmented and overwhelmed by the departmental structure to have a significant impact to date.

(e) New Brunswick and Alberta. To the extent that co-ordination in development planning has existed in both New Brunswick and Alberta, it has largely been of a gap-filling nature. New Brunswick expanded the operations of its Office of the Economic Adviser in 1962 from statistical

support to providing more co-ordination at the expediting level of the policy process. The Economic Adviser was then made secretary of the newly-created Treasury Board, and in his dual position he attempted to direct management, organization, and federal-provincial matters of policy to the Office, leaving the Treasury Board Secretariat primarily concerned about fiscal relations with Ottawa and budgetary performance of departments. The Office moved from one provincial problem to the next through the sixties. It provided industries with an official in Finance to assist them in making ADA applications; it served as a liaison with ADB research; it devised the Department of Economic Growth to handle aspects of development not covered by Trade and Industry; and it supervised the execution of the province's Equal Opportunity Program. The Office, however, was inclined to respond to problems as they arose and to allocate them to places within the civil service. Because of its small size (seven officials) it was not able to provide direction in terms of an overall provincial plan.

Co-ordination for long-term planning in New Brunswick was begun in 1969 by a group within the Office designated as a Development Policy Secretariat and divided to handle both economic and social policy formulation. Limited staff, newness, and lack of statistical data for the province still prevented the emergence of a planning framework or even an announced intention of overall planning. The Secretariat was also somewhat held back by the nature of Premier Louis Robichaud's Liberal Cabinet, entrenched in office through the decade, which was composed of several strong ministers to whom Robichaud gave considerable freedom. The premier was unwilling to impose planning upon departments, and this resulted in a continuation of the largely pragmatic response of the province to economic development. The Cabinet and Legislature were largely dominated by rural, pulp and paper, fisheries, and mining interests, and these primary enterprises, having low skill requirements, little need for tertiary industry and only limited economic "spinoffs" did not encourage social modernization or a newly systematic approach to government.

A similar problem of undertaking both industrial and human resource development motivated the Alberta Cabinet in 1967 to establish the Human Resources Development Authority (HRDA).[26] Twenty-five years of unprecedented economic expansion in that province had not been met by complementary social policy. The Authority was to co-ordinate existing social and welfare policy in Alberta designed to help people help themselves, and to initiate new programs for poverty or underprivileged people in light of better studies provided by the Economic Council and other sources on poverty, pockets of poverty, and urban unrest in North America.

The Authority was not intended to provide a total plan for the province as its responsibilities extended only to the social policies of government. Like the OEA in New Brunswick, it provided largely a gap-filling and management role in its co-ordination. It developed services, for instance, for native peoples not covered by other departments and sought to transfer these and any other programs it considered adrift to the appropriate departmental charge. Moreover, while the Authority was a Cabinet committee, in the notably *laissez-faire* Social Credit Cabinet, it was found to be politically a "lightweight" if it were to plan comprehensively. The four ministers involved, while in charge of departments with large budgets such as Education and Social Development, were young in a regime in office since 1935, in which length of service carried greater authority than size of budget.

The use of HRDA in a gap-filling role—as well as the willingness of the Cabinet to extend budgetary recommendations of the Budget Bureau into the setting of priorities—indicated the unpreparedness of a rich province, unused to establishing order for expenditures, for making a political response to periods of economic restraint.[27] The Cabinet transferred the task of establishing priorities to the Treasurer and HRDA. There was no provision for a comprehensive planning body. HRDA did have an equivalent group of economic planners in the form of the Budget Bureau but co-ordinated activity was a formal objective without actual substance. What "co-ordination" HRDA achieved was largely in new peripheral areas of its own making, not in the more urgent traditional fields for which it was created. It, for instance, eschewed the complex problem of co-ordinating the presence of at least six departments in the provision of education and training services in Alberta.

In the vacuum, the executive assistants to the premier and his ministers attempted a *de facto* organization to create policies for government and establish plans for an intergovernmental affairs department (which was only instituted late in 1971 by a newly elected Conservative government). They acknowledged, however, that they were hindered by lack of experience, insufficient data, and the protective and politicized attitude of departmental staff. Their activity was therefore largely to fulfil or initiate co-ordination of tasks which were properly the responsibility of—but untouched by—HRDA. As a result, the amalgamation of the Health and Social Development Departments and the creation of a Hospital Commission and Environmental Improvement Department were the result of policies designed by executive assistants and not by HRDA.

2. THE LIMITS OF COMPREHENSIVE PLANNING IN THE PROVINCES

In sum, the planning and co-ordination of policy on a comprehensive basis during the 1960s was evidently accepted in principle by poor provinces as a means of a concerted effort to catch up with the rich in economic development. But what actually emerged from the activities of planners and central co-ordination groups, while not identical in all provinces, suggested that their initial expectations were not realized. The interdepartmental experience of "vertical" policy co-ordination was rare; that is, the generation of continuity between the stages in policy making of selecting objectives, establishing priorities, planning strategy, developing programs, allocating money, and, finally, administrating policy. "Horizontal" management co-ordination and planning—that is, the development, interdepartmentally, of systematic procedures at any one of these stages—was more common, particularly in budget making, auditing, and personnel administration.[28] These evident difficulties in governments with the more extensive forms of vertical co-ordination as against horizontal co-ordination arose more from political motives than from technical reasons. At issue was the willingness of the politician to surrender traditional freedoms and spheres of influences to the uncertainties of the technocrats' plans.

Vertical co-ordination and planning had had only limited success because of the politician's ambiguity of emotions regarding the process and its conclusions. Quite characteristic of this period of the sixties was the disillusionment of planners when confronted by an absence of a positive government-wide response to their comprehensive documents. While this could be dismissed as a case of naive expectations on the part of planners untempered by the reality of the political system, frequently the situation had arisen because Cabinet had left the discovery and development of objectives and priorities to them, as if the means of decision making could somehow discover the ends.[29] The production of a comprehensive development plan based on this procedure did not necessarily begin, then, with prior Cabinet approval for the process or objectives of planning. Hence the conclusions reached could be considered not only unworkable but also illegitimate.

The COEQ and VEP and, to a lesser extent EIC, fell victim to this difficulty. Their plans were in a sense alien to an inarticulate Cabinet, and so without Cabinet support, the policy process had terminated at the planning level. Evidently, as the Maritime and Quebec experiences demonstrated, it was not even sufficient to protect the fragile priority-planning exercise by the political weight of the premier's office (to which they were usually responsible) in order to assure the conversion of plans to programs. Even if ministers were converted to integrated planning, it was essential that their deputy ministers down to their field officials be fully apprised of the new orientation which made the "rule book and catalogue of programs" approach unacceptable. In most provinces, moreover, the planners attached to the premier's office were the personal appointees of the premier holding power (as in Nova Scotia, New Brunswick, and Quebec) and lacked permanence or respect in confrontation with departments. Manitoba had gone further in ensuring an explicit and positive response of lower levels by infiltrating the civil service (posts of deputy minister and lower) with its political supporters. In most cases, however, co-operation had still to be squeezed from departments there.

Vertical co-ordination was further hindered by the ability of provincial departments to assert their intransigence. The planning process was both time-consuming and not highly visible, with the result that the establishment of a clientele support group—either within government or the private sector—was rarely very successful. In the interim, however, each department continued to serve its clientele so that, when the overall plan was delivered, the spirit of compromise over objectives and methods, although required, was not readily established. Each existing clientele reinforced departments against a loss or merging of their traditional services.[30]

A further reason for the failure of vertical co-ordination was the substitution of forms of horizontal co-ordination as an alternative. This occurred primarily at the budgetary or program level, whereby a new financial management technique or the co-ordination of administration was introduced as a substitute for the more thorough top-to-bottom flow of changes in functional boundaries, new priorities and innovations. Horizontal co-ordination, however, did not challenge the basic individuality of departments and they tended instead to work within their given functional responsibilities. Thus the activities of HRDA or OEA as gap–fillers were to meet problems left unattended when policies were designed by many departments, but they did not try to direct the mix of departmental policies which still remained largely a department's responsibility. Similarly, the new PPB system in provincial Treasury Boards, at best, secured a novel way of displaying departmental budgets but it did not necessarily achieve any greater interdepartmental co-ordination or the acceptance of more comprehensive objectives. In fact, even though PPBS tended theoretically to emphasize the flow from policy making to the administration of programs, its introduction to government at the departmental and not Cabinet level actually made it inimical to inter-departmental co-operation. Elevated to considerable prominence in Treasury

Board, the system stressed that departments were now more fully responsible, financially, for their decisions than under earlier Treasury Board practice. To the extent that management was preferred to planning, PPBS worked as a force against the co-ordination of a fully comprehensive policy process, while at the same time supporting this process within departments themselves.

In the provinces, then, the techniques of planning and co-ordination of development policies to speed the reduction of economic disparities did not overcome the existing pattern of and attitudes in the governmental process as fully as could be expected. There were similarly entrenched interests and intransigence in the federal regime, where the problem was further complicated by its dual responsibility to both rich and poor regions of Canada. Nevertheless, an impressive and effective solution was discovered at the federal level during the 1960s, and this will be looked at in the following chapter.

Chapter Ten

Federal Co-ordination for the War on Regional Disparities

As a method of integrating the various steps of selecting, designing, and executing policy, or as a method of achieving a degree of harmony between different functions, co-ordination had a longer existence at the federal level than in the provinces. Financial control, as one form of co-ordination, could be said to have started in the federal government with the passage in 1869 of the Department of Finance and Treasury Board Act. It should be recalled, however, that, except in wartime, the federal Cabinet had not used the form of highly-integrated and extensive co-ordination, covering all the functions and all the various stages of the policy process of government. Such comprehensiveness was also required for the attack on regional disparities. In fact, it was perhaps not until 1966, when Treasury Board developed the PPBS budgetary concept for federal policies, that a systematic and coherent horizontal co-ordination was progressively placed over the many programs devoted to aspects of regional poverty. This endeavour was greatly assisted by the vertical co-ordination achieved by the Privy Council Office and DREE. Until that time the legacy of post-war federal governments had been one of encouraging private economic activities, providing national income stabilization and social assistance, and allowing any further initiatives to come largely from the departmental level.

During the early sixties, when it came to the possibility of undertaking a concerted effort of government to reduce regional disparities, neither the Diefenbaker nor the Pearson regime was equipped to direct a comprehensive planning exercise had the occasion arisen. Neither leader was inclined by nature to raise his Cabinet's horizons above the immediate, daily crises. Diefenbaker, while sympathetic to the lagging regions, lurched from crisis to crisis and rarely secured a team effort or spirit in his Cabinet or officials. He continually interfered in his ministers' activities, so that any competence which they developed—reflected by technical and long-term plans—was repeatedly thwarted by the prime minister's interest in the short run and the political. Professionals, experts, and senior departmental officials, moreover, were not among his policy confidants. Pearson, while he was less domineering than Diefenbaker, was indecisive about the role of his minority government in the face of strong provincial challenges. He preferred to let his Cabinet and advisers reach their own compromises. He accepted compromise because he lacked conviction. Since policy decisions were cast at the lowest level of Cabinet consensus, they were decentralized and incremental.

Planning at Ottawa during much of the 1960s accordingly took place at various points in the policy process—finance, personnel management, administration—but not simultaneously at all levels and not within a comprehensive structure or policy framework. Federal planning for regional disparities in Canada initially took shape at the departmental level, and required that *ad hoc* horizontal arrangements be struck between various departments over specific programs that were of common interest. Gradually in the later sixties this "peer relationship" was provided with vertical co-ordination and direction from a level higher than departments. Three approaches thus made to encourage co-ordination had considerable relevance to questions of poverty and regional disparities, though the first two—a Special Planning Secretariat and the Privy Council Office—had mandates that extended beyond regional disparities. The SPS responsibility was to co-ordinate policies for poverty, whether regional, "pocket," or urban. The Privy Council Office provided a general secretariat service to Cabinet and its committees. The third example, DREE, was a further experiment, for this new ministry was both an ordinary department and an extraordinary super-ministry for the design and co-ordination of federal programs for specific regions of the country.

1. FEDERAL BODIES FOR CO-ORDINATION OF REGIONAL GROWTH POLICIES, 1965–1970

(a) The Special Planning Secretariat. The Special Planning Secretariat, established in early 1965 within the Privy Council Office (PCO) was, unlike ARDA or ADB, a body above strict departmental limits concerned with the problems of economic disparities. The PCO at this time was not a

particularly influential policy secretariat, as it was later to become under Prime Minister Trudeau. Pearson's practice of decentralizing decision making within his ministry meant that his Cabinet did not become a centre of general or future policy directives to departments. Without articulate Cabinet priorities the PCO was, accordingly, not placed in a position of having to provide a co-ordination of the individual efforts of departments. The weakness, and partial absence, of the Cabinet committee system removed a further need for the PCO to provide continuity. In short, departments were not asked to heed PCO directives or had few reasons to do so. In such an environment, the Special Planning Secretariat, a small group of nine civil servants in the PCO, had a monumental task of trying to co-ordinate and direct all departmental policies for Canada's "war on poverty."

In retrospect, one can see that the Secretariat's greatest success lay in its introduction of new thinking both to Ottawa and, through the War on Poverty Conference of 1965 which it sponsored, to the provincial and municipal governments. It emphasized that the problem of poverty demanded a response concerned with growth as well as welfare. It was clear that poverty had regional as well as individual characteristics; the Secretariat attempted to direct federal policy away from a single obsession with the symptoms of poverty treated by income security payments to individuals, and towards preventive programs for regions and areas in order to increase their economic growth and modernization. In its stress upon programs for labour mobility and for investment in the economy of poor regions rather than for the mere provision of welfare "floors" of income and services, it articulated and heightened the growing tension between the advocates of welfare policies for poor regions, coupled with labour mobility, and the advocates of considerable investment in the possible economic potential of those regions.[1] It served further to introduce to Canadians much of the experiences gained in the contemporary American war on poverty, including the use of comprehensive regional planning, the idea of rural self-help programs, and the turning of the federal government attention to urban ghettos of poverty.

In the intergovernmental context, the Secretariat's War on Poverty Conference succeeded in bringing together for the first time the diverse groups at three levels of government that were concerned with various aspects of poverty in Canada. No policy resulted directly from the Conference but it lent prestige to the attempts to improve TVTA, ADA, and ARDA that resulted in OTA, ADIA, and FRED respectively. At the provincial level, the conference added weight to the studies of poverty done by the Economic Council of Canada and contributed to the formation of HRDA in Alberta, to co-ordination for regional development in

Ontario, the elaboration of New Brunswick's Equal Opportunity Program, and the urgency of equivalent activities in other provinces.

At the federal level, however, the Special Planning Secretariat had little success in co-ordinating programs. Its resources were confined to a small staff under Tom Kent without funds or operational responsibilities. The personnel was oriented to ideas more than implementation, and it lacked a financial basis with which to challenge or entice departments.[2] Hence the Secretariat was expected to co-ordinate at no cost to departments those programs having to do with self help in poor areas which covered, in effect, *all* federal taxation and expenditure policies. The idealism of this mandate was sharply contrasted with an emerging realism in an initially similar mandate for the Atlantic Development Board which suggested the futility of this role—even *with* funds ADB still studiously avoided interfering with the activities of other departments.

The continuity of policy execution was impaired at this time by a weak Cabinet committee system and Privy Council Office so that the Secretariat had no "transmission belt" to the departments for its proposals. It had no means by which to extend its proposed reforms to others. Moreover, the idea of co-ordination raised the spectre of nine officials attempting to direct ministers' decisions within their own departments. Not surprisingly, this "completely naive notion" of tackling such a massive area in a novel, systematic, and technocratic manner was "absolutely abortive."[3] Attempts to establish interdepartmental committees met with less success than similar ARDA efforts, perhaps primarily because of the presence of funds in the ARDA coffers. The Secretariat, moreover, was unable to obtain prestige and power from its close connection to the prime minister, because of lack of direction of government policy. Kent left the Secretariat to become deputy minister of Manpower in 1966, and the SPS was finally reabsorbed into the PCO in 1967.

(b) The Privy Council Office. The change in stature of the PCO was a direct consequence of Pierre Trudeau's arrival as prime minister in 1968. Trudeau set, as an immediate reform of his government, the establishment of priorities and mechanisms for their review. The new leader crystallized at a political level the "new style" of executing governing responsibilities developed since 1964 by some federal civil servants and already evident in Finance's hard line and Treasury Board's Program-Planning-Budgeting System. Trudeau's attitude towards decision making in government was that it must be pervasive from the top downwards. Particularly it should be rational and systematic. It should, moreover, be made substantially more efficient and less time-consuming through better policy co-ordination at lower levels and well-informed, carefully-regulated Cabinet sessions.

One observer has commented that Trudeau required considerable time to himself, a fact that has had consequences for the PCO.[4] His own personal staff is large and highly organized, and this demands a corresponding response from the civil service. In fact, the present large and competent Prime Minister's Office and much-enhanced Privy Council Office both reflect a central point of Trudeau's thinking—that established forces (in this case the bureaucracy) must be challenged by "counterweights" (of either a political or new bureaucratic grouping of advisers). Thus, apart from expediting the heavy responsibilities of an active prime minister, these two bodies have deliberately been made large and inquisitive in order to prevent the "traditional way" of doing things from being the norm.[5] It should be noted also that Trudeau improved the frequency, size, and status of national party conventions—thereby using the party rank and file and thinkers as an alternative source of inputs and feedback to the political decision-makers.

To expedite his new style, Trudeau established active Cabinet committees to make lower level decisions and reduce the length of Cabinet meetings. The Cabinet was thus made less important as a scrutinizing (and hence decision-making) body by the committee process; often recommendations from a committee composed of senior ministers such as that for economic affairs, chaired by the minister of Finance, were already assured of Cabinet approval. The roles of Finance and Treasury Board were considerably enhanced by the committee system and the closer examination of policy proposals.[6] It was no longer possible, for instance, for new programs to be considered by the Cabinet without first receiving Treasury Board and Finance approval. Likewise, general Cabinet policy guidelines now most frequently went to Treasury Board for elaboration in greater detail and the selection of program priorities for optimum use of resources. The program departments were, therefore, removed several steps from policy decisions within the Cabinet. In effect, they were subject to the preferences of committee or budgetary groups prior to the political decisions made by Cabinet.

The PCO, as a common secretariat to all committees, was given correspondingly greater powers to direct departmental activities to the appropriate Cabinet committee and to ensure that all committees were well informed of progress elsewhere. The Office was to ensure that departments were working on current Cabinet priorities and was to provide for budgetary and departmental collaboration. The PCO is well situated and suited for such an overview; its "policies and priorities" section is the key to supplying the Cabinet with advice. Unavoidably a considerable amount of its time has been spent in directing a systematic and uniform federal attitude in relations with provinces—particularly in the light of the importance to the Cabinet of clarifying such relations. To this end most federal-provincial meetings are now observed by a silent PCO official attached to the federal delegation.

Strictly speaking, the PCO does not initiate policy proposals but merely expedites those of departments. It is true, however, that it may attempt to convert perceived social or community values into broad policies—such as those on bilingualism and regional development—and encourage departments to concentrate their new proposals within these guidelines. Equally, it may urge reform of a department's program, such as OTA, which has a poor performance record. In present circumstances this has become a responsibility of considerable potency. Trudeau's obvious respect for the Cabinet committee system places the PCO at the summit of staff advice flowing to the prime minister. Cabinet meetings no longer consist of ministers unveiling their pet projects for approval, but of a well-organized consideration of policy proposals which have cleared various prior levels of interdepartmental approval, through PCO guidance.

At the very least, then, the PCO constitutes for the program department one additional level of inspection and direction through which its proposals must pass on their way to the Cabinet. Its control of agenda, its communication of broad priorities and its rationalist approach can further regulate the appearance of departmental proposals that fall outside the priorities of Cabinet. Hence the pervasive influence of members of the Privy Council staff, many of whom are former Finance officials, has had a significant effect upon the breadth and length of perspective in departmental submissions, as well as on the integration of one department's proposals with activities in other departments. The activity of the PCO then, can very significantly affect research on the ultimate direction of a policy. In fact, the whole concept of policy making at Ottawa must now be greatly enlarged to include the so-called "neutral" role of the PCO as co-ordinator.

The PCO has had little tolerance for a lack of effective inter-departmental relations in the federal government. Nowhere has this been more evident than in policies for regional development. Where the question of building new airports had primarily been one of aircraft access for departments of transport at both levels of government, the activity of the PCO (and of the new Secretary of State for Urban Affairs) has now brought into the discussion the related questions of land use, housing, and urban growth, of economic stimulation and possible alternative modes of transportation. The inevitable result has been that the strictly transportation concerns have not been the only factors affecting the selection of sites. It is a reasonable speculation, too, that priority given to the location of a second airport at Montreal, instead of Toronto where the overcrowding is much greater, was not the first desire of the Department of Transport but rather one in accord with the two main policy priorities at Ottawa today —Quebec and regional disparities—both communicated by the PCO. Hence the activity of the PCO as a co-ordinator of a strong Cabinet committee system and as a general complaints department for the provinces has meant, for the departmental politician, the imposition of a significant analytical and synthesizing process upon his officials and even upon his own activities in the Cabinet. This may be technocracy carried to the extreme but it has assuredly been favoured by Trudeau.

(c) The Department of Regional Economic Expansion. DREE was a unique combination and culmination of the changes taking place at Ottawa during the Liberal regimes of the 1960s. Unlike many other new departments, it reflected not the undertaking of a new federal responsibility but the imposition of a new style and process upon existing functions. The creation of DREE in 1969 was a further result of the forces which had earlier formed the Special Planning Secretariat and later had enhanced the role of the Privy Council Office. Both the PCO and SPS had exposed to critical analysis the often narrow, inflexible, and uncoordinated behaviour of traditional federal departments. Likewise, DREE was a positive response to the new criteria of economic and financial efficiency developed by Finance and Treasury Board, which they found repeatedly frustrated by existing departmental programs for tackling regional disparities. Consequently the inability of these senior co-ordinating and planning bodies to secure sufficient changes in the approach of traditional programs, or to offer their own alternatives, had much to do with the establishment of the Department of Regional Economic Expansion.

Apart from the reduction of policies in the rural areas to alleviate regional disparities and the switch instead towards stressing industrial and urban growth, the motivation behind DREE reflected three priorities which had increasingly emerged at Ottawa, beginning in 1965. They were (a) the pursuit of efficiency in federal expenditures through a concentration upon medium-term (fifteen-year) economic objectives and the PPB system of resource management; (b) the achievement of a greater public visibility in federal expenditures and of a new constituency for federal services other than provinces in order to counteract centrifugal forces within the federation; and, (c) the direction of federal policies—even in nation-wide joint programs—towards definite *federal* goals.

DREE reflected not only the new methodologies that we have seen developing in government but also encompassed the two major targets of federal expenditures that were emerging by the mid-1960s; to recall, the alleviation of regional poverty and of Quebec's tendencies towards separation. Hence, when other departmental budgets were frozen or cut to control the inflation of 1968–71 (including the traditionally large spending Defence department), DREE was almost alone in being granted a substantial budgetary increase by Treasury Board.[7] Compared to the relaxed practices of earlier programs for dealing with regional disparities, the style and process of DREE could easily seem at times to be ruthless. It was indeed well-equipped to be aggressive when its minister and deputy minister were among the most powerful in Ottawa. Much of its influence besides, was derived from the strong support of Finance and Treasury Board for its initial creation. In turn, it was not timid in largely abandoning ARDA, FRED, and ADB concepts. And other departments such as Fisheries, Manpower, and even Finance found their policies challenged or directed in the field by DREE.

Within two years' operation, the young department demonstrated that it was increasingly effective at co-ordinating regional development policy and championing the economic cause among cultural, non-economic, and traditional forces in the federal government. Marchand, as the Liberals' trouble-shooter in Quebec, tended to see DREE as an omnibus department with the power to solve most of Quebec's problems. Hence, the department's activities were not strictly confined to industrial development or the federal jurisdiction. DREE's attainment of prominence in the federal departmental hierarchy brought to federal-provincial relations, however, a form of co-ordination inimical to past traditions of intergovernmental collaboration.

2. Intergovernmental Consequences of Federal and Provincial Policy Co-ordination

However significant, the discussion thus far of the efforts of government (both federal and provincial) to co-ordinate for regional economic growth has necessarily been placed in a rather limited setting. For the move to create bodies of co-ordination was as much a result of intergovernmental pressures as the desire for internal reforms within a particular level of government. In this intergovernmental setting the stresses that worked to produce co-ordination were varied. In some cases the extension of provincial and federal operations into fields of mutual interest often through shared-cost programs, aroused desires to replace merely external consultation with some forum for co-operation or even closer co-ordination of policy, in order to achieve maximum effectiveness through harmony. Thus it was that joint federal-provincial bodies were created as a result of FRED and ADB projects in the 1960s. This was a case of co-ordination and planning being executed by a federal and provincial co-operative effort between similar departments.

In a second set of cases, the establishment of policy co-ordination groups—at the provincial level—was really more of a defensive move to meet federal activity in provincial fields. To respond to the various aspects of the emerging hard line and new style of politics at Ottawa in the late sixties required comparable reforms at the provincial level, so that an adequate reply could be made to federal thrusts and federal discipline. In short, the provinces once again were not prepared to accept the notion that Ottawa knew what was best for them. This was one reason for the enhancement of provincial Treasury Boards to deal critically with the federal Treasury Board's demands for controlled growth rates in shared-cost programs. Further changes in the federal attitude to joint relationships in Manpower matters, constitutional reform, or social policy stimulated new or improved provincial reforms. In this respect, the Human Resources Development Authority in Alberta, the Continuing Program Secretariat in Manitoba, the Federal-Provincial Affairs Secretariat and the Taxation and Fiscal Policy Branch in Ontario, and the Department of Intergovernmental Affairs in Quebec all constituted, in part, a provincial response to federal co-ordination initiatives.

Yet, still further, a third set of provincial groups was established in answer to a chronic *lack* of federal co-ordination in some programs that affected a particular province. And in this regard the Cabinet Committee on Planning and Programs in Nova Scotia, New Brunswick's Office of the Economic Adviser, and Quebec's Intergovernmental Affairs department each in some degree developed from the provinces' frustration with the operations of *ad hoc* and unrelated federal policies within their own boundaries. Each also grew out of the desire of the respective province to feel better informed of where indeed it wanted to go and to accept from Ottawa only those programs that would contribute to its own provincial goals. The lack of co-ordination was particularly evident in federal industrial development policy in the Maritimes, where ADA and ADB had operated independently of each other and often at cross purposes. The establishing of industrial estates in Nova Scotia and New Brunswick was thus indicative of provincial efforts to concentrate the effects of scattered federal development throughout the two provinces.

In view of these considerations, one can see that DREE, while not the first accomplishment of federal co-ordination, was bound to have a crucial impact upon regional development policy since it so fully embodied the major political, administrative, and financial reforms carried out at Ottawa. These, then, were matched by hesitant steps in poorer provinces to undertake some planning for themselves with federal financial assistance. DREE's forceful behaviour in an intergovernmental setting accordingly had a profound effect upon the planning and co-ordinating capacity of the poorer provinces.

Put succinctly, DREE established two very clear lines of action in dealing with regional disparities: it was prepared to increase greatly the federal *scope* of activity, but only under the terms of a very definite *style* for provincial participation in the spending of federal funds through joint programs. Where federal expenditures were involved it was now decided that the design, performance and goals of joint programs would be in accord with federal criteria. Consequently, the continuation of the co-operative and even consultative federalism of the early sixties had been relegated to a notably lower priority by the federal government, which sought as its first objective, the greater efficiency, certainty, and effectiveness of its spending in both economic and political terms.

DREE's deputy minister, Tom Kent, was of course a vigorous proponent of a new style, as witnessed by his writing, speeches, the consistency of advice in the many posts he held and, especially, the character of DREE programs. Whether a visionary or anachronism, he personally was an important influence on Ottawa's policy, in removing the federal encouragement of provincial planning and even of operational co-ordination. His distaste for scattered decision making, for excessive levels of planning or co-ordination, and for programs with intangible results, created successors to ARDA, ADA, and ADB which bore scant resemblance to the earlier styles of government. His practice consisted in deliberately bypassing the co-ordination apparatus at the provincial level (often created through earlier federal encouragement) to deal directly instead with provincial departments or the private sector of the provincial economy. Even then provincial departments usually had the choice only of accepting or rejecting federal packages. Kent expressed his rationale as follows:

> . . . while the plan with provinces for development is a joint one in the sense that substantial sums of money are provided by the federal government to programmes that otherwise would not be possible, the federal government obviously has to be satisfied that these moneys are being properly spent.
>
> Obviously if there is a responsibility, the responsibility of any government is the responsibility for spending its funds.[8]

As this thesis was applied to DREE, the provinces were left only with a share of management of joint programs, not the decision making about general policy. Kent did not feel federal monies could be spent on provincial planning groups. Indeed he was not prepared to accept the view that problems bridged federal-provincial boundaries nor that, consequently, solutions also had to be joint.

The second novelty in DREE was that its scope of operations was to be as wide as Ottawa deemed the case under treatment to be. Constitutionally-assigned jurisdictions had to be treated as expendable luxuries if the provinces expected federal assistance for their problems. Experience in the past certainly suggested that the narrow departmental and constitutional constraints had robbed regional development programs of their full effectiveness. Thus, although the federal government in the late sixties was increasingly more willing to divert its funds to the reduction of regional disparities, this was to be without consideration of the formal divisions of the Canadian constitution.

It followed that this style and scope of DREE's activity had very serious consequences for the newly-established provincial planning bodies which, even without facing federal hostility, had often encountered unfavourable receptions within their own governments. Ottawa's direct dealings with provincial departments on an individual basis, and as contributors to federal plans, jeopardized provincial attempts to improve the integration of their own policies and to systematize the process of policy making in accordance with provincial goals. Even provincial efforts to formulate long-term objectives were challenged by what were, in effect, federal offers to enhance the existing empires and short-term policies of individual provincial departments. DREE gave no indication of its long term goals or the extent of its commitment; faced with this uncertainty and with the possibility Ottawa might yield to the pressure of the rich provinces at some point, the poor regions hastened to take up funds before they were withdrawn. But the federal industrial incentives in a poor province could very significantly affect the arrival and location of new industries and hence the overall mix of industries in the provinces. In certain instances they neutralized or contradicted the province's own incentives, which were much more modest and constricted by limited funds. DREE's activities, therefore, seemed to require greater not less, collaboration with a dominant federal power.

Because DREE's policies had such a profound effect upon economic development in poor provinces it is important to substantiate in greater detail the attitudes of its influential deputy minister who greatly limited provincial planning in economic matters. Before examining the specific examples of three provinces, we may recall that Kent preferred a situation where in joint agreements the federal government was not "locked" into long term arrangements. In 1970 he thus refused at first to propose a third five-year ARDA agreement with the provinces. Even when compelled by political forces he still insisted that each province should then bargain for the best individual settlement, and in all but Ontario's case Ottawa did not commit itself to a specific level of expenditure. The RDIA industrial incentive program, too, contained extensive leeway for ministerial discretion while the secrecy that shrouded Kent's activities in DREE increased the opportunity for flexibility and reduced the likelihood of his being tied down by public statements of his intent.[9] But in more specific detail, Kent's effective limiting of provincial planning as a factor in the committing of federal funds was best indicated by events in three provinces: Nova Scotia, Prince Edward Island, and Quebec.

One activity of Nova Scotia's Cabinet Committee on Planning and Programs was to produce in 1970, with the twin municipalities of Halifax and Dartmouth (a region designated for federal aid to infrastructure under DREE), an integrated plan of public works projects intended to develop a community in accordance with provincial and municipal preferences. The Secretariat to the Cabinet Committee, led by Poetschke, had been expressly established to enable the province to negotiate with Ottawa in the knowledge of where it wished to go. As a result, Kent discovered at a federal-provincial meeting in 1970 that *his* projects for the designated region could not alter the package upon which the province and municipalities had decided; furthermore, Nova Scotian departments refused to make bilateral "deals" outside this provincial package. The province, in short, rejected a predetermined collection of proposals from DREE and in turn insisted upon its own collection. Ottawa and the provinces had collided in efforts to fit one another into their plans as a specific and certain "input."[10]

The differences of views were sufficiently wide that Kent returned to Ottawa without signing an agreement. Subsequently he approached municipalities and departments in the province individually and encouraged them to submit to DREE a list of possible projects above and beyond immediate provincial priorities that they would like financed. From these he selected those in accord with his own preferences and presented them to the provincial-municipal planning committee as "the" DREE plan for the designated area. This resulted in a major political clash with the Nova Scotian ministers who had become committed to the official provincial-municipal plan and strongly resented Kent's interference with their officials and his selection of lower-priority items. The federal deputy minister yielded under strong political pressure and agreed to the original plan, although very little money was directed to the province for the remainder of the year. Kent subsequently refused to deal with Poetschke and his secretariat, even though they were officially designated as the provincial liaison with DREE.

Certainly there was a gulf between the two agencies. Poetschke held very different views from Kent about how to achieve economic development. The former attempted to force a philosophy for systematic and structural change upon a federal DREE policy directed by Kent primarily towards public works and jobs. Poetschke and his secretariat felt strongly that attitudes and processes in Nova Scotia had first to be changed and that proposed industrial incentives only constituted a subsidy to the existing faulty system. But because joint planning as an instrument of intergovernmental relations had been reduced by DREE there was no way these two philosophies could be harmonized except for the haphazard confrontation of proposal with counter-proposals—a wasteful duplication of both time and human effort in two parallel research organizations. Poetschke met considerable opposition not only from Kent but, as he has noted, from various forces in the province also.

> When the Nova Scotia government came to DREE for assistance in system building as well as public works, the local press admonished the Government to get in line with Ottawa. This the Government did and quietly went on with system building on their own without any federal assistance except for technical services from two or three departments and agencies.[11]

He further saw the vulnerability of his approach within his own government:

> . . . expectations of what government can deliver are unbelievably low, and in the absence of real credibility, the game of trying to punch the right buttons to get expenditure programmes will continue. Our experience over the last few months in Nova Scotia is that people and communities are willing to try the systems approach because they are fed up and desperate but with one hand ready to go back to the buttons at the first sign of a breakdown in servicing.[12]

In any case Poetschke's experiment ended in January 1971 when the new Liberal provincial premier disbanded his secretariat. This move may have been significantly influenced by Kent's inability to work with Poetschke and the considerable importance of DREE spending in the province. Clearly there had been little DREE spending during the last half of 1970, though whether Kent actually suggested to the newly-elected Premier Regan in December that the province was losing out on DREE funds is only conjecture.[13] Nevertheless it is interesting to note that two days after the secretariat was disbanded, DREE announced considerable additional spending in the province.[14] And what made Kent's complicity in the demise more likely than not was the evidence of similar behaviour in other provinces.

In Prince Edward Island, Gallagher and his Economic Improvement Corporation were urged in 1968 by federal ARDA staff to submit the province's proposal for a FRED plan before the signing of an agreement between Ottawa and Quebec for a FRED project in the Gaspé region arising out of the BAEQ study. ARDA officials were concerned that the size of the Quebec agreement for $250 million would definitely cool the enthusiasm of federal departments and Finance towards the FRED concept with the result that, while the Quebec agreement would be signed for political reasons, the Prince Edward Island proposal, which appeared to be very expensive, might be severely cut back. Premier Campbell was meeting opposition of his own within the provincial Cabinet, and was unwilling to take the Island's proposal to Ottawa while the provincial legislature was in session—which dragged on interminably during the spring of that year. It was not until June, after the Quebec plan had been signed, that the $725 million plan was submitted to (and stunned) the FRED Board at Ottawa.[15] Finance immediately gave notice that while not opposed to the FRED concept it would require considerable time to examine the magnitude and timing of the proposed expenditures.

The Island's proposal was clearly going to be delayed at Ottawa. Most federal departments were still reeling from the implications of the BAEQ agreement for their priorities and finances, and were not particularly eager to give an immediate positive response. At the same time the departure from Ottawa of Sauvé, the minister responsible for ARDA-FRED, and the national election of 1968 prevented any urgent or decisive action being taken upon the FRED project. Only by mid-July were Marchand and Kent chosen to replace Sauvé and his deputy, André Saumier, at the top of Forestry and Rural Development. And then Kent favoured dropping the whole FRED-ARDA approach in preference to an industrial development program.

In Prince Edward Island, Campbell had not budgeted for the delay in submitting the FRED plan caused by a long spring legislative session or by problems at Ottawa. He badly needed interim investment in his province during the summer. Eventually the federal ARDA staff was able to divert some ADB, ADA, and ARDA money towards certain physical and institutional projects of the proposed FRED plan as an interim measure for the Island.

The issue which destroyed the province's planning body, the Economic Improvement Corporation, was the administration of this interim package. ADB officials felt that the departments themselves should handle the physical projects (roads, a recreation complex, and ferry parking facilities). ARDA staff disagreed; they argued that the purpose of the plan and of EIC was to secure a new way of thinking and new processes in government. Because planning was a technique absent in the traditional procedure of the province's departments, the spending of FRED funds without EIC direction would have constituted a loss of the integrated plan with little hope that institutional changes would ever be implemented— particularly the reform of public administration. Premier Campbell and Gallagher met with the provincial Cabinet; after considerable persuasion, they secured agreement upon a draft press release drawn up by federal ARDA staff which placed EIC in charge of the institutional programs and made it co-ordinator of the physical projects. Saumier and his ARDA staff, however, misjudged the reaction of their new deputy minister, Tom Kent. Just as Campbell secured his Cabinet's agreement, Kent, who had only just read the draft release, called on the Island capital to delete all references to EIC. The programs fell back into individual departments. Needless to say, the provincial Cabinet could not disguise its glee, and Campbell realized further support of the EIC was futile. It was disbanded by 1970. The FRED plan was subsequently renegotiated with the province by DREE and the new agreement, signed in 1970, deleted many of the programs for institutional change, such as fisheries rationalization and civil service reforms, and effectively dropped the involvement of other federal departments.[16]

Quebec, however, was the main and most interesting point of concentration of DREE's activities as well as DREE's special talents of involving other federal departments in its regional development goals. Because Quebec was made a top priority of Trudeau's government, it was in the federal behaviour toward this province that one could discover that Kent's and Marchand's stern attitude towards provincial governments elsewhere had not been an exceptional or isolated phenomenon.

The extent of federal influence in the life of the Quebec economy was largely the cause of the demise of planning by the provincial government. The dilemma arose from the vicious logic of regional economic disparities. To secure a rapid development in the Quebec economy and catch up with English-speaking Canada, investment was required on a scale that was beyond the capacity of the provincial government and apparently in excess of private willingness to invest. Ottawa was prepared to supply a large part of the capital required for infrastructure and industrial incentives but—once again—on federal terms. If the province wanted the very large investment of funds in all aspects of its economy to come from Ottawa, rather than private sources, it was not to be by way of transfer payments to the provincial government but by directly-controlled federal spending. Several examples of this federal control can be set forth.

By 1971 the populated portion of the province, including the new designation of Montreal, was at least eligible for DREE's industrial incentive program (some areas of Quebec had further special status for aid to infrastructure and education).[17] It would seem natural that any new private plans for investment or expansion in the province (or any part of Canada, for that matter) would very likely be submitted to DREE in view of possible eligibility for federal grants. The designation of Montreal gave it a special attractiveness for investment over other heavily industrialized areas in central Canada. Moreover, the new incentives offered in the Montreal region were not added to the existing incentives in the rest of the province (although they *were* added to incentives for the Atlantic provinces). Therefore, the rest of Quebec was, by federal choice, dropped to a third rank position in DREE industrial incentives. In such a way DREE (that is, the federal government) decided upon not only the eligibility of and assistance to industry but very definitely the location and mixture of industry within the province—not to mention Canada at large.

DREE, however, was but one indication of the scope of federal unilateral activity in the province. The new Montreal airport being built by the federal Department of Transport had been located and was to be developed according to federal government preferences. It was to be linked with the existing airport by a new highway provided by the department. Both the valuable land bordering the road and the airport noise zone perimeter were available for development only according to federal criteria. (This comprised 88,000 acres; a new airport of identical class proposed for Toronto was to use only 18,000 acres.) Furthermore, federal control of harbours had been recently used to stimulate ship building and container ports in selected Quebec areas. Still further, the federal government had turned down a Quebec request for a special stabilization fund for provinces experiencing high cyclical rates of unemployment, arguing instead that the funds (which would have been unconditional grants) could be used in federal programs having greater impact.[18] Finally, Quebec was denied a substantial increase in its entitlement to unconditional transfers from Ottawa in the form of equalization payments. Its proposals to include municipal revenues in the calculations of provincial and local wealth were rejected by Ottawa as being too costly for the federal regime. It was acknowledged that an equivalent amount of money would be used conditionally under much increased DREE activity—and directed by the federal government.

In short, Quebec was virtually overwhelmed by the concentration of federal policies (specifically or disproportionately aimed at the province) which contained similar features of federal design and financial control.[19]

The activities of DREE and related federal policies, encouraged in other fields by the PCO's communication of the Cabinet's priority for Quebec, produced a situation where independent provincial action was constrained by federal funds that were not available without condition.[20] As the above account suggests, the conditions were sufficiently extensive and explicit so as to ensure that the future of economic development in the province would be decided in Ottawa not Quebec City.

The behaviour of DREE towards the provinces that has been outlined suggests *how* the federal government had more recently asserted itself in regional development. To explain more fully *why* Ottawa's presence was asserted thus, it is necessary to recall the two motivating forces mentioned earlier: the desire to control the growth and impact of federal expenditures in joint programs and the desire to reassert the federal presence in the country, in the light of the centrifugal effects of Quebec's separatist tendencies and the aggressiveness of rich provinces in resource development. Each of these factors will be considered in turn.

3. The Consequences of Program Budgeting for Intergovernmental Relations

The tendency of Ottawa in the late sixties to confront provinces with preconceived and tightly-defined proposals was derived in some part from the PPBS approach to policy making. The close regulation of the various steps in policy making—from policy guidelines through strategy to final programs—meant, however, that there was little provision for variations according to extra-departmental or extra-governmental forces.[21] Value was placed upon the system and ends of budgeting, not the process of interdepartmental negotiation. While PPBS purchased a measurable and integrated sequence of steps in a program it also tended to encapsulate the program by its internal and simplistic logic in a way that reduced the willingness for compromise that might alter the "efficiency" of resource allocation.

At the time it was applied by some Ottawa departments, PPBS was a method of wresting greater independence from the federal Treasury Board.[22] This diminished, in turn, a department's willingness to engage in interdepartmental or intergovernmental relations, to the extent that it meant a loss of control over its responsibilities and hence its independence from Treasury Board.[23] In its aversion to "incrementalism" in policy making, the federal government imposed a centrally-directed uniformity on the procedure of creating policy which had never existed before. This was particularly the case when DREE won its annual allotment from Treasury Board and sought to spend the full amount within the fiscal

175

year to avoid a year-end surplus and a possible lower allocation in the subsequent year. While this did not prevent the development of discriminate policies for different regions, the annual fight for budgetary allocations made DREE's outlook short term. An emphasis on spending reduced the attractiveness of joint (and time-consuming) planning and the provincial contribution was greatly reduced.[24]

Officials have suggested that in the vacuum of guidelines and priorities from Cabinet or in the presence of hopelessly general guidelines, PPBS became converted from a management tool to an end in itself. In such a situation, not only did it substitute for a selection of goals according to social values those which secured the greatest budgetary "efficiency," but also it set forth the language of success: a department that "spoke" this PPBS language got the most favourable reception from Treasury Board. As for regional development policy, the presence of PPBS here, as represented by DREE, brought undoubted clarity and uniformity to the display of program objectives and costs. There was considerable doubt, however, whether the objectives of infrastructure and jobs asserted by DREE were qualitatively improved enough to warrant the large increase in funds over the level consumed by former development programs.[25] Nevertheless, the greatest effectiveness of PPBS, hence the earning of Treasury Board's most favourable responses, involved processes such as labour training or generating industrial jobs which provided a quantitative indication of achievement.

The concern for visibility and quantity in program results evident in the fierce departmental competition for federal budgetary allocations restricted action to a narrow range of programs. DREE was not necessarily undertaking a better approach to regional development but rather one more concentrated. In fact, what was intended often to be a joint federal-provincial planning exercise deteriorated into negotiations over the best ways of showing the federal funds at work. Provincial officials in the Interlake FRED program, for example, found that DREE's interest in their projects was largely confined to the cost of performance of the program in dollar figures or the number of jobs produced, not whether the jobs or programs altered the quality of life, the useful skills of citizens, or encouraged the reorientation of interests. Prince Edward Island officials similarly complained of DREE's interest in "bricks and mortar" programs. The Atlantic Provinces Economic Council also observed that DREE had not altered but only reinforced the particular industrial composition of the Maritimes.

The obsession with this quantitative technique unfortunately restricted the appeal of policy decisions made on other grounds. ARDA and FRED programs, with their interest in structural and attitudinal change, were particularly vulnerable to the PPBS approach, as the education, participation and "animation" of rural people in their poverty problems produced results that often defied a dollar figure. The renegotiation in 1971 of the BAEQ-FRED plan by DREE eliminated social animation and joint planning in favour of greater expenditures on roads. In general, whatever were the merits of marginal cost or benefit-cost analyses, they could not measure the dynamic progress and improvement of a province's outlook in moving from project-oriented spending to integrated, comprehensive planning.[26]

The federal disinterest in the provinces as planning partners, as exemplified by DREE, was derived not solely from the influence of the PPBS technique of securing a hold upon expenditures and achieving the maximum effect from every dollar spent. The provision of roads, hospitals, schools, and industrial parks, while less exploratory than joint research, did lend a degree of solidity to federal expenditures and reflected a current (political) interest in more concrete policy. The control and direction of federal spending was a result of a growing desire at Ottawa to secure a greater visibility of federal policies. Along with the greater visibility which could be achieved by programs producing jobs, training labour, or building infrastructure, went a related effort to establish a new constituency of consumers of federal services greater than that comprised by provincial governments.

The reason for these changes of the last decade in turn stemmed, in the first instance, from the increasing strength and effectiveness of Quebec's separatist claims and, in later years, from the growing belligerency of rich provinces concerning the federal budgetary surplus and the way it was distributed in times of sluggish national expansion between fast and stagnant growth regions.[27] As the general mood of the "have" provinces became increasingly impatient with the uneconomic transfer of funds from one part of the country to others where the productivity yield was lower, Ottawa decided to get a firm grasp upon its expenditures in the smaller provinces and to design programs that were both defensible and productive. Tolerant, egalitarian feelings in rich provinces appeared by the end of the 1960s to be in the process of being replaced by a greater impatience to achieve labour mobility from poor regions, in order to release funds for the citizens of heavily and densely urbanized areas who increasingly felt that they were deprived and oppressed people in Canada and that tax revenues created in those regions should be returned to solve the problems arising from such a high tax-yield economy.[28]

Ottawa, moreover, sought a new constituency in the provinces—not their governments but their people—to combat the past habits of provincial regimes taking the full glory for joint expenditures under TVTA,

ARDA, FRED, and ADB. Through Manpower and DREE, Ottawa endeavoured to make the individual or industry, respectively, aware that application was made to the federal government, from which also the rewards flowed. This has resulted in specific provisions in each joint governmental undertaking for marking the capital project both during construction and permanently as a federally financed project. By diverting funds for planning from the provincial governments, Ottawa instead devoted its attention to these new consumers, while also lessening the ability of a poor province to respond in a highly competent or bold manner. In competing for the attention of the consumer and achieving greater efficiency in program design, finance, and delivery, the federal government sought to remove intermediate and unnecessary levels that provided for a "co-operative federalism" but did little for the delivery of service, except, as in the past, to obscure the federal component.

As a result of Ottawa's rationalization of regional development policies, the poorer provinces—which have always been unable to refuse federal expenditures without falling further behind the rich provinces—became virtual wards of the federal government. While granted ever increasing federal attention, they had to accept a federal outlook which, in many instances, seemed to concentrate upon a result—such as producing jobs—more useful for winning praise for Ottawa than contributing to the eventual self-sufficiency of the provincial government. While there was intergovernmental consultation in joint programs, increasingly it was through the negative inquiry of a federal post audit of provincial spendings and not through joint planning. Where federal paternalism ended and federal self-aggrandizement began during the 1960s was a question which yet requires extensive exploration, but in any event it was set aside by the poor provinces in their quest for assistance in the unending battle against regional disparities.

SECTION THREE

Assessment and Prospects

Chapter Eleven

Major Effects of Regional Development
Policies on Canadian Federalism

The issues and the legacies, the special agencies and the programs, which affected or directed Canadian regional development policies have been examined in preceding chapters, primarily in isolation from each other. It remains, in conclusion, to assess the aggregate and cumulative aspect of policies for regional development upon the politics and government of Canadian federalism as a whole. To recapitulate, our theme is one of transformation of the politics, philosophies, and institutions of Canadian federation through this form of government initiative and response. In their broadest setting regional development policies have introduced new thinking and new objectives, so much so that one concludes the federation has been transformed to a more precarious, more entangled system guided by the wrong principles. This chapter reviews the extent, means, and strength of such changes.

1. Expansion and Control by the Public Sector of Economic Development

It is readily apparent that over Canada's first century there was a notable expansion in the central government's treatment of regional deficiencies. Most striking was not just the extension of financial assistance from "original terms" through conditional grants to growth incentives but rather the change in federal attitude from cost consciousness to goal achievement. Such a change required stricter philosophies and institutions of control.

i) Expansion. It should be noted in passing that initiatives, which were predominantly federal, were reluctantly undertaken until about 1957 when they started to develop a momentum of their own and were subsequently hard to control. As has been indicated, the combination of personality (Diefenbaker, Hamilton, Gordon, Sauvé), philosophy (Keynesian and its modified version required for the 1957–63 depression), and institutions (regular intergovernmental meetings fed by research agencies), produced the novel policies of the 1960s.

Increasingly these federal initiatives were aimed at directing and not merely assisting economic forces. This was new public initiative, not just a redistribution of old solutions. Former private activities in land use, farm consolidation, urban development, resource exploration, the provision of infrastructure, training for skills, post-secondary education, and industrial location all became subject to increasing and vigorous government activity. Whether through the influence of incentives, comprehensive plans, or concerned politicians, the direction and pace of growth was no longer left solely to the private market forces or exclusively to provincial influence.

This forcing of the tempo and reversing of some of the trends in both national and regional economies created problems that affected both rich and poor provinces. Unavoidably some efforts led to irrational ventures in peripheral areas of a poor province's narrow resource base. In Saskatchewan a nationalized steel industry was unsuccessful; in Nova Scotia a goodly number of industries attracted by IEL failed. The effect of the RDIA program in other parts of Canada had indirect consequences even for the diversified and unregulated economies of rich provinces, since it lured footloose industries away from their original preferences for locating in these provinces to places in more depressed regions which occasionally proved to be a disadvantage.

ii) Experimentation in the Style and Scope of Controlling Disparities. The style and scope of federal policies to deal with regional economic disparities, differed notably between the first and last halves of the sixties.[1] A composite philosophy can be assembled from the significant federal attitudes towards the problems of the pre-1966 period; after that time Prime Minister Trudeau provided his own articulate view of the requirements of systematic and federal government.

Inflexibility and uniformity was characteristic of the earlier federal programs. In the first half of the decade Ottawa undertook to produce an economic climate conducive to investment and growth. It was a period in which a narrow federal concentration upon stabilization was extended to include policies for growth and structural deficiencies. It still evinced, however, the more traditional federal attitude that exceptional treatment of certain provinces could not be admitted openly. Evidence of this inflexibility could be seen in a dispute between Quebec and Ottawa over the former's request for an extension of a deadline of March 1963, within which the latter had agreed to pay seventy-five percent of a province's TVTA capital costs. Ottawa refused initially to bend the regulations for Quebec, although that province had benefitted very little from federal grants for vocational facilities both under TVTA and an earlier 1954 program because of Premier Duplessis' principle of rejecting federal money. When Jean Lesage became premier in 1960, he took almost three years to put the province's requirements in order, by which time seventy-five percent federal aid under TVTA was due to revert to fifty percent. That the new Liberal federal regime reversed the Conservatives' adamant rejection was an early indication of greater realism and flexibility coming to bear upon Ottawa's philosophy.[2]

In a similar manner, while the uniform approach of ADA might reduce unemployment impressively within designated centres in Ontario, it had little result in the Maritimes. Because other shared-cost programs, moreover, required a provincial matching of federal funds, poorer provinces had to divert revenues from their other expenditures more so than did rich provinces who were often already providing the service and for whom federal funds thus constituted a subsidy.[3] This of course was typical of the fiscal "settlements" throughout Canadian history. It led to the result that the earlier programs of the 1960s for national support against economic deficiencies, such as ARDA, ADA, and TVTA (which were to enlarge capacity and not alter it), were disproportionately advantageous to the richest provinces even though the most chronic sources of weakness lay in the poor provinces.

Next, these early programs were subject to only limited federal supervision. Ottawa was sufficiently cautious about its new expenditures, and the provinces sufficiently jealous of their jurisdiction over resources, that the former authority avoided influencing both provincial and private activity. Largely their programs consisted of unspecified transfers which did not require extensive consultation. A federal technical or design role in these programs was not central to their operation. ARDA and TVTA were left to provincial application, ADA to private decisions, and ADB to the unsystematic concerns of the secretary of state, J. A. Pickersgill. The federal role was to serve as a banker with few stipulations about operational or terminal performance, mainly because of a lack of critical internal tools for program assessment at Ottawa—as seen in chapters 6 and 8.

The approach of these initial programs, and especially of ADA and

ARDA, was scarcely remedial or preventive. The first aim of ARDA was to assist farmers in difficulty and that of ADA was to provide jobs, in the same location, where unemployment was disproportionately high. In both cases these schemes consisted of subsidies to the existing system. The technique of ADB was similarly to develop infrastructure, without concrete evidence that this was an urgent need or one conducive to growth.[4] In all three programs, and even with the capital construction aspects of TVTA, there was little evidence that officials or politicians had defined their objectives. Of course the newness of these policies meant to some extent that the initial absence of performance criteria was unavoidable unless all activities were to be stopped until conceptual clarity was achieved. Given the urgency of the need (as it was felt in Ottawa) any activity was better than none. Yet it was suggested by poor provinces that still too much was being done by subsidy to get the economy moving again and too little to open up new development prospects through innovation, a policy that could only favour the already rich.

The looseness of the general approach during the first half of the sixties coincided with satisfactory increases in Canada's aggregate growth. It produced pleasing national results but disparities between regions were left unchanged.[5] As a result, Ottawa undertook a more selective, intensified approach: during the second half of the decade, general programs for growth or isolated attacks on various symptoms of low income were replaced or supplemented by comprehensive strategy against the main causes of shortfalls in growth-deficient provinces themselves.

It can be seen that the initiation and refining of regional development policy produced a form of internal "administrative politics" which endeavoured to control the loose and inarticulate initial policy responses of the federal politicians to regional development problems. While initiation of government policy depended upon the input of public demand, whether through a Royal Commission, consultant's report, pressure group lobbying, or a politician's sensing of grassroots sentiment, usually the response was very general, leaving to the bureaucracy the task of forming detailed policy. The means of a solution were largely left to the state of administrative technology and politics within government at both levels. Politicians made the choice about when, but officials determined the how of a policy response.

Internal politics consisted primarily of the reduction of constraints: the departmental constraint (i.e., more than one department) and the constitutional constraint (i.e., more than one decision-making co-ordinate government). These two constraints were interwoven with each other and with the relative power and state of thinking of the individuals manning the various departments, agencies, and governments. Co-ordination became the attempt to overcome conflicts in thinking about solutions and executing programs. Essentially the mechanisms used were devices to control factors which might delay or prevent attainment of a stipulated policy objective through program activity. In Canada it involved the establishment of a systematic decision-making process, such as PPBS, reinforced by new finance and planning bodies, such as Treasury Boards, and made potent in an intergovernmental setting by the use of financial power in the form of conditional grants to coerce the provinces. As the administrative aspects of co-ordination were being implemented, thinking became more sophisticated, producing a "second generation" of programs characterized by greater central control in each government and increased federal financial regulation over the provinces through more stringent conditions, together with a reduction of policy spillover effects through a broadening of individual programs.

Control depends also on the power of persuasion or threat, and it elevates the importance of strong bureaucrats. In the presence of in-articulate demands from his political masters, the bureaucrat in the 1960s improvised his own solution. To the extent that he was influenced by a preference for problem solving and efficiency, the access and participation aspects of interdepartmental and intergovernmental relations were mini-mized by the bureaucrat, best typified as we have seen, by Kent's be-haviour. This eventually brought clashes with the more political elements in the federal government and in the provinces, thereby producing tension —tension which is examined in a later section of this chapter.

The regional development programs of the mid and late 1960s bore the marks of administrative politics. They sought to *solve* problems. All were in a sense more concentrated in their approach than their predecessors. The ARDA agreement shifted funds towards problems of rural *adjust-ment* rather than just the maintenance of farmers' incomes and employ-ment; the FRED projects were a comprehensive approach to the growth of the entire rural sector; the ADIA incentives were confined to regions most needful of new industries and, within them, to areas of economic potential; the OTA agreements were narrowed to adult retraining courses; and ADB began a (nominal) enquiry into a growth plan for the Atlantic region.

The flow of funds under these revised programs next was rationalized. They were directed towards the most needy regions.[6] None of the three rich provinces signed a FRED agreement or was given many RDIA areas designated for industrial incentives. Under RDIA it was the Atlantic provinces, Quebec, and the Prairies which were also the main recipients of the added category of "special areas" designation. Towns and cities in these provinces were additionally eligible for federal loans and grants necessary to economic growth and social progress. Further attention was directed to these provinces through different aspects of the new 1971–75 ARDA agreements not offered by Ottawa to the rich, as well as through the provision of "implicit equalization" in shared-cost programs.[7] (Ottawa will share fifty percent of "national average costs" of a program even though poor provinces have lower, and rich, higher, actual costs.) Of course it was evident that the evolution of policy towards these specific and tailor-made bilateral relations made it increasingly less meaningful to talk generally of relations between Ottawa and "the provinces."

Finally, administrative politics sought comprehensiveness. Although individual programs became more specific during this period, thereby reducing the spillover of funds in other jurisdictions on factors not central to disparity, there was a growing demand by officials for a broader package of policies. As economic knowledge became more complete, and pointed to the increasing importance of various sectors as impediments to aggregate prosperity, federal penetration into these weak areas was defined in the interests of national prosperity. Accordingly, the pursuit of greater effectiveness in these programs—in themselves a penetration into provincial jurisdictions—meant less and less federal concern for constitutional boundaries. Poor provinces were given funds in return for federal access to control over their exclusive responsibilities.

The interest in co-ordination and consolidation, evinced in the work of DREE and OTA, although started by bureaucrats, was at this time strongly supported by politicians, particularly by Pierre Trudeau. This top level support was instrumental to the pervasiveness of these philosophies on many fronts. The mid-sixties saw important philosophical contributions on federalism made by two other politicians: Jean-Luc Pepin, Liberal minister of Trade and Industry, and the then prime minister, Lester Pearson. All three men had backgrounds well suited for reflecting on federalism and the nature of governmental performance. Their views and attitudes established much of the strategy within which individual programs were initiated or changed.

It is, of course, too glib to refer to "Ottawa" or "the federal government" when discussing the policy initiatives of the times. The unity and common-mindedness implied by such terms was frequently sorely tested by two factors: the ongoing dynamics of politics engaged in by bureaucrats when responding to their politicians and the natural stress between departments when pursuing interactive policies. Accordingly the decisions reached and actions taken often represent compromise or an enforced truce; when the program reached the field or came under continuing stress it was not uncommon to find defection by the least enthusiastic party. DREE particularly encountered only token assistance from other ministries who were to be part of the PEI development plan.

186

In the past the federal Cabinet had been carried beyond its limits of understanding and confidence by bureaucratic schemes. The changes to TVTA, FRED, and ARDA were in part a result of political disaffection with the bureaucrats' grand designs. After 1966, however, leading federal ministers and bureaucrats were of one accord, and spoke on the same level. Uniquely, Cabinet led in this period, so that the philosophies of these personalities take on a special importance for a full understanding of the mid-sixties' attitude towards reform.

2. Ottawa's Changing Disposition towards Co-operative Federalism

Most participants in and observers of Canadian federalism have pointed to the development of co-operative or consultative federalism as a response of the 1960s to the mutually-overlapping interests of all governments in the greater sharing and harmonizing of fiscal and economic objectives at the policy level. While provinces wanted Ottawa to have a better awareness of, and give closer attention to their problems, the central regime desired increasing influence over the pace of economic activity in the provinces. Unfortunately, the term "co-operative federalism" has been used too loosely to cover a variety of relationships arising from very different concepts. Relations between administrations may simply consist of *consultation*, whereby one level of government is informed of the intended activities of the other; or, further, of *co-operation*, whereby efforts are made to harmonize programs of both governments to achieve the aims of each; or, still further, of *co-ordination*, whereby both levels of government decide upon a common objective and establish their policies to meet it.

As originally defined by Jean-Luc Pepin, in 1964,[8] "co-operative federalism" contained all three concepts. Subsequently co-operation and co-ordination have been less in evidence, although the term (and hence its tripartite conceptual imagery) is still used by Ottawa to enhance practically every type of federal-provincial meeting. In Pepin's eyes, it contained the following essential features:

> ... co-operative federalism is essentially a decentralizing force that ... brings about a certain decrease in Ottawa's role, at least the gradual withdrawal by the central government from essentially provincial sectors.[9]

> ... the distribution of tax income and taxation powers between Ottawa and the provincial capitals according to the principle 'to each level of government according to its requirements.'[10]

> ... that Ottawa should not introduce any more joint plans unless it has the provinces' consent.[11]

. . . preconsultation and continuous co-operation in the establishment of priorities of action.[12]

Pepin's concept was applied to a period during Pearson's administration when the federal government was prepared to "seek a compromise at the expense of conviction,"[13] largely as it groped for a solution to the grave problems of Quebec. We may recall that its response was to yield larger tax abatements, fund increased provincial activity (through TVTA, ARDA, and municipal works), accept Quebec's special pension plan for that province, permit opting-out from post-secondary education cost sharing, and offer the right of opting out from other shared-cost programs.

During the 1960s this uncontrolled proliferation of joint programs convinced many governments that Canada had lost a sense of direction in the distribution of responsibilities. Prime Minister Pearson first placed emphasis upon their temporary and joint nature in 1963. It was announced by 1966 that the federal initiatives in certain shared-cost programs would be phased out, while others would be open to the provinces to opt-out and new programs would cover only capital projects. This desire to clarify jurisdictions and return some powers to the provinces was not sustained, however, because of Quebec's repeated pressure for greater concessions. By 1966 Pearson was finally asserting his government's right to enter jurisdictions as it saw fit:

> This must especially be the case in the field of social security and welfare. Here legislative jurisdiction and administrative responsibility belong primarily but not exclusively to the provinces. The federal government however has an obligation in these fields to provide leadership and direction in matters of national concern and to establish national standards providing for interprovincial transfers.[14]

This was largely a result of discontent with excessive federal concessions to the provinces. Pearson admitted as much:

> If federal compromises in the interest of agreements, which are valid and wise merely increase the appetite for concessions as in Quebec which would not be valid or wise, and if the feeling develops that the federal government will always give way when pressed then this country is in for serious trouble. To avoid these dangers and fears we must make clear what the essentials of the federal position are.[15]

From 1966 on, the then newly appointed minister of finance, Mitchell Sharp, followed by other ministers, developed further the federal hard line as a reaction to earlier conciliatory approaches and their undercutting of central direction.[16] One will recall that the reasons for such a policy were three-fold: that the federal government needed a constituency other than provinces, that the level of federal expenditures was escalating intolerably, and that there needed to be a more deliberate ranking by Ottawa of its objectives. Accordingly, in practically every sphere of federal operations that touched upon provincial governments (not provinces) it was now clearly evident that the federal government refused to divert further federal funds or to permit a special political status for Quebec, and sought an extension of federal activities into jurisdictional "grey areas" along with a clarification of responsibilities in existing programs.

Pierre Trudeau's election as prime minister in 1968 not only lent political support to the hard line policy already urged by senior officials but also converted it into an aggressive political philosophy. Much of it was initially directed towards Quebec,[17] yet it was eventually used against other centres of provincialism. The hard line was extended from one of "go and raise your own taxes" in tax sharing, and the proposed termination of shared-cost programs, to encompass the whole relationship between forces working either for unity or diversity.

Trudeau in both his writings and speeches has emphasized the utility of provincial governments and has claimed that he is not a dogmatic centralist. While essentially true, this is not a full account, and it does not explain why many provinces feel a very real threat from the Trudeau conception of federalism. He supports provinces as legitimate participants in the federal state, in order to reject the socialists' historic tendency to dismiss decentralized powers out of hand. Conversely, he does not believe in rigid, legalistic, *a priori*, inalienable rights of either level of government but rather in a pragmatic approach. His is basically the plea of the liberal: that all interests are legitimate competitors for power but all must be prepared to compete; that is, that there should be an equality of opportunity, but not equality of condition. As a rationalist, he dislikes the sentiment of the constitutionalist as much as the dogma of the socialist:

> . . . it is not for the socialist to cast his lot irrevocably with one level of government as opposed to another.[18]

> My plea is merely for greater realism and greater flexibility in the socialist approach to problems of federalism.[19]

The prime minister's operative tools for determining the balance between unity and diversity have been rationalism and "counterweights."

> . . . the state will need political instruments which are sharper, stronger and more finely controlled than anything based on mere emotionalism

. . . in short if not a product of pure reason, the political tools of the future will be designed and appraised by more rational standards than anything we are currently using in Canada today.[20]

My political action or my theory—can be expressed very simply: create counterweights. As I have explained, it was because of the federal government's weakness that I allowed myself to be catapulted into it.[21]

Trudeau's counterweights, and his rationalism, had no more significant impact than in the field of regional development. Counterweights consisted of a reassertion of the presence of the federal government in direct service to peoples, and in particular a refusal to concede special powers to Quebec. Rationalism in the intergovernmental setting has comprised the extension of the PPBS technique to control joint expenditures, a respect for the process rather than the specific institutions of politics, and, indeed, the consolidation of scattered programs under DREE.[22] As one surveys the individual mechanisms for adjustments of federal-provincial relations, it can be seen that the impact of this philosophy has had very profound consequences for federalism, in particular for the ability of provinces to maintain their identity.

The crucial dilemma facing government policies for regional development in Canada has been posed by the federal system itself. As K. C. Wheare observed, a federation is essentially a political system for establishing and protecting the inviolability of aspects of both unity and territorial diversity in the governing of a state. Economic policy, however, may be contradictory to such political objectives. To the extent that Ottawa has redistributed tax revenues from rich to poor provinces, in its expenditures on disparities, it has been negating certain aspects of these disparities or diversities. Its growth policies, which include industrial incentives, have also been in a sense a reallocation of economic prosperity, or the potential for prosperity. In short, the actions of the central regime may have enlarged the aspects of unity and uniformity in the Canadian federation at the cost of economic diversity and the right of provinces to have that diversity protected from central "levelling" exercises.

The ferment at Ottawa, evident at the political level, has resulted in a series of initiatives and reforms not only in regional development programs, but also in related institutions and mechanisms of support. To assess fully the impact of federal activity after 1966, the health and vigour of diversity in the face of the political and technological forces making for uniformity now requires review.

3. Centralization Versus Provincialism

The balance between forces of unity and diversity, in the Canadian federation, has been a continuously changing one. It has been demonstrated in earlier chapters that the pendulum of power had swung periodically during Canada's first century, despite the intention of the founding fathers and the British North America Act of 1867 to fix it near the "centralized" end of its arc. At various periods provinces have been able to challenge the original belief of Confederation that the central authority knew best. This has been so because constitutional adaptation in Canada has increasingly proceeded by way of intergovernmental negotiation that turned on fiscal power and popular backing, rather than through legal interpretations settled in the courts.[23] The provinces thus were able, in periods that did not require centralization to meet external crises, to take an initiative in the public sector based upon popular demand for a developing of their constitutional responsibilities. Such was the case during the 1920s, marked as they were by the regionalization and fragmentation of the national economy. So also in the 1960s; the search for renewed prosperity after the recession of the late fifties centred upon an unparalleled exploitation of natural resources over which the provinces had an extensive jurisdiction. Ottawa then found itself initially in a supporting role—as previous chapters have indicated—one of picking up those responsibilities left by the provinces as too extensive or costly: for the unskilled, the aged, and needy, for agricultural rationalization, and generally for the poorer regions where all these responsibilities were particularly in evidence. In many of these areas Ottawa was even prepared to give the control of (and praise for) its expenditures to the provinces. Such a procedure was further aided by larger fiscal transfers through equalization payments, tax abatements, and a municipal loan fund, all of which assisted in meeting the ancillary costs of opening new industries or settling new territory.

In consequence of this trend, writers in the mid-sixties noted an apparent resurgence of "provincialism," or the decentralization of policy-making initiatives within the total public sector to the provincial governments. Two authors, Edwin Black and Alan Cairns, jointly summarized the trend from the viewpoint of 1966: "Today the pressures for decentralization have been so fired up by resurgent provincialism that many have questioned the very survival of the federal government as a *decisive* body."[24] It may well be argued, however, that this situation had markedly changed by the close of the decade, and also, that experience with regional development policies suggests that even the generally-accepted picture of the provincialism of the mid-sixties needs considerable refinement.

191

Certainly the term had to cover a wide variety of provincial action in the 1960s: everything from the making and carrying out of serious threats against Ottawa by Quebec to the rapid expansion of natural resource development in many provinces, development which was actually inconsequential in reference to federal responsibilities. "Provincialism," then, should be seen as a word used variously to describe three notable phenomena of the 1960s: the wresting of responsibilities for expenditures from Ottawa by Quebec, the provincial occupancy under some circumstances of a policy void left by Ottawa, and the extension of responsibilities in the public sector by provincial authorities on their own.

The surge of provincialism in the 1960s did not arise from a hard-fought victory won by provinces over federal powers but from a provincial undertaking of *new* governmental responsibilities in areas left unoccupied by Ottawa. The federal government, for its part, was experiencing a loss of confidence. Its traditional services—particularly in defence—had lost urgency under peacetime conditions and it had no definite notion of what to do next. In discussing the policy vacuum that had grown evident under the Diefenbaker and Pearson federal regimes, Paul Fox noted the following features:[25] (i) the recent series of minority governments that held federal office, reflecting the fact that "there is no consensus of Canadian opinion coming to bear at Ottawa"; (ii) the regionalization of the support for federal political parties, with the result that none had the ability to speak for the whole country; and, (iii) the lack of internal concord within each of the three "national" parties, so that none of them was unable to act "as a national broker to bring diverse and opposing interests together" to secure a consensus.

Provincialism for many provincial governments, therefore, really consisted in the discovery that in disenchantment with Ottawa popular opinion had turned to them for a solution to basic problems of income and growth.[26] While provinces willingly performed in their new limelight, for the poorer among them the effort was financially exhausting. What they next discovered was that, having climbed on the "anti-Ottawa" bandwagon, they had neither the facilities nor the determination of the French Canadians in Quebec to follow up their threats. In fact, many of the premiers who had bitterly complained of federal interference in 1962, by 1966 found themselves urging Ottawa not to take them too literally nor to set them free.[27]

Undoubtedly Quebec's Quiet Revolution lit and fed the flames of provincialism in the 1960s, striving as it did against the dominance of English Canada, primarily represented by the central power.[28] The fragmented state of national politics, in the period of minority governments from 1962 to 1968, coincided with the strong challenge to centralization

192

issuing from Quebec. To the Lesage and Johnson governments there, the survival of the French-Canadian culture required a greater access to revenues and the self-control of economic and social policies—not the isolation, low aspirations, and governmental frugality practised by the previous Duplessis regime. Their claims on Ottawa extended from a demand that a hundred percent of income tax revenue be returned to the province, to demands for the "provincialization" of every joint program, and even exclusively federal ones, that touched upon Quebec's social and economic life.

It is important to note that this was not the provincialism of the other provinces at the time. While many of their governments did express much milder distaste for similar features of Ottawa-centred federalism, none felt the situation desperate enough to take up a federal offer of 1966 to drop certain joint programs in return for equivalent federal fiscal transfers —except for Quebec. Ottawa then actually urged the provinces, in a definite timetable planned for them by the federal finance minister, Mitchell Sharp, to regain control over certain shared-cost programs. But the provinces concerned had already won significant concessions. Some joint programs had such loose and general terms that federal control was negligible. Under Pearson, indeed, further independence had been con- ceded by the return of the Canada Pension Plan fund to the provinces, by a new transfer in the field of post-secondary education that had few restrictions, and by the conversion of the operating tax collection agree- ment in order to end any suggestion by Ottawa of an "appropriate" provincial level of taxation.

For the rich and poor provinces alike, the provincialism of the mid- sixties did not mean taking the extreme step of opting out (once more except for Quebec). They lived comfortably within the relaxed central control of the time. For the rich, shared-cost programs amounted to a subsidy for certain responsibilities, thereby leaving funds free for other projects. For the poor, they provided national standards for growth at the rate of the richest provinces. Living with Ottawa's sharing of certain costs was more attractive financially to most provinces than the political assertion of jurisdictional propriety, especially in light of public opinion that appeared more interested in the provision and level of a service than in its proper constitutional origin. But as this sort of provincialism—and unequal rates of provincial expansion—began to produce greater dis- crepancies between rich and poor provinces, and as the federal stance under Pearson threatened to create a never-ending process of capitulation to Quebec, both senior officials and advisers at Ottawa and those in poorer and more remote provinces began to press for a strong reassertion of the central power. The federal regime thus responded with the extension of equalization in 1966 (which the poor provinces had asked for and the rich had sanctioned), and eventually with new conditional programs which proved, as always, a mixed blessing. Federal politicians, moreover, became less tolerant of Quebec's separatism,[29] and popular opinion put Trudeau in power in Ottawa in 1968 with an overwhelming mandate to be tough with the provinces—or so he evidently felt.[30] Even the rich provinces now joined in support of national policies for regional development, sparked initially by a sympathy for Quebec's desire to catch up. Ottawa resumed a central place, although not without a due appreciation of the phenomenon of provincialism which had reappeared in the days of its absence. This recognition of provincialism encompassed ideas of constitutional review, plans for consultative mechanisms, and tax sharing studies.

The resurgence of central power in the late sixties, while of a different nature from that exercised in earlier decades, nevertheless enables one to comment about the more resilient aspects of contemporary provincialism and also about its breaking points. Black and Cairns in their work of 1966 have described what they consider to be the factors on which provincialism (other than Quebec's Quiet Revolution) has been based. In considering their arguments in the light of our present study of regional development, one may note that they made only a limited attempt to indicate whether, or how, provinces exercised in intergovernmental relations the trappings of power they had acquired. In fact, it can be contended that these powers, arising notably from control over new resource exploitation, could not be fully utilized by the poorer provinces without the financial support of the central regime. The apparent strength of provincialism, therefore, was not equally available to all provinces, and rested not merely upon the existence of attributes of power but also on the use made of such potentialities, particularly when Ottawa in the late sixties re-established its competition for public favour in Canada. Accordingly, it is evident that modifications are needed in the current general view of provincialism, as the following new conclusions should make plain.

1. Threatening statements of provincial politicians have obviously not always resulted in any policy formulation. Even Quebec's categorical refusal of shared-cost programs did not prevent its agreement with TVTA, or BAEQ. Other provinces, while protesting ADA, Manpower, and DREE at the political level, did permit requisite federal funds to enter their jurisdiction and did allow smooth relations between central and local officials concerned with the program to continue. It is deceptive, therefore, to base evidence of provincialism *a priori* upon claims of

politicians (who might only be testing federal responses) that they wished to be unfettered.

2. The record plainly indicates that there is no such collectivity as "the provinces" in conflict with Ottawa. Even supposing all were philosophically opposed to federal policy, each province has a different breaking point—politically and financially—and each carries a different weight in its influence upon federal intentions. Ontario, one might expect, could seriously jeopardize the uniformity or financing of a national shared-cost program by its opposition, while those provinces (such as Prince Edward Island or Newfoundland) "kept" by Ottawa by virtue of heavy transfers, would have little freedom of manoeuvre. The experience is not consistent, however; Prince Edward Island won a FRED plan and Newfoundland a special grant by persistent pressure. Ontario lost a FRED plan, received few considerations from DREE, and failed to win concessions from OTA or ADIA. The Atlantic provinces were granted ADB, but lost the grand scale of FRED plans and TVTA. Initially, federal concessions to any one province were denied lest they set a precedent for all. As this became less of a concern, they were frequently denied by virtue of the cost of the expenditure involved, the size of the province notwithstanding. In any case, there was no one approach to a single collectivity in treatment.

3. Commentators on Canadian federalism have failed to read both sides of the greater federal flexibility in dealing with provinces. While, indeed, bilateralism may indicate greater concessions won by individual provinces, it may also serve as an entry for "divide and conquer" techniques in intergovernmental relations. Rarely have provinces been aware of each other's special relationships with Ottawa in shared-cost programs. As the number of meetings between Ottawa and all the provinces as a group has been reduced or changed in nature (as has been the case with DREE and Manpower), provinces have lost the opportunity to discover the informal, bilateral relations that have been established between Ottawa and each participant within the uniformity of the national formal agreement. Such a process has apparently worked to the disadvantage of both poor and rich provinces; the former have signed new ARDA agreements that are less generous than Ontario's, and the latter have not been able to gauge the size of federal redistributions of wealth from high to low income regions. The often different nature of relations between Ottawa and each province and the reluctance of each to reveal its own particular arrangements have created a situation whereby the provincial regimes cannot comment upon national development patterns apart from what Ottawa—i.e., the *federal* government—wishes to say they are. Thus

the apparent victory of provincialism may actually have fragmented collective action and left only Ottawa in a position to establish broad national objectives.

4. It is true, as analysts have observed, that the increasing competence and confidence of provincial civil services today often matches what has traditionally been almost an exclusive federal access to expertise. This may indeed reinforce provincial identity. But it does not necessarily intimidate Ottawa. It will be recalled that the federal government had no reluctance to enter adult training directly and wholly under the OTA, even though the provincial officials were far more experienced. Furthermore, while it has made many serious mistakes with Manpower (and in financial aid to post-secondary education) the central regime's intention to enter and remain within the supposedly provincial field of education appears undaunted. Likewise, the traditional sanctity of municipal affairs jealously preserved for a century from federal interference by the provincial governments, appears no longer to forestall Ottawa. The federal Parliament has created its own urban affairs ministry with the status of a full department, and has become more and more involved in tri-level consultations leading to resource, housing, transportation, pollution, and urban policies. Increasingly, it is making direct, unilateral offers to municipalities. All these developments, many relating to regional growth policy, once more indicate that the central presence has by no means given way to the provincial in modern Canadian federalism.

5. It has been argued that the mere size of Canada will always contribute to a strong provincialism. Certainly little evidence exists to suggest that Canadians have shed their acceptance of a mosaic society despite the regional development and welfare programs which have done much over recent decades to reduce accidental penalties arising from the location of one's birthplace. Ottawa, however, has been able to adjust in the late sixties to the continuing demand for flexibility in the application of programs while nevertheless returning the critical decision making in its regional policies to the national capital. Through regional desks in the Prime Minister's and the Privy Council Offices, through a larger field staff and regional offices (of DREE, for example), through the prime minister's frequent sorties into the country, and even through the succession of federal-provincial conferences, provincial, regional, and local feelings can more sensitively be felt at Ottawa than in times past. The geographic size of the country is no longer of the same importance in necessitating decentralization. While, indeed, there must be some form of decentralization, as commentators on provincialism argue, Ottawa feels that with closer and more frequent contracts, with telex services and

numerous trained field officials, this can be administrative and not policy decentralization. The distinction therefore is one between decentralization (intergovernmental) and deconcentration (use of field offices). The eclipse of unconditional by conditional transfers from Ottawa to the provinces (ever since 1960) would seem to reflect the federal intent not to have local/provincial governments set their priorities. Such a change is hardly symptomatic of increased provincialism.

6. At the provincial level, there can be no doubt that the development of natural resources within a province often has been impressive, imaginative, and has enhanced the provincial government, but the "spin-off" effects are still not well understood. The "failures" of the FRED plan in North Eastern New Brunswick and in Nova Scotia were largely a result of serious over-expectations about the peripheral effects of resource development. Natural resource exploitation, particularly, did not result in as large a multiplier effect in terms of new jobs or secondary industries as many felt would develop. In fact, DREE at times has encouraged large industries—such as steel works in Cape Breton Island—with very few jobs per dollar of incentive.[31] One reason for the formation of the Human Resource Development Authority in Alberta was to offset the one-sided and shallow benefits to society created by a booming natural resources economy. Provinces with new products, moreover, need considerable federal and commercial assistance in marketing and in guaranteeing a favourable dollar exchange rate. Resource development may actually make them more dependent upon Ottawa. The poorer ones additionally require help with the provision of infrastructure and skills. In short, resource development has not necessarily, or only, ministered to greater provincialism.

The final conclusion that can be drawn from all the foregoing material is that modern-day provincialism in Canada is a phenomenon which has encouraged deceptively simple and sweeping assessments. Perhaps the following aside, made by the previously noted observers of federal-provincial relations, Black and Cairns, will point the moral. Indeed it should be placed first, as a *conditio sine qua non* of provincialism, though it has also become the point of distinction between the relations of have and have-not provinces with Ottawa: ". . . maximum exploitation of potential provincial powers requires expanded financial resources and the fullest possible arena for provincial legislative action."[32]

4. INITIATIVE AND RESPONSE

In light of the above, one must be cautious about presuming a uniform and comparable capacity in provinces to respond to federal programs and structural reforms. As a consequence of the extended role of government during the 1960s, there was a related proliferation of formal federal-provincial consultative bodies. These institutional aspects of initiative and response also changed in nature, just as did the philosophies and attitudes mentioned above. Certainly meetings between officials and ministers of both levels increased in number, scope, frequency, and sophistication. During the mid-sixties it was often claimed, in fact, that these numerous federal-provincial meetings had actually replaced the function of the respective legislative bodies in federal-provincial policy making.[33] Commitments made between government officials or departments, through negotiations such as those of the FRED Board, were subsequently placed before their respective legislatures much as *faits accomplis*. Long-term agreements as provided by ARDA or TVTA, or the operations of an Atlantic Development Board or Area Development Agency, removed much of these federal and provincial activities from the annual budgetary control at either level. But all this changed in the latter portion of the decade, when the nature of consultation and the devolution of decision making from the centre was altered under the influence of DREE and Manpower schemes. As Ottawa developed mechanisms for knowing definitely where it wanted to go, "consultation" became the supplying of information, and devolution became largely an administrative phenomenon.[34]

Since 1966 provinces have lamented that opportunities for co-operative federalism, while increased in quantity and more elaborate, have actually declined in quality. This has resulted in recurrent forums of adversary politics, where each side reads to the other its preconceived position. Particularly with DREE and OTA, provinces have found themselves confronted with formal federal proposals presented in a manner of "take it or leave it," without discussions in intergovernmental meetings of any compromise.

Joint policy was only slowly hammered out in this adversary procedure of "proposal-rejection-reproposal."[35] This new style, although consistent with Trudeau's concepts of counterweights and greater rationalism in politics, was in contrast with the form of co-operative federalism as practised by Pearson, which was more full blown and involved meaningful co-operation and co-ordination as well as simple consultation. At the very least, joint meetings could expect to reduce the chances of misinformed governments, unnecessary duplications, and conflicts of services, and should increase the knowledge of how the other level of government will react to policy changes elsewhere. During the Pearson years, moreover, there was greater give and take, so that joint strategy, policy, and even mutual concessions could often be hammered out in the consultation process. But increasingly federal officials and ministers were compelled to wrestle with the problem,

> . . . whether it is more appropriate for a federal government to intro-
> duce into Parliament bills for activities in which the provinces are
> directly concerned, with the assumptions of course that provincial
> consultation will occur before the Parliamentary enactment, or whether
> it is more appropriate for the government to ask Parliament to ratify
> agreements previously reached with the provinces.[36]

In fact, the federal government has seen consultation with provinces as a form of policy legitimization, much as the legislative body itself performs, and not as consultation at the earlier stages of policy selection, priority setting, or program formulation, which is what the provinces have expected it to be.

The major reforms in Trudeau's office have contributed to this change and have extended beyond mere internal housekeeping. One aim has certainly been to avoid the "illicit intimacy" which close departmental liaison with provincial officials can produce. These countersteps have limited federal officials to definite mandates from the Cabinet for intergovernmental negotiations. The official's job has been returned to the more proper role of giving and receiving information for his minister. (This excludes those few officials, such as Kent, who remained free agents because of their quasi-political position.) The realm of political negotiation and compromise has very firmly been returned to federal ministers and to the powerful "supergroup" of select advisers around Trudeau who in concert have achieved greater integration of policies.[37] Accordingly, a minister has been limited by the Privy Council Office, Treasury Board, and Department of Finance from making extemporaneous concessions to the provinces. Because the federal position has been formulated in advance of a joint meeting with provinces, scope for flexibility has been limited. The federal willingness to negotiate has also been confined by Ottawa's habit in recent years of releasing its position to the press prior to federal-provincial conferences, which effectively has hardened the stands taken by opponents to that position. But this initiative has left provinces ill-equipped to respond in kind. At conferences it has led to frustrating experiences for many provinces who have been prepared to give their officials and ministers the power to bargain for the best results that can be obtained within the meeting. Federal and provincial strategies in such conferences were quite diametrically opposed. In many instances Ottawa now prefers to assemble compromise in bilateral meeting with individual provinces, while provinces prefer a multilateral bargaining setting.

This incompatibility between government styles of consultation has been exacerbated at the officials' level when reforms in one regime are not matched by similar reforms at another level of government. In the co-ordination and redirection of regional development programs under DREE, for example, the departmental reorganization was not complemented at the provincial level by a department closely connected with the subject, but at best by a secretariat attached to a Cabinet committee (or Treasury Board) or to the premier's office. In such a case these bodies usually lacked their own minister, a deputy, executive powers, or a fund. Often in response to DREE's initiatives—as was the case in Manitoba, and somewhat with HRDA in Alberta—they were unable to provide little more than a post-office role as they attempted to relate DREE's broad powers to deal with the problem of regional disparities to a myriad of provincial departments that covered various facets of a general problem, such as retraining. Most often provincial co-ordination groups lacked the planning capacity and political authority given by Trudeau to his own special bodies. Hence, the provinces frequently were not equipped in organization or outlook to respond to the more integrated and longer term approach of DREE, Manpower, or the PCO. When, for instance, DREE made expenditures in any year, x, they were derived from a federal budget set and approved eighteen months earlier; in contrast the Nova Scotia Resources Development Board claimed even in 1973 that its policy was still to have no policy. The mismatch between the long term outlook of DREE and the *ad hoc* approach of certain provinces was characteristic.

Consequently, the emergent relationships in the field of regional development have certainly *not* always been constructive for the operation of Canadian federalism. "Executive Federalism" depends upon the primacy of bureaucrats in policy making; their common professional interests at both levels is claimed to produce a harmonious federalism.[38] But, much increasingly has depended upon the provinces' political bargaining power at Ottawa, so that the influence of officials seeking uniform, nationwide programs has been progressively inhibited by the politician's reassertion of his responsibility for negotiation. While this returns to an admirable principle of democracy, it has imposed on federal-provincial relations the effects, beneficial or otherwise, of distinctive public personalities as well as the individual philosophies they hold. Diefenbaker's earlier pursuit of visions has been followed by Trudeau's pursuit of reason, Lesage and Johnson's willingness to go it alone, Marchand's interest in efficiency, and Kent's concern for central direction. These powerful personalities have, for some, constituted an almost impenetrable opposition. Furthermore, such persons often abruptly alter the emphasis of a government policy which is subsequently brought to joint negotiations.

Even at the intergovernmental bureaucratic level there are mismatches. If there have not been simultaneous or similar changes elsewhere, this has meant in some cases that federal Treasury Board officials find themselves talking to staff of provincial program departments rather than to their Treasury equivalents, or in other cases that federal program departments are reprimanded by provincial treasurers for talking directly to provincial departments. Joint advisory boards in DREE and Manpower committees have likewise brought together officials of different perspectives.[39] In consequence some joint programs have developed along a tortuous path of divergent propositions and oppositions.

Hard feelings between governments have developed, moreover, from these different perspectives to the extent that they have looked for dissimilar substantive results in negotiation or administration. It will be recalled that Poetschke (and others) felt strongly that DREE's commitment was to little more than public works and the enhancement of the federal image in the provinces. Provincial officials working with ADB and OTA entertained similar beliefs. Ontario's experience has been that "development" is at one time narrowly defined as infrastructure and at other times as inclusive of socio-economic projects—all involving unpredictable changes in timing and eligibility. Ontario has also felt in joint economic data exercises that Ottawa's interest in data collection was largely to score political points on the provinces by making its estimates public rather than to use the opportunity for serious and novel research on the impact of public sectors in a federation, and co-operating constructively to reduce high rates of growth in provincial expenditures.

Chapter Twelve

Three Challenges to Modern Canadian Federalism

By the 1970s regional development programs in Canada had reached a point where they represented an important leading edge of federal activity. As a significant portion of federal initiatives they now provide an instructive measure of the more general drift and transformation of Canadian federalism. It is possible that these developments are periodic and cyclical, but by the time of Canada's eleventh decade the policies studied here were yet symptomatic of three broad challenges to its federal system. First, there has been a change in emphasis among the various reasons for distributing powers in a federation; the horizontal assignment of relatively autonomous *spheres* of functional activity to one or the other government has been replaced by a vertical or hierarchical division of responsibilities within a function to two or more *levels* of government simultaneously. Second, there has been an entanglement of federal-provincial activities arising out of a confusion of roles and competitive intergovernmental policy making. Finally, the efforts to adjust and adjudicate traditional roles and competitive aspirations held by all governments have proceeded on a set of wrong principles, if federalism is to remain the objective. Each development must be considered in turn.

1. THE REDISTRIBUTION OF RESPONSIBILITIES BY PROCESS AND CONSTITUENCY

The swings between centralization and decentralization of power in the Canadian public sector have evidently been achieved largely through an incremental readjustment in the sharing of the policy-making process between federal and provincial governments. Since 1867, the Canadian federation has discovered a variety of ways of redistributing the processes, functions, and constituencies[1] of public authority, whether by constitutional amendment, *de facto* shared-cost agreements, or administrative provisions. During the 1960s further changes in roles were made to accord with the interest and values current at the time. They focussed primarily on the means by which government attained society's goals.

As criteria ruling the federal distribution of powers, access to and efficiency of government are two values on which politicians and officials may hold a variety of stands. Depending on the definition of either value, compromise may be necessary. Their maintenance becomes a question of balancing competing attributes, if by "access" is meant the provision of government at the most open, simplest level of participation which is felt to be significant for those involved, and by "efficiency," the provision of government able to meet the needs of society at the least cost in resource allocation.[2] Whether they are considered as either ends or means, harmony between them becomes difficult to achieve. John Stuart Mill at times suggested that both were complementary, because one was but a means to the other. The aim of government was to cultivate and distribute good citizenship through participation,[3] and this in turn would produce a demand for excellence in administrators. The results, he felt, would be efficiency in policy making. Yet at other times Mill conceded that, because of the various needs to be fulfilled by local government, not all of them could be served equally well without compromise.[4]

Mill's successors—which included policy makers in Ottawa—grappled further with what "need," "society," "effectiveness," and "efficiency" could mean in a Canadian setting. For instance, to divide responsibilities for planning, spending, or administration in regional growth programs in order to secure either efficiency or participation, one could consider the following varied criteria: (a) technical efficiency to achieve the lowest material input per unit of production; (b) economic efficiency to prevent the spillover of services to regions not bearing the costs of provision; (c) administrative efficiency, which requires a mixture of hierarchy and dispersion for effective problem solving; (d) promotion of local initiative and responsibility; (e) minimization of political "externalities," whereby a community sense is destroyed by the diversity consequent to a large region; and (f) claims of higher level values, such as nationalism or egalitarianism.

Tensions inevitably developed within and between governments in Canada, as a result of different attitudes towards the appropriate trade-off between political participation and aspects of efficiency in government.

Not surprisingly, the differences that arose within governments were between politicians and bureaucrats, the latter being chiefly concerned about the pursuit of efficiency and expert research, the former seeking to ensure the citizen's participation (or responsiveness to public expectations). Accordingly, the disagreements over ADA designations, the research operations of ADB, the selection of ARDA projects, and the reasons for terminating TVTA were consequences not of fundamentally different values held by various protagonists but rather of differences in emphasis given to commonly-held values.

Disagreement between governments occurred to the extent that internal bargaining resulted in different combinations of techniques for access and efficiency. On looking at early development programs it can be seen that the predominant interest was one of securing provincial government participation. The initial implementation of ARDA and TVTA was substantially influenced by constitutional, political, and institutional factors. Although Ottawa provided funds, it was prepared to recognize the province's existing rights and machinery in the fields involved. The FRED program was further concerned with local participation and self-help. And yet the implementation of ADA without provincial participation reflected a concern for efficiency in both technique and time. The planning division of ADB also recognized the need for technical and administrative efficiency, tempered by provision for specialized knowledge of local conditions secured through provincial collaboration.

It was the changes made to all these programs, and the related financial reforms of the mid-sixties, which reflected a new interest in efficiency rather than access. Administrative efficiency was now to be achieved by a reduction in the planning decentralization of Manpower and DREE programs. Decisions about design and eligibility in programs were returned to Ottawa. The contribution of local experts and the encouragement of local initiative and responsibility were treated as low priorities. Economic efficiency to reduce spillover effects and secure the lowest unit costs was achieved by tailoring programs so as to cover fully all the aspects of specific problems, but to treat them primarily in regions or areas of their most intense concentration. Hence, when all of the DREE programs were considered, their coverage ranged from total in the Atlantic provinces, to extensive in Quebec, and isolated in the rest of the country. Spending per member of the labour force by DREE ranged from a high of $89.00 in Nova Scotia to $1.25 in British Columbia. Three separate levels of incentives were applied to different regions in Canada.

This federal interest in rearranging the focus of central and provincial power assuredly met with provincial opposition. Minimizing production costs in services clashed with maintaining the provincial political structures of participation. The existing units sought to protect their traditional, historical (and political) identity within the federation without going as far as rejecting federal aid. In some cases they were able to get federal priorities set aside which for efficiency's sake would have required a certain merging of the provinces' functions into a regional unit of operation, particularly in the Maritimes and Prairies. The manpower mobility program was effectively discarded. DREE, too, disavowed massive labour mobility as an answer to regional expansion. On the contrary, its declared function was to find and create jobs of whatever nature, specifically in depressed regions.[5]

Whatever the individual concessions to existing provincial identities there was now a fundamental difference between the federal and provincial attitudes to stimulation of depressed economies. The federal government wanted a new constituency for its regional development schemes; one determined by the natural boundaries of commercial and economic activities in various parts of Canada and not those provincial political boundaries into which most federal economic policies had artificially been squeezed. Accordingly, Ottawa's frustration with a narrow response by the provinces to their initiatives was understandable. In their eyes too often provinces simply refused to make commitments to a modern, and larger, economic regional identification. Indeed both western and Maritime provinces made only token efforts to work together toward the more self-evident regional economy. Some efforts at a Prairie Economic Council and Council of Maritime Premiers proved to be only limited forums for discussion and did not lead to the transfer of political or economic authority to some transprovincial body. For example when Alberta bought the private regional air carrier, Pacific Western Airlines, which was based in Vancouver, it undertook to move its facilities to Edmonton although there were no route changes to explain this, only the prospect of more economic activity for that city.

The simple conclusion was to dismiss provincial governments as having legitimate economic interests, as Ottawa was inclined to do at this point when they wrote them out of DREE development planning. But precisely because they were responsible to distinct polities with distinct demands and aspirations did provinces require recognition, however inefficient an economic creation they might be. As most provinces continued to try their luck individually with Ottawa and as Ottawa in turn tried to bypass the parochialism of the provinces, a mutual state of frustration continued. In such a situation two fundamental questions remained unexplored: could federal regional development programs on merely a provincial scale really be efficient in terms of stimulating economic growth and stability? And since reducing regional economic disparities was essentially a task of compensating the regional losers in a national economy, should not this compensation be in the form of unconditional transfers to provincial governments which could then use the resources in pursuit of the political aspirations of the polity, since the lasting economic impact of federal transfers was marginal? By 1976 no government resolution was evident on either issue, although the vanguard of governmental economic thought, the Economic Council of Canada, was by now raising just such fundamental and realistic questions.[6]

The central regime's reaction was, therefore, increasingly to refuse to alter the regional organization of its departments, and to bypass the confusion or parochialism of provincial governments within regions in order to offer services which in scope and priority best met the requirements of federal standards for efficiency. There were political motives involved as well. The establishment of a virtually new constituency by Ottawa through increased direct spending, refusing the expansion of traditional transfers, and through elaborate provisions in DREE activities for the visible designation of all projects as clearly joint, constituted a new strategy in the assertion of central power. The result of this process has been not only a shift of some provinces from a role of designing the component parts of a federally-financed scheme to that of administrative agents within federal policy, but also the establishment of greater federal visibility in Canada for future tests of strength, particularly in provincial fields of resource policy and urban affairs.

What has not been made clear, or even frankly discussed in this evolution are the methods of the federal initiative. In fact, there seems to have been an inappropriate substituting of bureaucrats for politicians in the very process. To further its work of co-ordination within regions, Ottawa has in recent years greatly enlarged the DREE regional offices. It is claimed that this also will provide for greater local participation and sensing. These offices accordingly may be seen as a replacement for the earlier practice of providing considerable provincial government initiatives under ARDA and FRED. There are several critical points of difference, however. In some respects, local offices with federally-appointed staff are being offered as equivalents for provincially-elected legislatures as priority-setting, decision-making, and fact-finding instruments. These bureaucrats are as actively engaged with municipal councils as with provincial departments. They contribute a parallel information stream, along with provincial requests, to DREE decision making at Ottawa as to what might be cost shared. Not surprisingly, provincial constraints on its municipalities' activities can be neutralized to the extent Ottawa makes arrangements directly with municipalities to find locally cherished projects.

A dislocation of the purpose of federalism thus occurs when Ottawa claims that these units of *deconcentration* can substitute for *decentralization*. If both federal and provincial governments agree that regional issues should be decided regionally (or local, locally), but that they may require financial assistance from a national or provincial tax base respectively, the critical aspect of that procedure remains decision making. To suggest that large field offices feeding opinions to federal politicians provides improved local decision making is to emphasize improvement in efficiency; that is, that the scope of decision making can thereby be raised to more efficient dimensions represented by the territory or sectors served by such a field office. To propose that provincial legislatures or local councils should be the sole assessors of what is to be a "local interest" emphasizes instead the democratic and participatory aspect of decision making. What becomes of paramount importance here, is the capacity to be responsive rather than right. The latter of these two forms of "localizing" central funding decisions represents not the "best" method (technically) but the more democratic, if it is assumed the substitution of politician for bureaucrat indeed is such. (For of course this may in fact only work out to the substitution of provincial for a federal bureaucracy). There may be preferences for an efficient response to regional/local issues over a democratic one because of the current economic situation, or the fact that both national and provincial funds are being spent: there is a principle of accountability here, too. But the implications of a certain approach or priority still should not be confused, blurred, or casually passed over, as now seems to have become the case.

2. The Entanglement of Functions

Provinces have claimed that ADA, DREE, and OTA interfered with or pre-empted provincial responsibilities and jurisdictions. This tendency today is also evident in the fields of urban and consumer policy and for Quebec, at least, in cultural and social policy. Premiers have complained that initiatives, when unilateral, come without warning or negotiation and, when bilateral, come through shared cost programs that offer almost no real opportunity to refuse without penalty either their initiation, as the case of Medicare has shown, or their constraints, as was the case with post-secondary education financing, hospital insurance, and the Canada Assistance Plan. Indeed the proposed replacement for the CAP, a Social Services Act, is so much more restrictive of provincial freedom in its own jurisdiction that its acceptance by provinces may be only because the continuation of the CAP was not an option.

It would appear indeed that most new federal initiatives in these areas

are symptomatic of Ottawa's striving to remove past constitutional inhibitions and thereby remove restrictions upon the play of its interests
across the general spectrum of responsibilities in the public sector. Moreover, Prime Minister Trudeau's philosophy attaches little merit, *a priori*,
to any particular or traditional intergovernmental division of powers.
Accordingly, Mr. Barnett Danson, the former secretary of state for urban
affairs, proposed that "Trilevel (urban activity) is, I believe, most successful when there is a willingness on the part of all participants to discuss
real problems without concern as to who has prime responsibility."[7]
Equally, Mr. Trudeau reserved for the provincialist some of the bitterness
he has felt for nationalists; in 1973 he guided his fellow premiers with,
"[We] would promote a working, operational federalism: not a federalism
built on distant visions, legalistic positions, or old prejudices."[8] He
warned of ". . . the danger of adopting as a matter of course, centralization or decentralization as the prime or even exclusive criterion for the
orientation of federal provincial–relations."[9] Trudeau's attitude—consistent with his counterweights philosophy mentioned earlier—has been
that a more decentralized federal system would have to prove its merit
and demonstrate its worth by its operations. He thus gave warning of a
new twist to federalism in the 1968 Constitutional Conference: ". . . provincial interests cannot be represented *simply* through the device of transferring powers from the federal government to provincial governments."
This has been discomfiting for provinces, who have discovered that they
must remain in a state of constant alertness to Ottawa's newest attempts
to maximize its position in domestic politics.

The federal government is now better equipped to understand regional
issues and needs, through regional desks, regional offices, and itinerant
travels of ministers, thereby reducing the formal and informal relations
with provincial regimes as the prime means of input to or output of federal
policy in regional matters. These field functions provide a monitoring of
local interests. The prime minister's interest in "creative tensions" perhaps
further encourages his challenge of provincial empires. Accordingly,
Ottawa has sought to enter those fields in a manner consistent with its
notion of modern federal responsibilities, and particularly in regard to
the pursuit of economic progress.

When combined, this general interest in a higher public profile and the
greater competence in regional issues have enabled the federal government to set in place wide ranging economic levers (DREE, the National
Transportation Act, foreign investment policy, export policy), and to
establish the right to arbitrate interprovincial differences (demographic-
land use review, energy policy). Both of these developments will not only
place Ottawa uniquely and firmly in control of national economic policy

but also their very scope will significantly affect the provinces' responsibility for social policy and regional economic activity. In particular, the extensive and detailed federal involvement in housing, income security, and urban planning programs (not just policy) has meant that fundamental provincial responsibilities are bracketed by federal activities in these areas. (This leaves aside the current, but presumably temporary, federal involvement in wages and price control.)

For its part, the federal government has taken the initiative rather than made the response in almost any area of its choosing. In its exclusive jurisdictions, there has been more intensive use of those powers which would form a component of national economic planning, such as control of oil and gas marketing or banking regulation. In "grey" areas, such as control of corporate activity, federal powers over related matters have been extended to include in the area, for example, the regulation of foreign ownership or a policy on industrial competition. In provincial jurisdictions, the federal government has undertaken a comprehensive review of relevant issues, for instance, respecting mineral policy or demographic policy, and has retained the initiative on them in subsequent federal-provincial meetings. Still further, Ottawa has in recent years moved from matters of social policy to assembling the controls required to shape national economic development.[10] This shift has been taken quite independently of the precepts of co-operative federalism and is indicative of the freedom of action afforded by a healthy federal budget and an absence of any inhibitions over jurisdictional transfers.

Because Ottawa has set aside the jurisdictional approach to assigning roles (with the tacit acquiescence of most provinces), few provincial governments have been able or willing to reveal their specific intentions. As a result, neither side has been able to judge the limits of each other's actions in the federation apart from such broad declarations of interest as "portability of benefits," "uniform national standards," "provincial self-sufficiency," and "jurisdictional integrity." Trudeau has reintroduced "bilateralism" in his relation with provinces, just as Pearson's concessions to Quebec granted that province a *de facto* special status. Bilateralism is as much a federal refusal to extend its special arrangements made with one province to all as it is a provincial hope for a special private "deal." It has not only protected Ottawa from conceding a particular provincial victory to other provinces but it has also enabled the federal regime to penetrate into provincial jurisdictions as and when the opportunity presents itself. More significant still has been the fact that Ottawa remains the centre of its special or "flexible" relations with each province, affording the former exclusive knowledge of national policies and an overview of the balance between centripetal and centrifugal forces. While each province has been very much a party to this exercise of bilateralism (particularly as when it preceded the Victoria meeting of the Constitutional Conference in 1971), there are signs that its diminishing returns are now being seen. There is an increasing practice among provinces to caucus together the day before a federal-provincial conference, and to share with one another their individual experiences in dealing with Ottawa. In the same mood, premiers' conferences have become less social and more strategic in their tone.

Faced with this federal inclination to be vague about its overall intentions for economic development, particularly as they result in competitive action within provincial jurisdictions, the provinces, both rich and poor, have, in turn, come to challenge whether national economic policy can remain solely in federal hands, when the three levels of government in Canada have roughly equal expenditures. It is interesting to note that all the provinces—not only the rich—feel that Ottawa should share its decision making, because the federal activity is having such an effect on their own fiscal and economic policies.[11] While the poor provinces have been treated more generously by Ottawa, even they have not been prepared to accept this paternalism without comment. The need for Marchand to tell Maritime provinces not to complain about DREE's style,[12] and the proposal of Prince Edward Island for a National Planning Board[13] to give federal policy a long-term format, were both incidents which, developing in the case of Ottawa's most assisted provinces, indicated even their concern about the lack of adequately close co-operation.

Provincial and municipal interests have become increasingly concerned that the three levels of government do not neutralize each other's intentions inadvertently. Provinces continue to argue that it is the lack of advance planning, consultation, and co-operation between the two upper levels of government in national economic and fiscal policy which has led to needless program and staff duplications and over-spending in certain fields, recent examples being in seasonal employment activities and housing. Ottawa has rejected such requests for access to its policy making, however, claiming that eleven governments could not agree on national policies. (Although as noted above, the federal government was prepared to invite itself into the provincial planning areas of urban, mineral, forestry, and land-use policy.)

More recently Trudeau's wide-ranging initiatives have been met in kind by provincial initiatives. If provinces have been unsuccessful in securing a role in new national planning by the federal government which affects them intimately, they have, as an alternative, aspired to a national role unilaterally. Labelled by one observer as pretentious, this has consisted of provincial action in traditionally federal jurisdictions. The case of

211

Quebec's international activities in cultural and educational fields is an early and well-known example. Ontario instituted the notion of "full employment budgeting" in its 1971 Budget as an antidote to alleged federal failures in this regard. Alberta and Saskatchewan claim exclusive authority in the management and profits of non-renewable resources. Quebec has considered the production of enriched nuclear fuel, contrary to Canadian practice and is engaged in leading the province's struggle with Ottawa over regulation of communications. And Ontario recently employed its sales tax on cars in a manner having a discriminatory impact on trade.

What is inappropriate in federal and provincial actions in this situation is the unilateral and unstructured practice of one level following its own strategy for staking out spheres of interest. This has been a move away from the formalism of constitutional review toward a free play of federal and provincial interests seeking dominance in new and existing fields, whether or not they are a reasonable jurisdiction for the level involved. It constitutes justification by sheer economic or fiscal power rather than by the rights and privileges derived from a federation supposedly respecting diversity as well as unity. It makes the process of adjustment no longer an orderly one but an unrestricted competition in which the federal government has certain natural advantages. For example, unilaterally the federal government has terminated its revenue guarantee to provinces, imposed ceilings on its cost-sharing, and announced termination of shared cost programs. The funds so released will most likely be devoted to new high-profile federal urban programs.

The market place of short term competition for public favour and visible impact has replaced the multilateral, much more austere setting of constitutional review. Predictably the latter will not be attractive to politicians (at either level) without considerable, enlightened selflessness. In a sense, constitutional review is a zero-sum game played by politicians and advisers concerned with short term gains, not with the visions of another century of Canadian federalism.

In short, the developments of the sixties showed that most governments did not want as a solution to fiscal and economic problems the finality of a new Canadian constitution, but preferred improvised bargaining on issues of the moment. They also found, it is true, that what agreement they managed to reach—on spending powers, for instance—was scorned by the press as insignificant. Not surprisingly, when the constitutional charter of 1971 failed to receive universal support, Prime Minister Trudeau commented that "the federal government could live with the existing constitution" and that "most people in Canada are more interested in jobs than constitutional reform."[14] He had neatly caught the dilemma for those provinces which saw a reformed constitution as an answer to the changing quality of co-operative federalism: that neither the prime minister nor public opinion was greatly worried about clarity in the distribution of powers, while both were much more interested in the solution of current problems by the most effective economic means. It still seemed true, as Trudeau had written in 1968 of the Quebec cultural crisis: "In its last resort what really matters is that per capita income be increased as quickly as possible."[15]

3. WRONG PRINCIPLES

While perhaps a chance comment, Mr. Trudeau's essential stress on rapid economic growth and per capita incomes effectively ignores the communal, traditional, and social qualifications upon that growth in Canada. The technology required certainly makes no provisions for these factors,[16] and federalism has no necessary role in the attainment of the objective. Ottawa's restraint in its concessions to federalism, if long lived, will thus be critical, because the federal regime is so obviously central to setting the extent of diversity in the governing of this country.

The current federal attitude to shared-cost programs, further tax sharing, and extension of the revenue guarantee, in essence precludes larger intergovernmental transfers of an unconditional nature. But by conserving equivalent funds for its own unilateral activity (or nearly unilateral, as with DREE), the federal government has drawn a distinction between the provinces as areas and the provincial governments as authorities for being the recipients of its regional development expenditures. As Ottawa improves the size of its expenditures or the techniques for bypassing the provincial governments, the prosperity generated in a province will not necessarily be in accord with the priorities of its own provincial politicians—as the conflicts over ADA and DREE would seem to indicate.[17] Instead, the looked-for improvement will be in harmony with federal objectives. Thus, while economic disparities could well be reduced, so also, unintentionally or not, political and social diversity may be eliminated. This, in turn, raises the question whether there are, in fact, social and cultural diversities which are being overridden by the highly rational and efficient pursuit of economic modernization now practised by Ottawa. To the extent that there are, the federal government's techniques still make little provision for the treatment of some provincial regimes as other than regional administrators of federal departmental policies.

Clearly emerging from most of these new initiatives at the federal level and the responses developed by provinces is a concept of an intergovernmental relationship that will not enhance the federal system. PPBS, Trudeau's rationalism in politics, and the reorganization of government, all reinforce an affection for orderly, systematic, and hierarchical problem solving. A systems approach to problems breaks a complex issue into its component parts; not surprisingly those divisions may not coincide with the divisions of federalism, for the essentially organic premise of problem solving stands against the co-ordinative notion of federalism. The hierarchical arrangements of problem solving clash with the "separate spheres of interest" provisions of federalism.

Hence, the federal government, as it tries to mould traditions of Canadian federalism into the prescriptions of issue analysis and solution, finds considerable resistance because of a fundamentally different objective in each approach, and not one to be solved away by Mr. Trudeau's "harmonization" of policy or Mr. Danson's "elimination" of competition between governments. The federal use of "national standards" or "the national interest" as a new principle of paramountcy in areas of joint interest is derived directly from the logic of systems analysis: i) that all problems have their big, intermediate, and small scales, and ii) that a solution should know no bounds. However, it is a breathtaking jump of logic to assume that, because the problem is as described, the federation's response must be to shatter and fragment its traditions of accountability, spheres of authority, and responsive governments. The application of a hierarchical approach to government, as well as problem analysis, will consistently assign to provinces a truncated and intermediate "level" of activity within federal "national objectives" strategy. Already in urban affairs, mineral policy, forestry policy, land use policy, competitions policy, and demographic policy the federal government's initiatives reflect this conception of the federation. And as this book has shown, the precursor of this method of assigning roles has been the regional development activities of the federal government.

Largely responsible for this hydra-like reproduction of rational solutions for each problem area in Canada has been the fixation of Canadians upon a high standard of living and an economic measure of happiness or well-being (the GNP index primarily). The economic rationale has become predominant, and just as it has eroded the diversity, self-sufficiency, and authority of legislative bodies in the provinces, undoubtedly it has also borne much good fruit. But as federalism has served economics rather than conversely, fundamentally the emerging crisis becomes one of government, not one of solving regional development problems.

Canada has chosen to respond to issues, increasingly beyond mere regional development, in such a manner that economic disparity and political diversity become inversely related, so that the improvement in the former situation worsens the latter. This has occurred because of the liberal's distaste for the "distant visions, legalistic positions or old prejudices" that Mr. Trudeau mentioned earlier. Stated another way, however, this is an impatience with formalism, ponderous democratic processes, and institutions, or laborious efforts in modernizing tradition sensitively. A quick, efficient, least-cost, least-time response to issues has little respect for a federal system other than as a useful suboptimalization and administrative mechanism.

Indeed it is not formal constitutional reform or the respect between mutually complementary governments (which constitutionalism enshrines) that is today establishing future distributions of power. Instead, it is being decided by the incremental and bilateral approach of economists and political partisans. Intergovernmental competition, the establishment of immediate objectives, and the distribution of power itself, have been founded upon a narrow and short-sighted preoccupation with either the issue of tax revenue potential or the potential for greatest popular appeal. There has been only a token effort to reaffirm a working federation through self-imposed constraint on a government's jurisdictional aspirations. This is surely a backward approach to the ideal, which should be the distribution or revision of roles based on the relative capacities for responsive and effective legislative action possessed by several levels of government, followed by a subsequent allocation of revenue sources. Moreover, the fiscal arrangements themselves have been the result, not of intimate consultations and co-ordination of objectives, but of confrontations produced by a "propose and respond" technique. Unintentionally, perhaps, the country has accepted for itself a federation whose wandering future will be determined by a process of confronting Ottawa's fiats, based as they are upon predominantly economic considerations and general uniformity of services, by those provinces wealthy and concerned enough to make a stand. That the federal government has the greater fiscal power, makes the confrontation less than equal.

Of course there may well be no reason today to continue to provide for the representation of regionally different attitudes in Canada if there is a unitary trend in government either for reasons of economic efficiency or because of growing cultural uniformity (if the latter is indeed occurring), which would thus remove the operational need for a federal system. Perhaps, indeed, more effective representation of regional interests in the federal government or devolution of its bureaucratic powers can provide a satisfactory and lower key alternative to the entrenched rights of unity and diversity in the federal system. Certainly the central regime, by assuming that the pursuit of economic objectives alone can promote human welfare, has reduced greatly the significance of communal and non-economic matters. In consequence this has affirmed for Ottawa the redundancy of the need for a full-blown federal system.

To the extent, however, that a vigorous diversity is to be sustained, the federal methods used for reducing regional disparities have led to such an emasculation of self-determination in the poorer provinces that it well may be that their political regimes will not have the tools and revenues available to pursue an independent cultural or social policy through economic decisions, even if they should wish to do so. Professor Smiley pointed out in 1962 that "extension of the federal influence to matters within the legislative jurisdiction of the provinces" is made on the basis that "the amenity under discussion is one of urgent concern and *ipso facto* Ottawa should do something about it."[18] Buttressed by increasing fiscal leverage, acquiring still further economic levers through national policy reviews, and claiming the mantle of crisis federalism, the federal government has, with these advantages, carried the initiative in the incremental erosion of provincial authority.

What emerges from an incremental, informal, result-oriented adjustment of responsibilities and jurisdictions in our federation today is a major challenge to the accountability, responsiveness, and authority of provincial governments *qua* governments. Hierarchical problem solving creates increasingly a horizontal rather than vertical distribution of powers among three levels of government. Competitive federal-provincial activities produce similar results, though unplanned. In housing, urban development, health care, and resource management the function is no longer exclusively distributed, but rather within the policy area the governmental processes are: strategic and tactical planning, financing, administering, and adjudicating. Federal and provincial responsibilities weave through each other according to the stage in the process and the constituency affected. This division of power by process in a federation makes the "power to govern" extremely difficult to assemble for either level, as critical stages are lost to other governments. Or equally, successive enrichments of a program by different governments make the total service unwieldy, confusing, and diffuse. In such a setting the development of responsible government confined to its predominant mandates is frustrated by these most recent developments in Canadian federalism.

There is no villain in this situation. Governments at both levels have freely chosen to set aside the BNA Act and interpret spontaneously what they feel to be their mandates arising from their commonly-shared populace. Nor have they been prepared to stand, except for Quebec, upon the principle of the protection of diversity. The dynamic between governments has tended to turn upon each level's broad-scale policy initiatives, noble in the scope of response to problems, but consciously poor in recognition of the objectives of federalism or clarity of government mandates. Indeed it might be said that Canada's start as a pragmatic "quasi-federalism" in 1867 with strong central leadership has, after the periodic vicissitudes of provincialism over a century, returned full circle to federal initiative and leadership. To introduce a co-ordinate rather than hierarchical or organic form of federalism therefore would be to restrict and redirect the unbounded paternalism of the central government derived from the imperial-colonial roots of our federation and reinforced by the efficient means of responding to public issues.

The revitalization of the Canadian federal system depends on the character of leadership, not mechanisms for more meetings, more agreements, refinancing, or constitutional change. Just as in the mid 1960s Ottawa undertook to reassert the duality of Canadian political allegiance through the greater visibility and effectiveness of federal programs, so today it will be from the federal government that provincial autonomy and integrity will have to be affirmed.

But to achieve a practical division of responsibilities based on such considerations will require that qualities of enlightenment and self-restraint be critical factors in strategic thinking at both levels of government. It may then be possible that greater constitutional safeguards and greater reliance on interprovincial collaboration can serve as a positive means of ensuring the continued vigour of provincial activity in the face of the all-pervasive national standards concept.

In constitutional and contemporary issues there has been dramatic and intensive federal initiative—much of it critically important for sound economic management. The question, as always, is the issue of delimitation and priority. The question for Canada in the 1970s is whether diversity or unity should receive emphasis; if the former, it will be as a positive response to modern issues of community and regional consciousness rather than as a negative reaction to past tradition.

In its much-admired pursuit of economic and fiscal regional disparities, Canada has chosen to refine its methods instead of considering its overall objectives as a federation. Not only has this led to a narrow perspective from which to assess the effectiveness of the measures taken, but it threatens also to impose a fixed goal, which is one of uniformity. This one-dimensional activity has created one-dimensional citizens, as recipients of goods and services. Yet federalism provides an institutional structure with a potential for improved democratic proceedings: more openness, more awareness, more participation, more justice, and more commitment. For whatever reason federalism may have been adopted in the first place, it now could service the cause of making government less remote, big, and insensitive. In the process, the citizen would be required to be a participant in, as well as recipient of, governmental programs.

This is the enduring attraction of federalism: that despite its periodic abridgements in the case of emergency or rapid economic growth, it continually provides for important democratic forms which so attracted de Tocqueville and Montesquieu. Long past the possible end of cultural diversity or the relevance of territoriality, federalism can service both the individuality and small scales of human aspirations, as well as the national identity.

Notes

1. This point in respect of shared cost programs was made by J. A. Corry in *The Difficulties of Divided Jurisdictions,* Appendix 7 to the *Royal Commission on Dominion-Provincial Relations* (Ottawa: King's Printer, 1939).

2. "Economic growth" and "regional disparities" are interrelated terms, but not exclusively so. In the early decades of the Canadian union, disparities between regions or provinces were identified only in terms of deficiencies of revenues available to governments or deficiencies in the services they could provide. Hence the original settlement of Confederation included provisions to underpin the financial incomes of governments and in later years further transfers were added which concentrated upon the provision of comparable levels of services by the public sector in all provinces. In terms of these financial and service criteria, as they might be called, provinces could be distinguished as either "rich" or "poor" (colloquially "have" and "have not"). Since 1957 "poor" provinces have been further defined by virtue of the federal-provincial equalization formula. Equalization payments are made by Ottawa in instances where a province's average *per capita* tax yield (established by applying a national average tax rate to one or more selected provincial tax bases) falls below a national average. "Disparities" is a term now used increasingly to describe not only fiscal or service deficiencies but the potential for economic growth as well. By examination of fiscal, service, or economic data it would seem but a quantitative task to judge the discrepancy for growth potential between regions and thereby classify provinces as either rich or poor. The fact is, however, that the responsibility for growth has been placed in the charge of many governments and many departments with different philosophies and little individual or combined experience in systematic policy making. This has produced a variety of interpretations and conflicts. Consequently there have been understandable differences over not only the means of achieving growth but also the form and extent of that growth. Some provinces have defined the territory in which growth is to be achieved to imply the boundaries of their own jurisdiction. Hence the pursuit of that optimum growth—particularly to the extent that it has involved funds

from the central regime—has not necessarily harmonized with Ottawa's concept of growth as a national or trans-provincial phenomenon. This study does not weigh the argument for whether provincial economies do in fact exist or whether they are more regional/urban in character. But it does explore the strains developed between federal officials, committed increasingly to the latter interpretation, and provincial personalities wedded to the former. To the extent that the latter persists as a source of provincial identity, although not true in fact, two problems persist. As provinces define themselves as distinct economies they tend to obscure the more factual dimensions in which each one is distinguished from the other on social and political grounds. Next, effective regional development policy is probably impossible when it is grounded on an inappropriate notion of what the regional components of the national economy are. For further discussion of cultural identities and the clash of regional-provincial economic boundaries see, respectively: J. Wilson "The Canadian Political Cultures: Towards a Redefinition of the Nature of the Canadian Political System," *Canadian Journal of Political Science*, VII, 3, (September, 1974), pp. 439–83; A. Raynauld, "Objectives, Limitations and Results of Regional Development Policy," a speech to the Atlantic Canada Economic Association, Fredericton, Oct. 3, 1975. The specific aspects of disparities in Canada are discussed in ch. 3, Appendix A, below.

3. Economic Council of Canada, *Second Annual Review* (Ottawa: Queen's Printer, 1965), p. 136.

4. Structural deficiencies are the lack of appropriate decision making and evaluating processes (and institutions) relevant to the need to improve the performance of the economy. In addition to these procedural aspects of structural deficiencies, the term also describes the inappropriate combination of an economy's resources if growth is to be the objective.

5. For variation, "Ottawa" is used to represent "the federal government."

Notes to Chapter Two

1. D. G. Creighton, *British North America at Confederation*, Appendix 2 to the *Royal Commission on Dominion-Provincial Relations* (Ottawa: King's Printer, 1939), p. 54.

2. *Parliamentary Debates on the Subject of Confederation of the British North American Provinces* (Quebec: Parliamentary Printers, 1865), p. 93.

3. Ibid., p. 69.

4. *Dominion Sessional Papers*, 1885, vol. 10, no. 34, p. 139.

5. Ibid., 1886, vol. 13, no. 76, pp. 8–14.

6. W. Eggleston and C. T. Craft, *Dominion-Provincial Subsidies and Grants*, a study for the Royal Commission on Dominion-Provincial Relations (Ottawa: King's Printer, 1939), p. 33.

7. Canada, *Statutes of Canada*, 2 Geo. V, ch. 3 (Agricultural Aid Act, 1912), 3–4 Geo. V, ch. 5 (Agricultural Instruction Act, 1913), 8–9 Geo. V, ch. 21 (Employment Office Co-ordination Act, 1918), 9–10 Geo. V, ch. 54 (Highway Act, 1919), 9–10 Geo. V, ch. 73 (Technical Education Act, 1919). Most were prepared prior to but were pre-empted by the First World War.

8. Canada, *Royal Commission on the Natural Resources of Alberta and Saskatchewan* (Ottawa: King's Printer, 1935); *Royal Commission on the Transfer of the Natural Resources of Manitoba* (Ottawa: King's Printer, 1929).

9. Canada, *Royal Commission on Maritime Claims* (Ottawa: King's Printer, 1927).

10. See also, D. Clark, *Fiscal Need and Revenue Equalization Grants* (Toronto: Canadian Tax Foundation, 1969).

11. Canada, *Royal Commission on Financial Arrangements between the Dominion and the Maritime Provinces* (Ottawa: King's Printer, 1935).

12. Nova Scotia, *Royal Commission-Provincial Economic Inquiry* (Halifax: King's Printer, 1934).

13. Canada, *Royal Commission on Dominion-Provincial Relations* (Ottawa: King's Printer, 1939).

14. Ibid., p. 78.

15. Ibid., p. 80.

16. *Canada, Dominion-Provincial Conference* (Ottawa: King's Printer, 1941), p. 45.

17. Canada, *Dominion-Provincial Conference on Reconstruction*, August 6, 1945 (Ottawa: King's Printer, 1946), pp. 55–108.

18. Canada, *White Paper on Employment and Incomes* (Ottawa: King's Printer, 1945).

19. Alvin Hansen, *Fiscal Policy and Business Cycles* (New York: Norton, 1941).

20. Canada, *White Paper on Employment and Incomes*, p. 59.

21. When statistics eventually became available there was seen to be little evidence for this optimism; see, Economic Council of Canada, *Second Annual Review*, p. 105.

22. "The federal government would seem reluctant to step any further into the provincial field of development. The greater the participation, the greater will be the centralizing influence. The question of areas that are falling behind in development is a political fundamental. The whole question is not purely financial."

"There is no inclination to deny the federal government's interest in the general growth but getting mixed up in provincial financial matters is another thing again."

Statements made by federal officials at the Preparatory Committee for the Federal-Provincial Conference, 1955, unpublished minutes.

23. M. Lamontagne, "The Role of Government," in G. P. Gilmour, ed., *Canada's Tomorrow* (Toronto: Macmillan, 1954), pp. 117–152.

24. *Proceedings of the Conference of Federal and Provincial Governments* (Ottawa: King's Printer, 1950), p. 23.

25. See ch. 5.

26. W. Magnusson, "Regional Economic Planning and Canadian Federalism," B. Phil. thesis, Oxford University, 1969, pp. 31–32.

27. P. Meerberg, "Controversial IEL may be at turning point in 13-year life," *Chronicle-Herald* (Halifax: Jan. 7, 1971), p. 7.

28. See Premier Frost's proposals for a permanent "fact finding" committee, Federal-Provincial Conference, Preliminary Meeting (April 26, 1955), unpublished minutes, p. 17.

Notes to Chapter Three

1. Canada, *Royal Commission on Canada's Economic Prospects* (Ottawa: Queen's Printer, 1957).

2. For a clearer explanation of these complex provisions, and in particular, Quebec's special grievances, see, A. M. Moore, H. Perry and D. Beach, *The Financing of Canadian Federation* (Toronto: Canadian Tax Foundation, 1966), pp. 28–44.

3. This can be demonstrated by the rapid growth of conditional grants, which have eclipsed unconditional grants since 1960.

4. See C. S. MacNaughton, *Ontario Budget 1970*, Budget Paper B (Toronto: Department of Treasury and Economics, 1970).

5. From a 1965 vantage point, the Economic Council of Canada reflected upon the use of the new approach, "This framework of potential growth serves to underline two important general observations concerning economic growth and productivity. The first is the fact that while the *potential* growth of the Canadian economy is basically determined by the quantity, quality and efficiency of use of productive resources—factors which affect the capacity of the economic to *supply* increased output—actual growth may deviate sufficiently from potential as a result of the change in demand." Economic Council of Canada, *Second Annual Review*, p. 49.

6. W. L. White and J. Strick, *Policy, Politics and the Treasury Board in Canadian Government*, (Don Mills: Science Research Associates, 1970), p. 59; P. C. Newman, *Renegade in Power* (Toronto: McClelland and Stewart, 1963), p. 35; John Meisel, "The Formulation of Liberal and Conservative Programmes in the 1957 Canadian General Election," *Canadian Journal of Economics and Political Science*, XXVI, 4 (Nov. 1960), p. 565.

7. Newman, *Renegade*, p. 91. See also on this period, Denis Smith, *Gentle Patriot* (Edmonton: Hurtig, 1973).

8. Newman, *Renegade*, p. 93.

9. Expenditures by the Department of Agriculture under the Tories increased 240 percent from $84 to $286 million. Newman, *Renegade*, p. 142.

10. Newman, *Renegade*, p. 92.

11. Canada, *Royal Commission on Taxation*, vol. II (Ottawa: Queen's Printer, 1966), p. 79.

12. Bruce Doern explores the evolution of the Privy Council and Prime Minister's Offices from this era to 1969, noting the development of a very complex role for both, *The Structure of Policymaking in Canada* (Toronto: Macmillan, 1972), ch. 2.

13. Economic Council of Canada, *First Annual Review*, pp. 9–10, 17; also chart 6.

14. See, on structural readjustments, Canada, Senate, *Report of the Special Committee of the Senate on Manpower and Employment* (Ottawa: Queen's Printer, 1962), p. 2; also Appendix A to this chapter.

15. Meisel, "Formulation of Liberal and Conservative Programmes," pp. 570–71.

16. See ch. 4 for details; the bypassing of the deputy minister, the use of outside consultants, and the special position of the ARDA secretariat in the interministerial setting were examples of this minister's response to novelty.

17. A full examination of what constituted "below average performance" in certain provinces can be found in T. K. Shoyama, "Public Services and Regional Development in Canada," *Journal of Economic History*, XXVI (December 1966), pp. 498–513.

Notes to Appendix A

1. *Canadian Policies for Rural Adjustment*, Special Study No. 7 of the Economic Council of Canada (Ottawa: Queen's Printer, 1967), ch. 2.

2. Ibid., p. 29.

3. Canada. Senate, *Report of the Special Senate Committee on Manpower and Employment* (Ottawa: Queen's Printer, 1961), p. 49.

4. Ibid., p. 11.

5. Ibid., p. 11.

6. Ibid., p. 8.

7. Economic Council of Canada, *First Annual Review*, p. 42.

8. Ibid., *Second Annual Review*, p. 16.

9. Ibid., *First Annual Review*, p. 43.

10. Ibid., p. 43.

11. H. E. English, *Industrial Structure in Canada's Internal Competitive Position* (Montreal: Private Planning Association, 1964), p. 2.

12. Economic Council of Canada, *Second Annual Review*, p. 105.

13. Atlantic Provinces Economic Council, *The Economy of the Atlantic Region in Perspective* (Fredericton: APEC, 1961), n.p.

14. Economic Council of Canada, *Second Annual Review*, p. 126.

15. Ibid., p. 136.

16. All data is taken from the *National Finances* (Toronto: Canadian Tax Foundation, annual) where various federal statistical presentations are developed in an easily readable form.

Notes to Chapter Four

1. This has been claimed as a characteristic method of Canadian decision making in social services. See J. Porter, *The Vertical Mosaic* (Toronto: University of Toronto Press, 1965), p. 370.

2. The sections of TVTA included: capital construction, high school voca-

tional training, technical training, training of the unemployed and disabled, student aid, and vocational teacher training.

3. R. D. Ford was made director of the Canadian Vocational Training Branch of the federal Department of Labour.

4. In fact so limited was talent that Labour's director of research, Jack Francis, was made assistant deputy minister of the new Department of Regional Economic Expansion in 1968; once again, a new deputy minister of DREE was drawn from Labour in 1971.

5. A confusing situation; see, Canada, Senate, *Report of the Special Committee of the Senate on Manpower and Employment* (Ottawa: Queen's Printer, 1961), pp. 13–14. Economic Council of Canada, *Eighth Annual Review* (1971), p. 123.

6. In fact, under the TVTA Quebec had twenty institutions compared with Ontario's seven that were eligible for grants under the Trade and Occupational Training Section.

7. A more detailed but more specific study of the history of manpower training policy as it evolved between Ontario and Canada is now available: J. S. Dupré et al., *Federalism and Policy Development* (Toronto: University of Toronto Press, 1973).

8. G. P. A. McDonald, "Labour, Manpower and Government Reorganization," *Canadian Public Administration*, X, 4 (Dec. 1967), p. 486.

9. Canada, House of Commons, *Debates* (Ottawa: Queen's Printer, Dec. 9, 1961), p. 678.

10. Canada, *Committee of Inquiry into the Unemployment Insurance Act* (Gill Commission) (Ottawa: Queen's Printer, 1962), p. 167; also, Senate Special Committee, *Report*, "There is a regrettable lack of integration between the operations of the Employment Service and the research and policy making activities of other governments including the Department of Labour," p. 9.

11. Economic Council of Canada, *First Annual Review*, p. 178.

12. Ibid., p. 182.

13. S. Young, "Latest communique: all quiet on the Canadian front," *Globe and Mail* (Toronto: October 29, 1965), p. 7. On Tom Kent in his quasi political-bureaucratic role, see J. Lamarsh, *Memoirs of a Bird in a Gilded Cage* (Toronto: McClelland and Stewart, 1969); D. Smith, *Gentle Patriot* (Edmonton: Hurtig, 1973).

14. Privy Council Office, *Federal-Provincial Conference*, October 24–28, 1966 (Ottawa: Queen's Printer, 1966), pp. 48–52.

15. See detailed account in *Report: Intergovernmental Liaison on Fiscal and Economic Matters* (Kingston: Institute of Intergovernmental Affairs, 1968), pp. 127–29. Also R. Simeon, *Federal-Provincial Diplomacy* (Toronto: University of Toronto Press, 1973), pp. 85–86.

16. Canada, House of Commons, *Debates* (April 25, 1967), p. 15324.

17. The PPBS concept of program management is discussed in ch. 8.

18. One report labelled the new attitude as a "microcosmic orientation toward society . . . job placement and retraining is viewed as though it were a lever or dial for adjusting the monolithic labour force to technical innovations in an everchanging economic machine." Association of Colleges of

Applied Arts and Technology of Ontario, *Report of Action Committee on Manpower* (mimeo, n.p., 1969), p. 7.

19. Economic Council of Canada, *Eighth Annual Review*, pp. 120, 125.

20. Indeed, it was reported that Premier Johnson of Quebec signed only a "temporary" agreement in 1967 because of these constitutional problems, but necessitated by a critical lack of provincial funds. See, Simeon, *Federal-Provincial Diplomacy*, p. 179.

21. *Report of the Action Committee on Manpower*, pp. 1, passim; see also Economic Council of Canada, *Eighth Annual Review*, p. 130.

22. T. Kent, "Intergovernmental Responsibility for Manpower Training," a paper presented to the Institute of Public Administration of Canada (mimeo: Sept. 1967), p. 12.

23. Economic Council of Canada, *Eighth Annual Review*, pp. 145, 147.

24. The Treasury Board is a committee of senior Cabinet ministers that decide the annual allocation of government resources among competing objectives. A detailed analysis of the role of the Treasury Board is found in ch. 8.

25. Consultation with provincial officials.

26. Economic Council of Canada, *Eighth Annual Review*, p. 97.

Notes to Chapter Five

1. See, for instance, H. Buckley and E. Tihanyi, *Canadian Policies for Rural Adjustment*, Special Study No. 7, Economic Council of Canada (Ottawa: Queen's Printer, 1967); J. N. McCroirie, *ARDA: An Experiment in Development Planning*, Special Study No. 2, Canada Council on Rural Development (Ottawa: Queen's Printer, 1969).

2. See reference to Merril Menzies, ch. 3, p. 40; also Canada, *Resources for Tomorrow Conference*, Background Papers, I (Ottawa: Queen's Printer, 1961–2), especially D. W. Carr, "Resource Adjustment in Agriculture: Effects of the Legislative and Administrative Framework," pp. 123–42.

3. Canada, Senate, Special Committee on Land Use, *Proceedings*, 1960–1963 (Ottawa: Queen's Printer).

4. Canada, House of Commons, *Debates* (May 22, 1961), p. 5194.

5. Preamble of act.

6. Canada, House of Commons, *Debates* (March 23, 1961), pp. 3260–64.

7. See Senate Special Committee on Land Use (Dec. 3, 1963), p. 38.

8. A. T. Davidson, "Notes for talk on ARDA," at Canadian Forestry Association Annual Meeting (Ottawa: mimeo., March 20, 1962), p. 3.

9. For similar behaviour in Prince Edward Island, see, Senate Special Committee on Land Use (Dec. 3, 1963), p. 44; also "ARDA and ADB Slowness Make Islanders Unhappy," *Financial Post* (Toronto: Dec. 28, 1963), p. 27.

10. The Atlantic provinces in fact only used fifty percent of their allotment under the first five-year agreement; Davidson, in Senate Standing Committee on Banking and Commerce, *Minutes of Proceedings* (May 10, 1966), p. 185.

11. McCroirie, *ARDA: An Experiment,* p. 89.

12. Consultation with officials.

13. Canada, House of Commons, *Debates* (Oct. 25, 1967), pp. 3475, 3488.

14. Conversation with officials; also referred to in, L. P. Apedaile, "Rural and Agricultural Development: A Federal-Provincial Point of View," a paper delivered to the Canadian Economics Association Conference (Winnipeg, 1970), p. 2.

15. V. Mathews and L. Apedaile, "Action, Agencies, Advocacy and Analysts," *Canadian Journal of Agriculture Economics,* XIX, 1 (July, 1971), pp. 1–11.

16. J-B. Bergevin, "Gaspé: A Case Study in Regional Planning," *Canadian Public Administration,* IX, 1 (March, 1966), pp. 86–95.

17. G. Coulombe, "Planning and Socio-Economic Structures (Quebec)" in Ontario, Department of Economics and Development, *International Conference on Regional Development and Economic Change* (Toronto: Queen's Printer, 1965), pp. 65–72.

18. See, Canada, Senate, Special Senate Committee on Poverty, *Proceedings,* No. 6 (May 20, 1966), pp. 91–96.

19. See also, for a further description of the following events, J. Guay, "L'Heure des Realisations," *Le Magazin Maclean* (Nov. 1969), pp. 23 ff.

20. F. Howard, "Roland Parenteau: gearing for five-year drive toward prosperity," *Globe and Mail* (Toronto: April 11, 1967), p. B5; and C. Vincent, "Discours au Congress Conjoint du Conseil d'Orientation économique du Bas Saint-Laurent et du Conseil Regional d'Expansion économique de la Gaspesie et des Illes-de-la-Madeleine." (Chandler: mimeo, 28 mai 1967.)

21. Bergevin, "Gaspé," pp. 92–3.

22. See, speeches given by C. Vincent, minister of Agriculture and Colonization on ARDA at Amqui, Quebec (mimeo, April 29, 1968); also, P. Dozois, "Inauguration of Fishing Centre of Rivière-au-Renard" (mimeo, Sept. 26, 1967), and D. Johnson, "Text of a speech given at conveyance of BAEQ Report to the Quebec Government" (mimeo, July 20, 1966).

23. Constitutional Conference, *Proceedings* (Ottawa: Queen's Printer, 1968), pp. 227–49.

24. The inflexibility of CMHC's national policies is now well documented in M. Denis and S. Fish, *Programs in Search of a Policy* (Toronto: Haakert, 1972), ch. 5.

25. Buckley and Tihanyi, *Canadian Policies for Rural Adjustment.*

26. Consultation with officials; referred to by André Saumier, Senate Committee on Poverty (May 20, 1969), p. 189.

27. Evidence of the tension can be found in a paper by Ted Duncan "A Rationale for Development Planning," prepared in the last days of the Department of Forestry and Rural Development (Ottawa: mimeo, July 23, 1968).

28. Conversation with officials; T. N. Brewis in Standing Committee on Regional Development, *Proceedings* (May 3, 1971), p. 9:30.

29. Conversation with officials.

30. Canada, House of Commons, Standing Committee on Regional Devel-

opment, *Minutes of Proceedings* (Ottawa: Queen's Printer, Dec. 14, 1970), p. 2:27. They have been replaced largely by infrastructure projects.

31. Meeting alluded to in Canada, House of Commons, *Debates* (Feb. 3, 1970), p. 3176.

32. See chs. 8 and 10 for an examination of this change in other departments.

Notes to Chapter Six

1. See Prime Minister Pearson's comments, Canada, House of Commons, *Debates* (June 3, 1963), p. 803.

2. Most provinces established consultative economic bodies (some of which are discussed in chapter 11); the Manitoba Development Authority, Nova Scotia Voluntary Planning Board, New Brunswick Research and Productivity Council, Quebec Economic Advisory Council, Saskatchewan Economic Advisory and Productivity Council, and the Ontario Economic Council.

3. Canada, *Royal Commission on the Automotive Industry* (Ottawa: Queen's Printer, 1960), p. 53 and "The Case of the Missing Word," *Globe and Mail* (Toronto: October 26, 1960), p. 6.

4. *Report of the Special Committee of the Senate on Manpower and Employment* (Ottawa: Queen's Printer, 1961), p. 4.

5. Examples were attempts at a steel complex in Saskatchewan or secondary industry in Nova Scotia. See, F. Robertson, "IEL Facts May Help if Liberals Lift Wraps," *Globe and Mail* (Toronto: Oct. 15, 1970), p. B-5.

6. Canada, *Report of the Royal Commission on Government Organization* (Ottawa: Queen's Printer, 1962), vol. 3, pp. 36ff.

7. These became eventually the criteria of later federal industrial incentives.

8. *Report of the Royal Commission on Government Organization*, vol. 3, p. 22.

9. See quote in text pertaining to footnote 13, below.

10. See the statement made in Canada, *Resources for Tomorrow Conference Background Papers*, "The kind of institution required for effective regional planning is one that recognizes the urban centred region as a proper sphere of action . . . and which equips the people of the region to plan effectively for themselves," p. 402.

11. Canada, House of Commons, *Debates* (June 3, 1963), p. 803; italics supplied.

12. Ibid., *Debates* (June 27, 1963), p. 1644.

13. Canada, Commons Standing Committee on Industry, Research and Energy Development, *Proceedings* (Nov. 8, 1966), p. 292.

14. The ADIA legislation offered specific grants as industrial incentives in a wider range of area than ADA; RDIA expanded area coverage to regions and added more types of industries, eligible for a still more generous grant.

15. Hon. C. S. MacNaughton, *Ontario Budget 1970*, Budget Paper B.

16. "Roberts says Ottawa draining Ontario of its wealth," *Toronto Daily Star* (April 17, 1971), p. 1.

17. Canada, House of Commons, *Debates* (June 12, 1966), p. 5892.

18. Commons Standing Committee on Industry, Research and Energy Development (Nov. 8, 1966), pp. 302–3.

19. Toronto director of National Employment Service (now called Canada Manpower Centres) on Toronto radio interview, Feb. 17, 1971.

20. T. N. Brewis, *Regional Economic Policies in Canada* (Toronto: Macmillan, 1968), p. 141.

21. H. Larsen, *A Study of the Economic Impact Generated by ADA-Assisted Manufacturing Plants Located in the Province of New Brunswick* (University of New Brunswick: mimeo, March, 1968), I, p. 5, fn. 1.

22. Ibid., V, 34–5.

23. Ibid., VII, 1–2.

24. *The National Finances*, 1970–71 (Toronto: Canadian Tax Foundation), ch. 11.

25. P. C. Newman, *The Distemper of Our Times* (Winnipeg: Greywood, 1968), p. 16.

26. Ibid., p. 31.

27. See note 13.

28. Canada, House of Commons, *Debates* (June 3, 1963), p. 803.

29. Press Release, Sept. 6, 1963.

30. Department of Industry, "Function and Organization," Release for meeting with provinces, Dec. 10, 1963 (n.p.), p. 1.

31. Ibid., p. 3.

32. Saskatchewan and Nova Scotia excepted.

33. Conversation with provincial official; the change pertained to provisions for mortgages.

34. H. I. Macdonald, Briefing note to Premier Robarts, May 27, 1965 (private papers).

35. For example, in "special areas" DREE can pay 100 per cent of the cost of roads, schools, sewerage, water supplies, and recreation facilities.

36. See note 28 and quote in text, above.

37. Commons Standing Committee on Regional Development, p. 2:14.

38. Finance may have "won" the designation of Montreal, from DREE. See ch. 8, p. 133.

39. "Incremental" in this thesis is used to describe the piecemeal approach of government to its overall public sector activity whereby this total activity is built up from the individual activities of deparments, not distributed from a central planning document. Hence this is aggregative rather than distributive policy making.

Notes to Chapter Seven

1. The original ADB legislation was passed in 1962 by the Diefenbaker government. Six months later it was redrafted by the new Liberal regime and operated until 1969.

2. The economic impact of ADB is a separate question; see T. N. Brewis, *Regional Economic Policies in Canada* (Toronto: Macmillan, 1968), chapter 8.

3. A. K. Cairncross, *Economic Development and the Atlantic Provinces* (Fredericton: Atlantic Provinces Research Board, 1961); T. Wilson, *Financial Assistance with Regional Development* (Fredericton: APRB, 1964). These economists were hired not for their intimate knowledge of the Atlantic region but for the impressiveness of their names on the reports.

4. Canada, *Royal Commission on Canada's Economic Prospects* (Ottawa: Queen's Printer, 1957), p. 410.

5. The "Board" approach was favoured by the Conservatives (along with the device of Royal Commission); Flemming had proposed an Economic Development Board before the election defeat in 1963. It was the precursor to the Liberals' Economic Council of Canada.

6. Newman, *The Distemper of Our Times* (Winnipeg: Greywood, 1968), p. 214.

7. Ibid., p. 215.

8. Canada, House of Commons, *Debates* (Dec. 4, 1962), p. 2290.

9. Ibid., p. 2291.

10. E. P. Weeks, "The Atlantic Provinces: A Case Study" in, Ontario Department of Economics and Development, *International Conference on Regional Development and Economic Change* (Toronto: Queen's Printer, 1965), pp. 73–84.

11. Conversation with officials.

12. In fact Saskatchewan provided numerous planners to other governments in Canada after 1964 when the new Liberal regime in the province disbanded much of the CCF's planning apparatus.

13. See New Brunswick in, Canada, Constitutional Conference, *Proceedings* (Ottawa: Queen's Printer, 1968), p. 361.

14. Conversation with officials.

15. "Joe happy with Ottawa reception," *St. John's Telegram* (Jan. 26, 1971), p. 1.

16. However, New Brunswick definitely requested that this be encouraged; see Constitutional Conference, *Proceedings* (1968), p. 361.

17. Atlantic Provinces Economic Council, *The Atlantic Economy* (Fredericton: APEC, 1967), pp. 63–75.

18. Nova Scotia Voluntary Planning Board, *Annual Report and Economic Review* (Halifax: Queen's Printer, 1967), pp. 93–4.

19. Conversations with officials; alluded to in *The Atlantic Economy*, p. 15.

20. The history of the Program Development Agency is discussed in ch. 9 in detail.

21. This issue is further discussed in chapter 10; see also Atlantic Development Board, *Annual Report* (Ottawa: Queen's Printer, 1968), p. 22.

22. DREE undertook to finance a major container port at Halifax and an industrial "multiplex" at Saint John, N.B.

23. Atlantic Provinces Economic Council, *Fifth Annual Review* (Fredericton: APEC, 1971), p. 91.

24. B. Little, "DREE: Maritimers want more say in the planning, but . . . they fear complaining too much," *Financial Times of Canada* (Toronto: Sept. 13, 1971), pp. 18–19.

Notes to Chapter Eight

1. See ch. 4.

2. Bennett's "personal gambles" include, according to officials, the construction of a resources railway and nationalization of hydro-electric power. His "second looks" include the revision of his stands on controlling teacher and doctor costs and his reversal of the decision not to nationalize private electric companies.

3. P. Jewett, "Political and Administrative Aspects of Policy Formation," in T. Brewis, *et al., Canadian Economic Policy* (Toronto: Macmillan, 1961), p. 300.

4. Canada, *Report of the Royal Commission on Government Organization* (Ottawa: Queen's Printer, 1962), III, pp. 22, 24.

5. Ibid., p. 32.

6. W. L. White and J. C. Strick, *Policy, Politics and the Treasury Board in Canadian Government* (Don Mills: Science Research Associates, 1970), p. 42.

7. Jewett, "Political and Administrative Aspects," p. 306.

8. See, J. F. Graham, "Areas of Economic Stress in the Canadian Federal Context" in W. D. Wood and R. S. Thoman, eds., *Areas of Economic Stress in Canada* (Kingston: Queen's University Industrial Relations Centre, 1965), p. 15; and J. Parizeau, "What are the areas of responsibilities of provincial governments under a programme of constitutional decentralization or co-operative federalism?", a paper presented to A National Conference on Economic Unity (Banff: mimeo, 1967), p. 4. Keynesians were declared simple-minded only to the extent that they could not foresee restrictions to the free flow of labour and capital which had been imposed by deliberate federal policy favouring certain regions. As a consequence the Keynesian belief that there could be no regional isolation from national policies in an open market situation simply did not hold.

9. See ch. 3, Appendix A, for a discussion of the factors accounting for the poorer economic performance of certain regions. One general requisite was a rise in people's aspirations to encourage better participation in social reform and more forceful demands for a change.

10. P. C. Newman, *The Distemper of Our Times* (Winnipeg: Graywood, 1968), p. 22; D. Smith, *Gentle Patriot* (Edmonton: Hurtig, 1973), p. 137.

11. P. C. Newman, *Renegade in Power* (Toronto: McClelland and Stewart, 1963), p. 95.

12. G. B. Doern, "Recent Changes in the Philosophy of Policy-making in Canada," *Canadian Journal of Political Science*, IV, 2 (June, 1971), pp. 246ff.

13. This is a greatly simplified statement; it is not to suggest that budgetary

reforms were not progressively concerned with objectives, only that the failure to articulate macro objectives did not thwart the reform of lower level program objectives and performance criteria.

14. See, for a description of other aspects of the Treasury Board, M. Hicks, "The Treasury Board and its Clients," *Canadian Public Administration*, XVI, 2 (Summer, 1973), pp. 182–205.

15. Cost efficiency may be defined in terms of the "capacity of an organization to achieve results with a given expenditure of resources—in short the ratio between organizational inputs and outputs" while "Effectiveness is more broadly defined to be the degree of success . . . in goal achievement." For elaboration, see, James Cutt, "Efficiency and Effectiveness in Public Sector Spending: The Programme Budgeting Approach," *Canadian Public Administration*, XIII, 4 (Winter 1970), p. 397.

16. Conversation with officials. A similar point is put more elaborately by A. Wildavsky, "Rescuing Policy Analysis from the PPBS," *Public Administration Review* (March/April, 1969), pp. 189–202. In the Canadian setting, see, A. W. Johnson, "Management Theory and Cabinet Government," *Canadian Public Administration*, XIV, 1 (Spring, 1971), pp. 73–81.

17. See the federal Budget, *Debates* (June 3, 1969), pp. 9419–20.

18. Conversation with federal finance officials.

19. L. Watkins, "Regional disparities remedies meeting nation-wide disfavour—Marchand," *Globe and Mail* (Toronto: August 17, 1971), p. 33.

20. Canada, House of Commons, Standing Committee on Regional Development, *Minutes of Proceedings* (Ottawa: Queen's Printer, 1970–1), pp. 5:23, 2:21.

21. Ibid. (December 15, 1970), p. 3:7. Areas in Quebec outside Montreal interestingly were not given an added incentive.

22. Ibid. (December 14, 1970), p. 2:9.

23. Doern, "Recent Changes," p. 260.

24. "Opting out" is the term used to describe the federal offer in a number of conditional grant programs to allow provinces to regain exclusive control of the field while Ottawa would continue to provide aid unconditionally through equalized transfers or greater provincial access to tax revenues, i.e. through abatements of a portion of federal personal income taxes.

25. Conversation with officials; *per capita* debt in 1965 and 1966 rose 18 percent over the previous year while own source revenues grew at 9 and 16 percent respectively. See also, *Globe and Mail* (Toronto: October 26, 1966), p. 8.

26. Saskatchewan, *Report of the Royal Commission on Government Organization* (Regina: Queen's Printer, 1965), p. 192.

27. The province was able with abundant revenues to exhaust its allocations under the TVTA program, for instance, a full year and a half before termination.

28. See, "Men who direct the Prairie economies," *Globe and Mail* (Toronto: March 3, 1967), p. B-5.

29. The experience of Manitoba is more complex and will be examined in ch. 10.

NOTES TO PAGES 137–148

30. H. I. Macdonald, "The Solemnization of an Institutional Marriage," *Ontario Economic Review*, VII, 2 (March/April 1969), pp. 2–14.

31. B. Doern, "Horizontal and Vertical Portfolios," in Doern & Wilson *Issues in Canadian Public Policy* (Toronto: Macmillan, 1974).

Notes to Chapter Nine

1. See ch. 5 for a discussion of the use of *animation sociale* as well as public and private collaboration in the development of FRED projects.

2. H. Quinn, *The Union Nationale* (Toronto: University of Toronto Press, 1963).

3. Tremblay reported to Lesage in 1959, before the latter became premier, to bring a new look to the Liberal Opposition.

4. For greater detail on the origins and structure of COEQ, see R. Parenteau, "The Quebec Economic Advisory Council," *Canadian Public Administration*, VIII, 2 (June, 1965), pp. 166–71.

5. Much of the following detail is derived from conversation with officials, but also, F. Howard, "Roland Parenteau: gearing for five-year drive toward prosperity," *The Globe and Mail* (Toronto: April 11, 1967), p. B–5.

6. Conseil d'orientation économique du Québec, *Documents de base en vue de la planification* (Québec: Imprimeur de la Reine, 1962); for another account of COEQ see, R. Parenteau, "L'expérience de la planification au Québec (1960–69)," *l'Actualité Economique*, XLV (jan–mars 1970), pp. 679–96.

7. J. N. McCroirie, *Arda: An Experiment in Planning*. Special Study No. 2, Canada Council on Rural Development (Ottawa: Queen's Printer, 1969), p. 80; also COEQ, *Les Exigences de la planification economique* (Québec: Imprimeur de la Reine, 1964).

8. For a criticism of COEQ see, Québec, Assembly, *Comité des Credits* (Québec: l'Editeur Officiel du Québec, 23 mai, 1967), pp. 595–612.

9. Québec, *Report Annuel du Conseil d'orientation économique du Québec* (Québec: Imprimeur de la Reine, 1966); see also, Québec, Assembly, *Credits du ministère du Conseil executif* (Québec: l'Editeur Officiel du Québec, 3 juillet, 1970), p. B632.

10. For greater detail see, Parenteau, "L'expérience," p. 694.

11. Committee on Manitoba's Economic Future, *Manitoba 1962–75* (Winnipeg: Queen's Printer, 1963).

12. A similar case of this strangulation, at Ottawa, is described in W. L. White and J. C. Strick, *Policy, Politics and the Treasury Board in Canadian Government* (Don Mills: Science Research Associates, 1970), pp. 39ff.

13. "Organization for Developmental Planning," confidential planning document, May 25, 1968, mimeo.

14. Subsidies to an out-of-date system could be aid to industries which suffered a permanent location disadvantage, subsidies to marginal farmers, fishermen, and miners, or subsidies to housing when in fact local zoning laws limited the rate of house building and hence increased the price of houses. See, T. Duncan, "A Rationale for Development Planning," Rural Develop-

ment Branch (Dep't of Forestry and Rural Development: mimeo. July 23, 1968).

15. Economic Council of Canada, *Second Annual Review*, p. 126.

16. L. E. Poetschke "Regional and Rural Adjustment—Problems and Policies," a paper delivered to a conference of the Canadian Economics Association (Winnipeg: mimeo., Nov. 14, 1970), p. 13.

17. Ibid., p. 16.

18. As late as August 5, 1970 general confusion and suspicion in other departments necessitated a memo by the Secretariat to a conference of deputy ministers in response "to a number of questions raised about the authorities and role of the Cabinet Committee . . . and its Secretariat" (unpublished Secretariat document).

19. Cabinet Committee on Planning and Priorities, *A Development Plan for Nova Scotia* (Halifax: mimeo, 1970), p. 12. Italics supplied.

20. M. Keddy "Development plan sparks bitter debates," *Chronicle-Herald* (Halifax: April 24, 1970), p. 4; also "Regan axes Committee," *Financial Post* (Toronto: Jan. 16, 1971), p. 7.

21. "Premier decides to 'phase out' Secretariat," *Chronicle-Herald* (Halifax: Jan. 7, 1971), p. 1.

22. Ibid.

23. *The Report on Maritime Union Commissioned by the Governments of Nova Scotia, New Brunswick and Prince Edward Island* (Halifax: Queen's Printer, 1971), p. 86.

24. B. Game, "Development plan is major issue in PEI's election," *Globe and Mail* (Toronto: May 8, 1970), p. 27.

25. Already 65 percent of the province's 1970–71 budget came from federal transfers. See, "Province gets major portion of revenues from Ottawa," *Financial Post* (Toronto: May 2, 1970), p. 14.

26. L. Richards, "Human Resources Development in Alberta." A paper delivered to the Annual Meeting of the Canadian Political Science Association (St. John's, June 1971).

27. British Columbia had no bureaucratic body for establishing comprehensive priority recommendations during the 1960s; Ontario in 1970 established a Cabinet Committee on Policy Development with no provision for secretariat support. A full secretariat, the Cabinet Office, was introduced as part of the 1972 C.O.G.P. (Committee on Government Productivity) and effected extensive reforms of the Cabinet committee structure.

28. "Vertical" and "horizontal" are terms used by A. H. Hansen, *The Process of Planning: A Study of India's Five Year Plans 1950–64* (London: Oxford University Press, 1966), pp. 361–62. See also Doern, in Doern & Wilson, *Issues in Canadian Public Policy* (Toronto: Macmillan, 1974), ch. 12, for a related usage.

29. See, on a similar problem in federal urban policy, N. Lithwick, "Political Innovation: A Case Study," a paper delivered to the Faculty of Architecture, University of Toronto (Nov. 1971), p. 18. Doern, in *Political Policymaking* (Montreal: Private Planning Association, 1971) makes a useful distinction between "policymaking" and "decisionmaking."

30. Parenteau, "L'expérience," p. 693.

Notes to Chapter Ten

1. See also Economic Council of Canada, *Second Annual Review*, p. 99, and ch. 7.

2. The Ministry of State for Urban Affairs had a similar experience. See, N. H. Lithwick, "Political Innovation: a Case Study," *Plan*, XII, 1 (April, 1972), pp. 46–55.

3. Observations of a senior finance official at Ottawa.

4. W. Stewart, "The 30 Men Trudeau Trusts," *Maclean's*, LXXXII, 10 (Oct. 1969), p. 43.

5. For greater detail see, G. B. Doern, "Recent Changes in the Philosophy of Policy-Making in Canada," *Canadian Journal of Political Science*, IV, 2 (June 1971), pp. 243–64.

6. M. Hicks, "The Treasury Board of Canada and its Clients," *Canadian Public Administration*, XVI, 2 (Summer 1973), p. 189ff.

7. G. B. Doern, "Recent Changes," p. 223, provides a more detailed analysis of the "winners" of the 1970–71 estimates. For an indication of Quebec's favoured position in federal spending see, H. Shea, "DREE—dream hasn't quite come true," *Chronicle-Herald* (Halifax, July 8, 1971), p. 8. Also it should be recalled that Quebec was granted a costly new airport and was the major beneficiary of equalization payments increases since 1966. From 1969–75 DREE spent 46 percent of its funds in Quebec.

8. Canada, House of Commons, Standing Committee on Regional Development, *Minutes of Proceedings* (Ottawa: Queen's Printer, 1970–1), pp. 12:9, 12:11. The exchange between federal and provincial representatives in this committee on this date (May 12, 1971) are a poignant testimony of the incompatibilities of two approaches to the same problem.

9. Earlier chapters have indicated that expressions of grand visions had made ADB and ADA subject to considerable critical provincial comment.

10. See, Keddy, "Development plan sparks bitter debate," *Chronicle-Herald* (Halifax: 24 April, 1970), p. 4; also, L. Chudy, ". . . and N.S. the Special Headache," *Financial Times* (Toronto: July 6, 1970), p. 12.

11. L. E. Poetschke, "Regional and Rural Adjustment—Problems and Policies," a paper delivered to a joint meeting of the Canadian Economics Association and the Canadian Council on Resource Development (Winnipeg: mimeo, 14 Nov. 1970), p. 17.

12. Ibid., p. 16.

13. Conversation with officials. See also, D. Conrad, "How Federal Planner Tom Kent is Killing the Maritimes," *The 4th Estate* (Halifax: Jan. 21, 1971), pp. 1, 10–11.

14. "DREE Announces New Spending," *Chronicle-Herald* (Halifax: Jan. 11, 1971), p. 1.

15. J. Mcandrews, "Massive development for PEI target set out in White Paper," *Globe and Mail* (Toronto: April 7, 1967), p. B-9.

16. "$725 Million Plan Triggers PEI Election," *Financial Post* (Toronto: May 2, 1970), p. A-4.

17. M. Goldblatt, "Ottawa Outlines $20m aid to Slow Regions," *Globe and Mail* (Toronto: March 12, 1970), p. B-1.

18. P. E. Trudeau, "Notes for Remarks by Prime Minister on Fiscal Arrangements," to the Federal-Provincial Conference (Ottawa: mimeo, Nov. 16, 1971), p. 6.

19. Other examples include special consideration of Quebec in Manpower and Transportation policies. New controls were placed on a redrafted DREE replacement for the FRED-BAEQ scheme in Gaspé whereby joint planning and social development projects were replaced by road-building projects.

20. Kent, however, claimed humbly that, ". . . the only power the federal government has is to say that this is not a programme within the objectives of the development plan." Standing Committee on Regional Development, *Minutes*, p. 12:10.

21. See A. Schick, "Systems Politics and Systems Budgeting," *Public Administration Review* (March–April 1969), pp. 137–51. See also, Economic Council of Canada, *Eighth Annual Review* (Ottawa: Information Canada, 1971) which devotes chapters 3 and 4 to this topic.

22. W. L. White and J. C. Strick, *Policy, Politics and the Treasury Board in Canadian Government* (Don Mills: Science Research Associates, 1970), p. 109.

23. For a public statement of his disenchantment with this empire-building in Urban Affairs, see the speech of the federal director of research who resigned in protest of a similar condition, N. Lithwick, "Political Innovation: A Case Study"; also consultation with federal officials.

24. Doern, "Recent Changes," pp. 260ff.

25. Atlantic Provinces Economic Council, *Fifth Annual Review* (Halifax: APEC, 1971), esp. pp. 88–91.

26. See Parenteau, "L'expérience de la planification au Québec," *l'Actualité Economique* XLV (jan–mars 1970), pp. 679–96, for the emphasis that he placed as a defeated planner upon the urgency of changing expectation and encouraging compromise as the primary steps to any success of planning within government or for the private sector.

27. See statements made by Ontario, Alberta, and British Columbia to the Federal-Provincial Conference, Nov. 1971.

28. "Robarts says aid given have not provinces by Ottawa maybe 'roasting golden goose'," *Globe and Mail* (Toronto: April 17, 1971), p. 14.

Notes to Chapter Eleven

1. This is only a rough approximation but the beginning of the hard line examined in chs. 8 and 10 was in 1965. While the boundary between the two periods might be vague, the difference in behaviour was not.

2. Canada, House of Commons, *Debates* (1963 Session), pp. 3135–7, 4728–37, 4782–9, 4859–74, 4882–96.

3. On the "Subsidy-Substitution" effect of shared-cost programs see, D. V. Smiley, *Conditional Grants and Canadian Federalism* (Toronto: Canadian Tax Foundation, 1963), p. 45.

4. Economic Council of Canada, *Fifth Annual Review* (1968), p. 176; also H. Larsen, *A Study of the Economic Impact Generated by ADA–Assisted Manufacturing Plants located in the Province of New Brunswick* (Fredericton: University of New Brunswick, 1968).

5. Economic Council of Canada, *Second Annual Review*, p. 106.

6. Under OTA, for instance, Ottawa spent $57.45 per labour force member in the Atlantic region but only $22.20 in Ontario, Economic Council of Canada, *Eighth Annual Review*, p. 97. DREE expenditures in industrial incentives were more than seventy percent east of Ottawa, with Nova Scotia receiving ninety dollars for every dollar spent in British Columbia.

7. See the development of this concept in, Hon. C. S. MacNaughton, *Ontario Budget 1970*, Budget Paper B (Toronto: Department of Treasury and Economics, 1970).

8. Jean-Luc Pepin, "Co-operative Federalism," *Canadian Forum*, XLIV, 527 (Dec., 1964), pp. 206–10. Pepin was later made minister of Trade and Commerce in 1966.

9. Ibid., p. 208.

10. Ibid., p. 210.

11. Ibid., p. 209.

12. Ibid., p. 208.

13. P. C. Newman, *The Distemper of Our Times* (Winnipeg: Graywood, 1968), p. 86. See also on this period, D. Smith, *Gentle Patriot* (Edmonton: Hurtig, 1973).

14. Canada, House of Commons, *Debates*, January 20, 1966, p. 72.

15. Ibid., p. 73.

16. See Hon. G. Favreau, "National Leadership in Canadian Federalism," a speech given by the president of the Privy Council, in G. Hawkins, ed., *Concepts of Federalism* (Toronto: Canadian Institute of Public Affairs, 1963), pp. 46ff. Also see "What Size of Rudder," editorial in *Canadian Tax Journal*, XIV, 5 (Sept.–Oct., 1966), pp. 402–410. Richard Simeon lists five objectives adopted by Trudeau's government: respect for the Constitution, end the shared cost mess, end special status, clear up federal-provincial revenue sources, extend support to the poor, and equalization. *Federal-Provincial Diplomacy* (Toronto: University of Toronto Press, 1973), p. 67.

17. D. Smith, *Bleeding Hearts . . . Bleeding Country* (Edmonton: Hurtig, 1971), ch. 7.

18. P. E. Trudeau, *Federalism and the French Canadian* (Toronto: Macmillan, 1968), p. 147.

19. Ibid., p. 125.

20. Ibid., p. 203.

21. Ibid., p. XXIII. See also, D. Smith, "The Political Catechism of Pierre Elliott Trudeau," *Canadian Forum*, XXI, 608 (Sept. 1971), pp. 13–20.

22. Denis Smith comments on Trudeau's Hobbesian preference for a strong

state. The inattention to Lockean concerns for liberty results in an inattention to the coercive outputs of government. See Smith, *Bleeding Hearts*, p. 84. More generally this is a variant of the "good process makes good policy" philosophy. As Lowi demonstrates, such an approach ignores the coercive aspect of the outputs of politics. See T. Lowi, *The End of Liberalism* (New York: Norton, 1969), ch. 2. In Canada, Bregha in *Public Participation in Planning Policy and Program* (Toronto: Queen's Printer, n.d.) suggests several important variants upon the theme of participation and consultation.

23. J. R. Mallory, "The Five Faces of Federalism," in P-A. Crepeau and C. B. Macpherson, eds., *The Future of Canadian Federalism* (Toronto: University of Toronto Press, 1965), pp. 3–15.

24. E. R. Black and A. C. Cairns, "A Different Perspective on Canadian Federalism," *Canadian Public Administration*, IX, 1 (Mar. 1966), p. 34. Italics supplied. See also P. W. Fox, "Regionalism and Confederation" in Ontario Advisory Committee on Confederation, *Background Papers and Reports, Vol. 2* (Toronto: Queen's Printer, 1970).

25. Fox, "Regionalism and Confederation," pp. 12–14.

26. Most took up industrial incentive programs with a vengeance. D. V. Smiley, *Constitutional Adaptation and Canadian Federalism Since 1945*, document of the Royal Commission on Bilingualism and Biculturalism (Ottawa: Queen's Printer, 1970), p. 32.

27. Contrast Smiley, ibid., p. 64, with provincial statements in the Tax Structure Committee, *Federal-Provincial Tax Structure Committee* (Ottawa: Queen's Printer, 1966), pp. 61ff.

28. On the Quiet Revolution see, D. V. Smiley, "Two Themes of Canadian Federalism," *Canadian Journal of Economics and Political Science*, XXX, 1 (Feb. 1965), pp. 80–97; F. R. Scott and M. K. Oliver, *Quebec States Her Case* (Toronto: Macmillan, 1964).

29. Smiley, *Constitutional Adaptation*, p. 135.

30. In fact, further increases in equalization payments, 1972–77, were initially refused by Ottawa which stated its intention to use the funds in conditional or unilateral programs. Constitutional Conference, 1971, unpublished minutes.

31. W. Stewart, "Baby, it was cold inside," an interview with Eric Kierans —a former federal minister of Communications, *Maclean's Magazine*, LXXXIV, 7 (July, 1971), p. 66; also Canada, Department of Regional Economic Expansion, *A Summary of Regional Development Incentives Offers Accepted* (Ottawa: Department of Regional Economic Expansion, June, 1971), p. 7.

32. Black and Cairns, "A Different Perspective," p. 42. See Quebec's *sine qua non*: C. Morin, *Quebec versus Ottawa* (Toronto: University of Toronto Press, 1976), pp. 70–71.

33. L. Lapierre, "The 1960s" in J. M. S. Careless and R. Craig-Brown, *The Canadians 1867–1967* (Toronto: Macmillan, 1967), p. 355.

34. Canada, Standing Committee on Regional Development, *Minutes of Proceedings* (Ottawa: Queen's Printer, 1970–1), p. 4:13.

35. Further problems are listed in *Report: Intergovernmental Liaison on*

NOTES TO PAGES 199–211

Fiscal and Economic Matters, p. 125ff. The renegotiation of health care by the Hon. John Munro was an example of a confrontation form of federal-provincial politics, as was Finance Minister Turner's Budget announcement (June 23, 1975) that health care ceilings were to be imposed on joint programs.

36. Smiley, *Constitutional Adaptation*, p. 83.

37. For the surface ripples of the great internal turbulence wrought by this process see, A. W. Johnson, "Management Theory and Cabinet Government," *Canadian Public Administration*, XIV, 1 (Spring, 1971), pp. 73–81 and M. Hicks, "The Treasury Board of Canada and its clients," *Canadian Public Administration*, XVI, 2 (Summer 1973), pp. 182–205.

38. See Smiley's argument for the harmony produced by "executive federalism," *Constitutional Adaptation*, ch. VII. See in contrast Mr. Reisman's comments on the declining primacy of the deputy's influence on the Finance minister. *Globe and Mail* (Dec. 4, 1974), p. B–1.

39. In the OTA program this was critical. See J. S. Dupré et al., *Federalism and Policy Development* (Toronto: University of Toronto Press, 1973), chs. 4, 8.

Notes to Chapter Twelve

1. A. Maass, "Division of Powers: An Areal Analysis" in A. Maass, ed., *Area and Power* (Glencoe: Free Press, 1959), p. 10.

2. P. Ylvisaker, "Some Criteria for a 'Proper' Areal Division of Governmental Powers," *Area and Power*, pp. 34ff. Also, M. Janach, "Efficiency and Effectiveness in the Ontario Government," B.A. thesis, Glendon College, York University (Toronto: Frost Library, 1974).

3. J. S. Mill, *On Liberty*, ed., A. D. Lindsay (London: Dent, 1962), pp. 347–48.

4. Ibid., pp. 347ff, esp. 353.

5. Standing Committee on Regional Development, *Minutes* (Dec. 14, 1970), p. 2:16.

6. A. Raynauld, "Objectives, Limitations and Results of Regional Development Policy," a speech to the Fourth Annual Conference of the Atlantic Canada Economics Association (Fredericton, mimeo.), October 3, 1975.

7. Hon. B. Danson, "Opening Statement to Ontario Regional Trilevel Conference" (Ottawa: Ministry of State for Urban Affairs, April 12, 1976), p. 2. Italics supplied.

8. Rt. Hon. P. E. Trudeau, "Notes prepared for the Opening Statement, First Ministers' Conference" (Ottawa: Prime Minister's Office, May 23, 1973), p. 8.

9. Ibid., p. 7.

10. See the important "leak" of federal strategy, D. Crane, "Trudeau Aims to Narrow Rich-Poor Gap," *Toronto Star* (Toronto, Nov. 7, 1975), pp. A10–A11.

11. See provincial submission to the Federal-Provincial Conference (Nov. 1971).

12. P. Teasdale, "Maritimes condemn plan to aid regions," *Toronto Daily Star* (Aug. 17, 1971), p. 14.

13. Prince Edward Island submission to the Federal-Provincial Conference, Ottawa, 1971. See also, Atlantic Provinces Economic Council, *Fifth Annual Review* (Halifax: APEC, 1971).

14. Prime Minister's Office, "Transcript of the Prime Minister's Press Conference" (Toronto: Men's Press Club, June 23, 1971), p. 12.

15. D. Smith, *Bleeding Hearts . . . Bleeding Country* (Edmonton: Hurtig, 1971), p. 113.

16. J. Ellul, *The Technological Society* (New York: Vintage, 1964), ch. 4.

17. L. Watkins, "Regional Disparities Meeting Nation-wide Disfavors—Marchand," *Globe and Mail* (Toronto: August 17, 1971), p. 33.

18. D. V. Smiley, *Conditional Grants and Canadian Federalism* (Toronto: Canadian Tax Foundation, 1963), p. 25.

Index